Degenhard Meier

Post-Investment Value Addition to Buyouts

GW00493216

GABLER EDITION WISSENSCHAFT

Entrepreneurship

Herausgegeben von
Professor Dr. Malte Brettel, RWTH Aachen,
Professor Dr. Lambert T. Koch, Universität Wuppertal,
Professor Dr. Tobias Kollmann, Universität Duisburg-Essen,
Campus Essen,
Professor Dr. Peter Witt, Wissenschaftliche Hochschule für
Unternehmensführung (WHU), Vallendar

„Entrepreneurship" ist ein noch relativ junger Forschungszweig, der jedoch in Wissenschaft und Praxis stetig an Bedeutung gewinnt. Denn Unternehmensgründungen und deren Promotoren nehmen für die wirtschaftliche Entwicklung einen zentralen Stellenwert ein, so dass es nur folgerichtig ist, dem auch in Forschung und Lehre Rechnung zu tragen.

Die Schriftenreihe bietet ein Forum für wissenschaftliche Beiträge zur Entrepreneurship-Thematik. Ziel ist der Transfer von aktuellen Forschungsergebnissen und deren Diskussion aus der Wissenschaft in die Unternehmenspraxis.

Degenhard Meier

Post-Investment Value Addition to Buyouts

Analysis of European Private Equity Firms

With a foreword by Prof. Dr. Malte Brettel

Deutscher Universitäts-Verlag

Bibliografische Information Der Deutschen Bibliothek
Die Deutsche Bibliothek verzeichnet diese Publikation in der Deutschen
Nationalbibliografie; detaillierte bibliografische Daten sind im Internet über
<http://dnb.ddb.de> abrufbar.

Dissertation RWTH Aachen, 2005

1. Auflage Februar 2006

Alle Rechte vorbehalten
© Deutscher Universitäts-Verlag/GWV Fachverlage GmbH, Wiesbaden 2006

Lektorat: Brigitte Siegel / Nicole Schweitzer

Der Deutsche Universitäts-Verlag ist ein Unternehmen von
Springer Science+Business Media.
www.duv.de

Umschlaggestaltung: Regine Zimmer, Dipl.-Designerin, Frankfurt/Main
Druck und Buchbinder: Rosch-Buch, Scheßlitz
Gedruckt auf säurefreiem und chlorfrei gebleichtem Papier
Printed in Germany

ISBN 3-8350-0228-7

Foreword

From 1999 onwards a steady decline in the performance of buyout investments in Europe has occurred. The traditional levers to value creation – high financial leverage and multiple expansion – are common knowledge in the private equity industry and therefore no longer a source of competitive advantage. In addition, financial leverage has declined due to stricter solvency margin requirements imposed by the Basel II accord. The return on equity achieved by a private equity firm has therefore decreased along with lower ratios of financial leverage. Furthermore the magnitude of multiple expansion – the positive differential between exit and purchase multiple – has declined or even become negative, so that multiple expansion can only selectively be achieved as a result of adept management of the acquisition and divestment process. As a result, the future success of buyout investments in Europe will depend on the ability of private equity firms to improve the operating performance of their portfolio companies post-acquisition.

This is the central theme of Degenhard Meier's dissertation. The goal of his thesis is to identify the success factors of post-investment value creation and their relative importance. Degenhard Meier achieves this goal in an impressive manner. In a first step, he identifies the dimensions of post-investment value addition characterizing the interaction between private equity firms and their portfolio companies. The dimensions of interaction are then combined with a theoretical framework in order to derive plausible hypotheses. Degenhard Meier tests the hypotheses in a very innovative way: he takes the current discussion on alternative methods to structural equation modeling as a basis and develops the discussion further by shedding light on partial least squares – a variance-based approach to structural equation modeling. The dissertation therefore not only advances practitioners' knowledge of the post-acquisition phase of buyout investments but is also of significant value to the research community. Surely an ample number of doctoral students will refer to this comprehensive description of partial least squares modeling.

However, also the practical implications of this doctoral dissertation are highly interesting: Degenhard Meier is the first scholar to clearly show the beneficial effects of hands-on involvement of private equity firms on an empirical basis. Moreover, he is able to give specific recommendations on how to implement a hands-on involvement approach. Summarizing, the dissertation of Degenhard Meier is highly interesting to both private equity practitioners and management scholars alike. Practitioners find a methodologically solid backup for implementing a hands-on involvement strategy and solid suggestions on how to implement it. And management scholars find one of the first comprehensive applications of partial least squares analysis, which is going to be applied by numerous followers in the future.

This doctoral dissertation will therefore surely find the broad audience that it deserves.

Malte Brettel

Acknowledgements

First, I want to express gratitude to my academic advisor and first referee Univ.-Prof. Dr. Malte Brettel. He was always available for discussions and provided many valuable suggestions that helped to craft this thesis. I want to thank him in addition for creating a highly effective and fun environment for my studies. I am also grateful to my second referee Univ.-Prof. Dr. Wolfgang Breuer for many valuable comments on a preliminary version of this dissertation.

Second, I would like to thank all the private equity professionals that participated in this study. Clearly, private equity professionals are part of one of the most secretive industries that exist. It is therefore highly appreciated that more than one hundred professionals took the time to fill in this dissertation's survey. Hopefully the results of this study will compensate study participants with an adequate return on their time invested.

Third, I would like to thank all those friends and colleagues that helped me in designing this study. I want to thank Dr. Moritz Hagenmüller for the dicussions that lead to shaping the research question of this thesis. I am grateful to Cyril Jaugey for many insightful discussions on the research design. Dr. Ekkehard Franzke and several anonymous private equity professionals helped as sparring partners in the design of this study's questionnaire. I am in addition grateful to Professor Dr. Michael Hänlein for his introduction to partial least squares analysis as well as the intricacies of formative and reflective indicators. I would like to also thank the fellow members of the "Männerschwimmgruppe" for pushing my physical endurance. It certainly was a critical success factor in the compilation of this thesis.

Fourth, I am grateful to Bain & Company for both providing the funding for this thesis and the opportunity to use the facilities of the Munich office.

Finally, I want to thank my family. The support and understanding of my wife Susanne Meier was central in writing this thesis. Surely she has carried far more than her fair share in running our family. I am also grateful to my parents Elisabeth and Dr. Eberhard Meier for their continuous motivation and generous financial support of my studies.

Degenhard Meier

Contents

1 **Introduction**   **1**

1.1 Relevance of Post-Investment Value Addition to Buyouts 1

1.2 Research Gap and Research Questions 2

1.3 Research Design and Structure 4

2 **Context and Definitions**   **6**

2.1 Positioning of Thesis in Entrepreneurial Finance 6

2.2 Definitions 10

    2.2.1   Private Equity Firm 10

    2.2.2   Buyout 14

    2.2.3   Value Addition 17

    2.2.4   Post-Investment Phase 21

2.3 Conclusion 22

3 **Framework for Structuring the Analysis of Post-Investment Value Addition to Buyouts**   **23**

3.1 Evaluation of Frameworks Used for the Analysis of Post-Investment Value Addition by Private Equity Firms 23

    3.1.1   Neoclassical Financing Theory 24

    3.1.2   Property Rights Theory 26

    3.1.3   Transaction Cost Theory 27

    3.1.4   Agency Theory 29

    3.1.5   Knowledge-Based View 32

    3.1.6   Corporate Governance View 33

    3.1.7   Procedural Justice Theory 35

    3.1.8   Investment Controlling 36

    3.1.9   Summary Evaluation and Conclusion 37

3.2 The System-Based View of Controlling developed by Horváth as a Suitable Theoretical Concept 38

3.3 Discussion of the Application of the System-Based View of Controlling on the Relationship between Private Equity Firm and Portfolio Company 41

4 **Methodology of Data Analysis**   **44**

4.1 First-Generation Multivariate Research Techniques are Not Suitable 44

4.2 Structural Equation Modeling Basics 46

4.3 Variance- and Covariance-Based Approaches to Structural Equation Modeling 49

5   Derivation of Hypotheses and Design of the Survey Instrument   57

5.1 Derivation of Hypotheses 57

    5.1.1 Activities of Private Equity Firms.. 57

    5.1.2 Organization of Involvement 60

    5.1.3 Information Systems 61

    5.1.4 Actors 64

    5.1.5 Summary of Hypotheses and Research Model 67

5.2 Design of the Survey Instrument... 68

    5.2.1 Fundamental Considerations 69

    5.2.2 Activities of Private Equity Firms.. 70

    5.2.3 Organization of Involvement 72

    5.2.4 Information Systems 73

    5.2.5 Experience of Private Equity Professionals 75

    5.2.6 Usage of External Resources.. 76

    5.2.7 Value Added to Buyout.. 77

6   Data Collection and Analysis   81

6.1 Data Collection.. 81

6.2 Data Analysis.. 84

    6.2.1 Representativeness of Study... 85

    6.2.2 Analysis of Non-response and Informant Bias 86

    6.2.3 Evaluation of the Measurement Model: Validation of Constructs................ 87

    6.2.4 Determination of the Significance Criterion: Statistical Power Analysis 106

    6.2.5 Estimation of the Structural Model: PLS analysis 110

7   Discussion   114

7.1 Interpretation of Results 114

    7.1.1 Influence of Post-Investment Concepts on Post-Investment Value Creation 114

    7.1.2 Operationalization of Post-Investment Concepts... 116

7.2 Implications for Practitioners 118

7.3 Limitations of the Analysis and Areas of Further Research............................... 120

8   Summary   122

Appendix   123

Cover letter... 123

Survey instrument 125

References   131

X

Figures

Figure 1: The three dimensions of entrepreneurial finance. 10

Figure 2: Legal setup of a private equity partnership 13

Figure 3: Number of studies using certain frameworks as a basis for researching post-investment value addition by private equity firms. 24

Figure 4: Corporate governance view of the corporation 34

Figure 5: System-based view of controlling developed by Horváth 41

Figure 6: Structural equation model composition.. 48

Figure 7: PLS algorithm 53

Figure 8: Research model. 68

Figure 9: Data analysis steps using PLS... 85

Figure 10: Response rate by country surveyed. 86

Figure 11: Process of validating formative and reflective constructs in PLS structural equation models.. 97

Figure 12: Type I and Type II errors... 107

Figure 13: Statistical power analysis.. 109

Figure 14: R², Q², significance and size of path coefficients of structural model.................. 113

Tables

Table 1: Dimensions of post-investment value addition analyzed by prior studies 3

Table 2: Dimensions of post-investment value addition covered by theories used so far for the analysis of post-investment value addition by private equity firms 38

Table 3: Impact of post-investment involvement on value added to portfolio company (+: positive relationship; O: no relationship; -: negative relationship) 59

Table 4: Impact of informal organization of the relationship between private equity firm and portfolio company on value added. (+: positive relationship; O: no relationship; -: negative relationship) 61

Table 5: Criteria for the identification of formative indicators 91

Table 6: Criteria for the assessment of reflective constructs' trait validity 95

Table 7: Reliability coefficients of the construct "completeness and intensity of portfolio company reporting" 100

Table 8: Reliability coefficients of the construct "quality of portfolio company information" 101

Table 9: Reliability coefficients of the construct "performance of portfolio company information systems" 101

Table 10: Reliability coefficients of the construct "usage of external resources" 102

Table 11: Reliability coefficients of the construct "value added to buyout" 102

Table 12: Correlations of constructs and reflective indicators (correlations of indicators with their respective constructs in bold) 103

Table 13: Square root of average variance extracted (diagonal) and correlations of constructs (off-diagonal) 104

Table 14: Weights and VIFs for the construct "activities of private equity firms" 105

Table 15: Weights and VIFs for the construct "organization of involvement" 105

Table 16: Weights and VIFs for the construct "frequency of interaction with the portfolio company" 106

Table 17: Weights and VIFs for the construct "experience of private equity professionals" 106

Acronyms

AVE	average variance extracted
ES	effect size
EVCA	European Venture Capital Association
CTA	confirmatory tetrad analysis
EBO	employee buyout
EBIT	earnings before interest and taxes
e.g.	for example
et al.	et alii (and others)
f	and the following page
FCI	Finance and Capital for Industry
ff	and the following pages
IBO	institutional buyout
ICFC	Industrial and Commercial Finance Corporation
i.e.	that is
IRR	internal rate of return
LS	least squares
LV	latent variables
MBI	management buyin
MBO	management buyout
MEBO	management and employee buyout
ML	maximum likelihood
N	sample size
NPV	net present value
n.s.	not significant
OBO	owner buyout
P&L	profit and loss statement
pfc.	portfolio companies
PLS	partial least squares
SEM	structural equation modeling
UK	United Kingdom
US	United States
VC	venture capital
VIF	variance inflation factor

1   Introduction

1.1   Relevance of Post-Investment Value Addition to Buyouts

Buyouts can be defined as the "purchase of a controlling stake in a company (or a division) from its owners, usually financed with a combination of equity and debt and with strong involvement of specialized financial investment companies"[1], the so-called private equity firms.[2] Along with the fast growth of private equity firms' funds,[3] buyouts have evolved in Europe as an increasingly important source of financing for established companies: capital invested in buyouts by European private equity firms has increased from €1.9 billion in 1992 to €16.9 billion in 2002 at an annual growth rate of 24%.[4] Given that private equity firms also offer valuable contributions beyond financing, it is not surprising that buyout transactions are claimed to have a positive economic and social impact.[5]

Buyouts have traditionally been characterized by a lack of information on individual investment characteristics or their performance. As a result the "mechanisms through which buyouts create – or destroy – value remain to a large extent the proverbial black box"[6]. Prior research usually claims three levers to drive value creation in buyouts: financial leverage, multiple expansion, and operating income growth.[7] Financial leverage of buyouts – the ratio of debts to assets – has declined in recent years and may remain at low levels due to the strict solvency margin requirements imposed on lending banks by the Basel II accord.[8] The importance of financial leverage as a lever of value creation in buyouts – anyway questionable from a theoretical point of view[9] – has therefore declined. Along with a decline in stock market valuations from the year 2000 onwards, multiple expansion – the positive differential between

---

[1]   Berg/Gottschalg (2003), p. 3.
[2]   For an in-depth definition of the terms "private equity firm" and "buyout" see chapter 2.2.1 and 2.2.2, respectively.
[3]   See EVCA (2003).
[4]   See EVCA (1997), p. 83; EVCA (2003), p. 66.
[5]   The European Venture Capital Association (EVCA) found in a survey among 300 portfolio companies of private equity firms that companies would no longer exist or developed more slowly without the buyout in 84% of all cases, that the number of employees has increased since the buyout in 61% of all cases, and finally that the average salary of employees increased in 62% of all cases (see EVCA (2001), pp. 4ff). As a matter of fact the findings presented by the EVCA are just an indication of the beneficial social and economic impact. Given that company survival, the increase in number of employees and the increase in average salary of employees have not been benchmarked relative to the industry averages in the respective countries, it remains unclear whether buyout companies have actually had a positive economic and social impact beyond their non-buyout peers.
[6]   See Gottschalg et al. (2005), p. 1.
[7]   For a deeper and formal discussion of the levers of value addition to buyouts see chapter 2.2.3.
[8]   For a review of the Basel II accord see Deutsche Bundesbank (2004), pp. 75ff.
[9]   See Miller (1991), pp. 474ff.

exit and purchase multiple – has declined as well or even become negative.[10] In view of uncertain future multiples and continuing low levels of financial leverage, value creation in buyouts will depend on the ability of private equity firms to improve the operating performance of their portfolio companies post-acquisition: "Whereas in the past leverage and rising markets were delivering the uplift in a successful LBO, today it is down to the general partners working with management to transform businesses. And no one is saying this is going to be easy. It's going to take longer, be harder and the odds are going to widen."[11]

1.2   Research Gap and Research Questions

Prior studies conducted on post-investment value addition by private equity firms share at least one of the following three shortcomings. First, almost all prior studies either focus on early stage portfolio companies[12] or have no focus at all on specific financing stages[13]. It has been shown, however, that private equity firms act differently in different financing stages.[14] The findings of studies that focus on early stage portfolio companies or that lack any focus on a specific financing stage can therefore be regarded only as indicative for private equity firms engaging in buyout financing. Therefore, the first objective of this thesis is to answer the following question: which post-investment concepts do have a significant influence on value added to buyout?

---

[10] See Knoblauch (2002), p. 5.
[11] PrivateEquityOnline.com (2003).
[12] That is, on portfolio companies that have just been started up or on recently founded portfolio companies that are in the process of expanding their business. See MacMillan et al. (1989); Landström (1990); Fredriksen et al. (1991) and Fredriksen et al. (1997); Rosenstein et al. (1993); Fried/Hisrich (1995); Barney et al. (1996); Sweeting/Wong (1997); Fried et al. (1998); Brinkrolf (2002); Ruppen (2002); Busenitz et al. (2004).
[13] See Sapienza/Timmons (1989) and Sapienza (1992); Sapienza et al. (1996); Schefczyk/Gerpott (1998) and Schefczyk (2000); Burgel/Murray (2000); De Clercq/Sapienza (2002); Kaplan/Schoar (2003); Reißig-Thust (2003). There are only two studies focusing on portfolio companies in the buyout financing stage: Kraft (2001) and KPMG/Manchester Business School (2002).
[14] Schefczyk (2000), pp. 305-306 shows that activities of private equity firms investing in early or late stage portfolio companies are significantly different.

2

Dimensions analyzed by studies on post-investment value addition by private equity firms	Activities	Organization	Information systems	External resources	Internal resources
MacMillan (1989)	X				
Sapienza/Timmons (1989) and Sapienza (1992)	X		X		
Landström (1990)	X				
Fredriksen et al. (1991) and Fredriksen et al. (1997)	X				
Fried/Hisrich (1995)		X			
Barney et al. (1996)	X				
Sapienza et al. (1996)	X		X		
Sweeting/Wong (1997)	X				
Fried et al. (1998)	X				
Schefczyk/Gerpott (1998) and Schefczyk (2000)	X	X	X		
Burgel/Murray (2000)					X
Kraft (2001)				X	
Brinkrolf (2002)	X				
Ruppen (2002)	X		X		
KPMG/Manchester Business School (2002)			X		X
DeClercq/Sapienza (2002)					X
Kaplan/Schoar (2003)					X
Reißig-Thust (2003)	X	X	X		
Busenitz et al. (forthcoming)	X				
Total mentions	13	3	6	1	4

Table 1: Dimensions of post-investment value addition analyzed by prior studies

Second, prior research has analyzed only individual dimensions of post-investment value addition by private equity firms – e.g. focusing on activities, organization and information systems –, neglecting other dimensions – e.g. external and internal resources.[15] There is no study analyzing all dimensions of post-investment value addition concurrently, thereby revealing the relative importance of individual dimensions. Hence, the second objective of this thesis is to provide additional insights into the question: what is the relative importance of different post-investment concepts?

Third, prior research has made use of basic research techniques such as multiple regression or correlation analysis that are restricted – among other limitations – to the analysis of observable variables.[16] Given that post-investment constructs – such as the experience of private equity professionals – are unobservable variables that have to be operationalized by an array of indicators – such as private equity experience or professional services experience – structural equation modeling (SEM) techniques have to be used. SEM techniques allow measuring of unobservable variables with the help of an array of indicators. Consequently, the third objective of this thesis is to answer the question: which indicators should be used to operationalize post-investment concepts such as the experience of private equity professionals?

---

[15] See table 1.
[16] Out of the studies on post-investment value addition mentioned above, only Schefczyk (2000) and Reißig-Thust (2003) made use of structural equation modeling, which allows to analyze the relationship among several latent variables operationalized by multiple indicators.

Summarizing, this thesis intends to answer the following research questions:

1. Which post-investment concepts do have a significant influence on value added to buyout?
2. What is the relative importance of different post-investment concepts?
3. Which indicators should be used to operationalize post-investment concepts such as the experience of private equity professionals?

1.3 Research Design and Structure

Research in business administration is usually built on one or more of the following generic research strategies: First, factual-analytic research structures complex relationships in a qualitative, verbal way.[17] Second, formal-analytic research analyzes problems with the help of abstract mathematical models.[18] Third, empirical research generates insights on the basis of real world observations.[19] Researchers do not have to use one of the strategies in isolation, however. On the contrary, combining several strategies to advance research in business administration is recommended.[20] "Applying different approaches from varying perspectives, exploring and experimenting, enriches the opportunities to formulate and find answers to those intriguing questions embedded in a vivid and exciting area."[21]

As a consequence of this suggestion, a pluralistic research strategy is adopted by this thesis. It starts with factual-analytic research deriving hypotheses: with the help of the system-based view of controlling serving as a theoretical framework, prior research on post-investment value addition by private equity firms is structured and hypotheses are derived. Each hypothesis is subsequently tested – i.e. accepted or rejected – on the basis of an empirical analysis.

---

[17] "Die Forschungsinteressen des sachlich-analytischen Forschers richten sich grundsätzlich auf die Durchleuchtung komplexer Zusammenhänge und die Erarbeitung von Handlungsgrundlagen. Bei dieser Erarbeitung stützt er sich aber auf Plausibilitätsüberlegungen und empirisch festgestellte Teilzusammenhänge, ohne eine eigene, systematische empirische Überprüfung anzustreben, oft sogar, ohne sich überhaupt auf eine Überprüfbarkeit vorgeschlagener Theoreme einzustellen." (Grochla (1976), p. 634).

[18] "Die formal-analytische Forschung ist im Gegensatz zu den beiden anderen Forschungsstrategien stärker an der vereinfachten und mehr oder weniger abstrakten Beschreibung von Problemstrukturen interessiert. [...] Dieses Anliegen besteht allgemein darin, Vorgehensweisen aufzuzeigen, um die jeweils behandelten Probleme auf der Ebene der gedanklichen Problemlösung einer möglichst rationalen Entscheidung zuzuführen." (Grochla (1976), p. 634).

[19] "Die empirische Erforschung von Organisationen ist vor allem durch das Bemühen um eine systematische Erfahrungsgewinnung gekennzeichnet. Diese Erfahrungsgewinnung richtet sich nach bestimmten Methoden, die etwa im Bereich der empirischen Sozialforschung bzw. der induktiven Statistik niedergelegt sind." (Grochla (1976), p. 634).

[20] See Grochla (1959), pp. 65ff; Grochla (1976), p. 637.

[21] Häckner/Hisrich (2001), p. 183.

4

With regard to the research structure, this thesis proceeds along eight chapters. The first chapter discusses the relevance of the thesis, outlines research gaps and research questions and finally describes the research design and structure adopted.

The second chapter then shows the positioning of the thesis within the entrepreneurial finance stream of research and defines all relevant terms for the thesis. The purpose of this chapter is to give an introduction into entrepreneurial finance in general and the pillars framing this thesis – private equity firms, buyouts, the post-investment phase and value addition – in particular.

The third chapter begins with a discussion of criteria for the selection of a suitable framework for structuring the subsequent analysis. Frameworks used by prior studies to analyze post-investment value addition are then evaluated along those criteria. As frameworks used by prior studies do not meet all criteria established before, a system-based perspective is adopted as a framework for structuring further analysis.

The fourth chapter starts with a discussion of first-generation (e.g. multiple regression analysis, factor analysis, discriminant analysis or principal component analysis) and second-generation (e.g. structural equation modeling) multivariate research techniques. Then variance- and covariance-based approaches to structural equation modeling are contrasted with a special emphasis on distributional and scale requirements, sample size requirements and finally formative and reflective indicator specifications.

In the fifth chapter hypotheses are derived relating all constructs of post-investment interaction between private equity firm and portfolio company as independent variables to "value added to buyout" as dependent variable. Given that variables are not directly observable, the operationalization of variables with suitable indicators is subsequently discussed.

The sixth chapter starts with a description of the mail survey process adopted. The data obtained by the mail survey is then analyzed with regard to its representativeness and tested for a potential non-response or informant bias. Next, the measurement model is analyzed, evaluating formative and reflective constructs separately. After determining the significance criterion, the structural model is finally estimated using partial least squares analysis.

In the seventh chapter, the results of the statistical analysis are interpreted. Based on these results, implications for practitioners are derived. Finally, the limitations of the analysis and areas of further research are discussed. The thesis ends with a summary in chapter eight.

2 Context and Definitions

2.1 Positioning of Thesis in Entrepreneurial Finance

This thesis belongs to the entrepreneurial finance stream of research in business administration. In order to give an idea of the positioning of this thesis in entrepreneurial finance, a brief introduction into entrepreneurial finance will be given followed by the positioning of this thesis within the field of research.

Entrepreneurial finance is a relatively recent discipline in business administration: Professor William A. Sahlman was the first to teach an entrepreneurial finance elective. He introduced the elective at Harvard Business School in 1985. Today, four out of the nine leading United States (US) business schools have an entrepreneurial finance elective in their course offerings.[22]

Due to the novelty of this field of research, a consistent definition of entrepreneurial finance has not yet emerged: it is a field of research "characterized by a variety of terms, various scientific perspectives, different methodological approaches, and a broadening of the problem area addressed in the studies"[23].

A compelling effort to structure the medley of definitions for entrepreneurial finance has been undertaken by Achleitner. She structures existing definitions of entrepreneurial finance along three dimensions: the perspective of the firm/the entrepreneur, the perspective of the intermediary (the private equity firm) and the perspective of the investor.[24]

The focus of entrepreneurial finance research is on the perspective of the firm or the entrepreneur. It discusses the levers to value creation in entrepreneurial firms: "if 'entrepreneurship' is

---

[22] See Achleitner (2001), p. 9 and Sahlman (1997). Entrepreneurial finance is also a relatively recent academic field of study in comparison to entrepreneurship, which was established already in the late 1940s: the first course of entrepreneurship was offered at Harvard Business School in 1947 by Myles Mace and the first conference on small business issues was held at St. Gallen University in 1948 (see Cooper/Weil (2003), pp. 2ff.

[23] See Häckner/Hisrich (2001), p. 183.

[24] See Achleitner (2001), pp. 10ff. Another attempt to structure the entrepreneurial finance field of research has been undertaken by Denis (2004), pp. 301ff. He mentions "four primary areas of inquiry [of entrepreneurial finance]: (i) alternative sources of capital, (ii) financial contracting issues, (iii) public policy, and (iv) the dynamics of private equity returns." The approach of Denis to structure entrepreneurial finance research is, however, less compelling, as it is neither collectively exhaustive nor mutually exclusive. Says Denis (2004), p. 303: "these four areas are not meant to be an exhaustive set of issues but, rather, represent the primary areas that have been studied to date."

about relentless pursuit of opportunity without regard to the resources currently controlled and 'finance' is about cash, risk and value, then 'entrepreneurial finance' is about the pursuit of opportunities to create value"[25]. The analysis of the perspective of the firm/the entrepreneur in entrepreneurial finance is usually structured along the financing stages of a firm (see also figure 1):[26]

- Seed financing is provided to determine whether a business idea deserves further consideration and investment.

- Start-up financing is provided to develop and test-market a product, build the management team and refine the business plan.

- The advent of the expansion stage is characterized by the start of serial production, product marketing and sales activities. The expansion stage ends when the original providers of equity sell their shares or terminate their portfolio company.

- Buyout financing has the purpose of changing ownership in a mature or declining company to implement value adding measures. A detailed definition can be found in chapter 2.2.2.

According to Achleitner, the perspective of the firm/the entrepreneur by itself constitutes entrepreneurial finance in a narrow sense. Entrepreneurship in a broader sense includes also the perspective of the intermediary and the perspective of the investor.[27]

Research on the perspective of the intermediary can be structured along the steps of the private equity investment process. The investment process has so far been analyzed extensively for private equity firms focusing on early and expansion stage (venture capital[28]) investments,[29] however, rarely for private equity firms focusing on buyout investments. Since both private equity firms investing in early/expansion and later stage firms share many characteristics, the sequence of investment process steps will be similar.[30]

---

[25] Sahlman (1997), p. 4.

[26] See Sahlman (1990), p. 479; Achleitner/Fingerle (2003), pp. 5-6.

[27] See Achleitner (2001), pp. 14ff.

[28] Venture capital is usually defined as "[funds] primarily devoted to equity or equity-linked investments in young growth oriented firms" (Gompers/Lerner (1999b), p. 3). In the past the terms private equity and venture capital have been distinct in the US – venture capital referring to investments in portfolio companies in the seed, start-up and expansion financing stages and private equity referring to investments in portfolio companies in the buyout financing stage – while being "generally used interchangeably" (EVCA (1998), p. 5) in Europe. This has changed, however: "recently, some investors have been referring to venture investing and buyout investing as 'private equity investing'" says the NVCA (2004). And also the EVCA (2004) says: "Venture capital is, strictly speaking, a subset of private equity and refers to equity investments made for the launch, early development, or expansion of a business". This thesis will therefore use the term private equity to include investments of all financing stages – seed, start-up, expansion and buyout.

[29] See for example Bygrave/Timmons (1992), Fried/Hisrich (1988), Gompers/Lerner (1999b), MacMillan et al. (1985), Sahlman (1990), Sweeting (1991), Tyebjee/Bruno (1984), Wright/Robbie (1998).

[30] "Both invest funds on behalf of other institutions and although there is a degree of heterogeneity in the forms they take, both are often, especially in the US, organized as limited partnerships. Both cases involve relationship investment with management, managerial compensation is oriented towards equity and there are likely to be severe penalties for underperformance" (Wright/Robbie (1998), p. 532). Given the similarities mentioned, above all the organizational form, it seems reasonable that the sequence of investment process steps will be similar for private equity firms investing in early/expansion stage and later stage portfolio

Tyebjee and Bruno were among the first researchers to develop a model of the investment process of private equity firms, including five sequential steps: deal origination, deal screening, deal evaluation, deal structuring and post-investment activities.[31] Fried and Hisrich enlarged this view by adding the creation of the private equity firm and the liquidation of its investments to the investment process.[32] Wright and Robbie included feedback loops.[33] Gompers and Lerner then created the idea of the private equity investment process as a continuous, multidimensional cycle:[34]

- Raising of funds: In this phase general partners acquire capital from limited partners, primarily institutional investors such as pension funds and insurance companies.[35]

- Deal generation: within this phase viable investment opportunities are explored that can be funded at acquisition prices generating the target rate of return.[36]

- Screening: portfolio companies are selected from available investment opportunities in a two-stage process:[37]
  - First, investment opportunities are matched with pre-defined screening criteria.
  - Second, investment opportunities are investigated in depth and a valuation is made.

- Approval and structuring: structuring a deal involves contract negotiations with all parties involved in a certain deal, e.g. other equity investors, banks or the management team.[38]

- Post-investment: after all relevant contracts are signed, both investor and management team start working on increasing the value of the portfolio company.[39]

---

companies. However, there will be a difference with regard to the type of enterprise they invest in, the relationship between investor and investee and the financing structure (see Sahlman (1990), pp. 473ff; Achleitner/Fingerle (2003), pp.3ff; Brinkrolf (2002), p. 13; Graf et al. (2001), pp. 25f; Kraft (2001), p. 45; Schefczyk (2000), p. 37; Sahlman (1990), p. 479). As a consequence, the execution of individual process steps will be significantly different. Therefore, an abstract description of the investment process steps will be chosen.

[31] See Tyebjee/Bruno (1984), pp. 1051ff.
[32] See Fried/Hisrich (1988), pp. 23f.
[33] See Wright/Robbie (1998), p. 536.
[34] See Gompers/Lerner (1999b). The description of the individual stages of the investment process will be biased towards the limited partnership that has been identified as the dominant organizational form of venture capital firms. However, most of the stages of the investment process will be identical for different organizational forms.
[35] See Fried/Hisrich (1992), pp. 29f; Hagenmüller (2004), pp. 1ff; Lerner (2000), p. 146; Schröder (1992), p. 122-125. It may be discussed, whether establishing the investment firm or raising a new fund is the beginning of the investment process. In literature, fundraising is usually regarded as the beginning of the investment process (see Brettel (forthcoming), p. 83).
[36] While practitioners are aware of the importance of deal generation, so far only limited research has been conducted in this field (see Bygrave/Timmons (1992), pp. 13f; Murray (1995), pp. 1077ff.; Wright/Robbie (1998), p. 536).
[37] See Korsukéwitz (1975), pp. 39-155; Pichotta (1990), pp. 35-154; Wright/Robbie (1999), pp. 14ff; Brettel (2002), pp. 305ff; Cullinan et al. (2004), pp. 96ff.
[38] See Fried/Hisrich (1988), p. 24; Norton/Tenenbaum (1992), pp. 20ff; Trester (1998), pp. 675ff; Kaplan/Strömberg (2003), pp. 281ff; Brettel et al. (2004), pp. 431ff.
[39] The post-investment phase is discussed in detail in chapter 2.2.4.

- Exiting the investment: investors sell their equity stake in order to realize capital gains or losses.[40]
- Return capital to investors: after liquidating investments, capital is returned to investors, whereby profits are shared among general and limited partners as determined in the partnership agreement.

Apart from the perspective of the firm/the entrepreneur and the intermediary, entrepreneurial finance in a broader sense also includes the perspective of the investor. Research on the perspective of the investor can be structured along the asset management investment process.[41] So far, the perspective of the investor has not been analyzed comprehensively in the context of entrepreneurial finance. In general, the asset management investment process is made up of four steps:[42]

- Research generates information as input for portfolio management decisions.
- An asset management strategy is formulated specifying a combination of assets resulting in the best possible risk/return tradeoff.
- The asset management strategy is implemented either through an index oriented management style (passive) or a management style with the goal to outperform the index (active).
- The performance of the asset management strategy is measured by comparing the risk/return profile of the portfolio with the relevant index.

Given the interrelatedness of many questions in the field of entrepreneurial finance, Achleitner suggests adopting the broader definition of entrepreneurial finance, covering the perspectives of the portfolio company/entrepreneur, the perspective of the intermediary and the perspective of the investor as shown in figure 1.[43]

---

[40] See Barry et al. (1990), pp. 447ff; Barry (1994), pp. 3ff; Prester (2002), pp. 1ff.
[41] See Achleitner (2001), p. 15.
[42] See von Maltzan (2000), pp. 860ff; Mössle (2000), pp. 872ff. Whenever necessary, references to the specifics of the private equity asset class shall be given.
[43] See Achleitner (2001), p. 15.

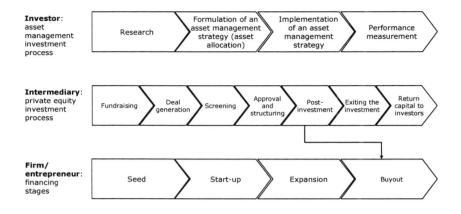

Investor: asset management investment process

| Research | Formulation of an asset management strategy (asset allocation) | Implementation of an asset management strategy | Performance measurement |

Intermediary: private equity investment process

| Fundraising | Deal generation | Screening | Approval and structuring | Post-investment | Exiting the investment | Return capital to investors |

Firm/ entrepreneur: financing stages

| Seed | Start-up | Expansion | Buyout |

Figure 1: The three dimensions of entrepreneurial finance.[44]

This doctoral dissertation fits into the three dimensions of entrepreneurial finance as follows: the perspective of the intermediary is analyzed with respect to one step of the investment process – the post-investment phase. The post-investment phase is, however, not analyzed for all possible financing stages. Given the differences between individual financing stages mentioned above, this thesis will focus exclusively on portfolio companies in the buyout financing stage.

2.2 Definitions

Analyzing academic literature on the value addition of private equity firms to their portfolio companies, it becomes quickly clear that there is no one and only definition for the terms defined in the following. Nevertheless it will be attempted to contrast different researchers' definitions and to give a clear idea of what aspects of the presented definitions are relevant for this thesis.

2.2.1 Private Equity Firm

Private equity firms are usually defined as intermediaries between investors and companies looking for capital. As an intermediary, private equity firms serve three main functions:[45]

---

[44] Based on Achleitner (2001), p. 16. See von Maltzan (2000), pp. 860ff and Mössle (2000), pp. 872ff for an overview of the asset management investment process; Gompers/Lerner (1999b), pp. 1ff discuss the private equity investment process as a continuous, multidimensional cycle; see Sahlman (1990), p. 479 for the private equity financing stages of a firm.

1. Investment function for investors.
2. Financing function for portfolio companies.
3. Control and support function for portfolio companies

Private equity firms can be segmented along three dimensions – first of all by the sources of their funds:[46]

- Independent private equity firms are organizations not connected with the investors supplying their funds other than occasionally via minority shareholdings. Examples of independent private equity firms are Apax Partners, Bain Capital, Kohlberg Kravis Roberts, Permira or the Texas Pacific Group.
- Captive private equity firms raise their capital from their main shareholder. Shareholders are typically investment banks or insurance companies. Examples of captive private equity firms are Allianz Private Equity Partners, Barclays Private Equity or Morgan Stanley Capital Partners.
- Semi-captive private equity firms raise their capital from both a main shareholder and outside investors. An example for a semi-captive private equity firm is EQT that has raised its capital both from its main shareholder, the Wallenberg family, and from outside investors.
- Public private equity firms raise funds mainly from public sources or publicly held companies. Examples for public private equity firms are Invest Northern Ireland or Mittelständische Beteiligungsgesellschaft Hessen.

From the private equity firm segments mentioned above, all but public private equity firms are taken into account in this thesis. Public private equity firms are neglected, as they have as primary objective the promotion of employment or of the economy in general as opposed to realizing capital gains.[47]

Second, private equity firms can be segmented by their specialization on certain deals:[48]

- Region: most private equity firms start focusing on individual countries. Although the process of internationalization is cumbersome, many firms have been successful in es-

---

[45] See Bader (1996), p. 17; Kraft (2001), p. 39. Bader and Kraft mention a total of five main functions of private equity firms. Unfortunately those five main functions are not mutually exclusive. First, the screening and valuation function for private equity investments is part of the overall investment function for investors. In order to adequately allocate their investors' funds, private equity firms have to screen and evaluate potential investment opportunities. Second, the liquidation function to realize capital gains is part of the overall investment function for investors as well. Private equity firms have to exit their investments in order to realize capital gains and return all funds to their investors.

[46] See Schefczyk (2000), p. 17. A detailed description of individual segments can be found in Temple (1999), p. 58.

[47] See Reißig-Thust (2003), pp. 25f.

[48] Specialization strategies are discussed by Norton/Tenenbaum (1993), pp. 431ff.

11

tablishing a European-wide or even worldwide presence.[49] The focus of this study is on European deals.

- Industry: the European Venture Capital Association (EVCA) differentiates 17 industry sectors as possible specializations of private equity firms: communications, computer related, other electronic related, biotechnology, medical/health related, energy, consumer related, industrial products and services, chemicals and materials, industrial automation, other manufacturing, transportation, financial services, other services, agriculture, construction and other.[50] This study has no limitations with regard to industry sectors.

- Financing stage: as shown above, seed, start-up, expansion and buyout financing are distinguished. The focus of this study is on buyout financing. Other financing stages are not taken into account.

- Deal size: private equity firms handle a considerable spectrum of deal sizes: on the one hand, investments of less than €100.000 are not uncommon in seed and start-up finance. On the other hand, billion dollar buyouts are not unheard of. More often than not, deal size will increase from seed to buyout financing stages.[51] Within buyout financing, no limitation with regard to deal size was made.

Third, private equity firms can be segmented by the degree of their involvement in portfolio companies. Two generic strategies have been described in venture capital contexts: hands-on firms are characterized by an overall high involvement in their portfolio companies, whereas hands-off firms can be recognized by their laissez faire attitude towards portfolio companies.[52] Private equity firms with all of the above-mentioned management styles are researched in this study.

Independent of private equity firms' sources of funds, specialization or involvement in portfolio companies, most private equity firms are organized in the legal form of limited partnership (see figure 2).[53] It is important to discuss the legal setup of private equity firms due to the powerful incentives associated. A limited partnership has two types of partners: the private equity firm serves as general partner, takes the risk of raising funds and takes full responsibility and liability for managing the private equity fund. In return for organizing the private equity partnership and contributing a small percentage of the fund's total capital (typically

---

[49]   Dixit/Jayaraman (2001), pp. 40ff discuss three internationalization strategies adopted by private equity firms: organic growth, affiliates and specialized funds.
[50]   See EVCA (2003), pp. 291-293.
[51]   See Bygrave/Timmons (1992), p. 16.
[52]   See Cohen (1985), pp. 37-39; Sweeting/Wong (1997), pp. 125ff; Kümmerle et al. (1998), p. 27.
[53]   See Bygrave/Timmons (1992), p. 10; Wright/Robbie (1998), p. 532; Gompers/Lerner (1999a), p. 6.

1%),[54] private equity firms receive as a fixed component an annual management fee (typically 2%)[55] and as a variable component a significant part of the capital gains realized on investments (typically 20%), called carried interest.[56] The performance-based variable compensation creates strong incentives for general partners to realize capital gains on their investments. However, general partners are kept from taking excessive risks. Having to commit capital to the fund – often representing a significant part of their personal net wealth – general partners will carefully balance risk and return of potential investments.

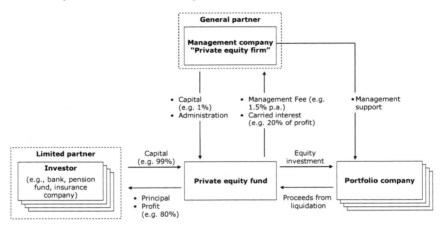

Figure 2: Legal setup of a private equity partnership[57]

Institutional investors (banks, corporate or public pension funds, insurance companies, endowments or foundations and non-financial corporations) or high net worth families and individuals are the limited partners.[58] In order to retain their limited liability status, limited partners may not become involved in day-to-day fund management. Limited partners contribute the majority of the fund's capital (typically 99%) and receive in exchange, besides the principal committed to the fund, a major part of the capital gains realized on investments (typically 80%).

Private equity funds have a "finite life of about ten years, which may be extended by up to two years with the consent of the majority of the shareholders",[59] after which all the investments made have to be realized and principal as well as capital gains distributed among lim-

---

54 Sahlman (1990), p. 488 reports that general partners typically contribute about 1% of the capital raised by a fund, the remaining 99% being contributed by limited partners.
55 During the first years of a limited partnership, total capital committed is the basis for the calculation of the management fee. After four to five years the basis for the calculation of the management fee is changed. Then capital invested forms the basis for the calculation of the management fee (see Barger (2002), pp. 3-4).
56 See Gompers/Lerner (1999a), pp. 14ff; Barger (2002), p. 2.
57 See Bilo (2002), p. 20.
58 See Fenn et al. (1997), pp. 70ff.
59 Gottschalg et al. (2003), p. 32 ; see also Gompers/Lerner (1999a), p. 6; Barger (2002), p. 2.

ited and general partners. Private equity firms often manage more than one private equity fund concurrently, "raising a new fund three to five years after the closing [...] of the fund-raising process for the previous fund".[60]

Concluding, private equity firms are defined as intermediaries between investors and companies looking for capital. Private equity firms can be segmented by the sources of their funds, their specialization and their involvement in portfolio companies. This study focuses on independent, semi-captive or captive private equity firms that engage in buyout financing in Europe. The most common legal setup of a private equity firm is the limited partnership creating strong incentives for general partners to add value to their portfolio companies.

2.2.2 Buyout

Buyouts are not a recent phenomenon in Europe. The origins of buyouts in Europe go back to the United Kingdom before World War II: "In 1931 the Macmillan Committee was set up to investigate the then economic malaise. Among other things, it looked at why small and medium sized businesses in the United Kingdom (UK) found it so hard to access capital. While the committee, whose members included such notables as John Maynard Keynes, spent much of its time considering international trade and the problems of the Gold Standard, it did also conclude that there was a funding gap that needed to be addressed by the government. Two organizations, Finance and Capital for Industry (FCI) and the Industrial and Commercial Finance Corporation (ICFC) were eventually set up immediately after the war as a result of this initiative. FCI was intended to lend larger amounts, and to play a part in the restructuring of key industries, while ICFC [...] was to address the funding needs of smaller companies."[61] It was, however, not before the 1990s that buyout investing took off in Europe. During the 1990s several large US buyout funds entered Europe, spurring an unprecedented growth of buyout investments from €1,5B in 1990 to €16,9B in 2002.[62]

Buyouts are typically defined on the basis of the following characteristics: private investors, including a specialist private equity firm, members of the management team[63] and sometimes also employees buy a significant equity stake[64] in a company or subsidiary of a company. Whereas the private equity firm typically acquires enough equity to control the company,

---

[60] Gottschalg et al. (2003), pp. 32-33. For a detailed description of the legal form of limited partnership as form of private equity firm organization see Bilo (2002), pp. 19ff.

[61] Temple (1999), pp. 20-21.

[62] As an example, two of the most prestigious US buyout firms, Kohlberg Kravis Roberts and Texas Pacific Group, entered Europe in 1995 and 1996 with the acquisition of the Italian motorcycle manufacturer Ducati and the acquisition of the British newspaper company Reed Regional Newspapers, respectively (see n. a. (1996), p. B5; n. a. (1995), p. B2). Regarding the magnitude of buyout investments in Europe see EVCA (1997), p. 83; EVCA (2003), p. 66.

[63] See Easterwood et al. (1989), p. 30.

[64] See Wright et al. (1993), p. 90 and Achleitner/Fingerle (2003), p. 3.

management team and employees will hold minority stakes.[65] Private investors will cover, however, only part of the purchasing price, borrowing the rest from "banks and from buyers of subordinated public debt, which in the 1980s became known as junk bonds"[66]. The private equity firm professional is an active investor,[67] "who actually monitors management, sits on boards, is sometimes involved in dismissing management, is often intimately involved in the strategic direction of the company, and on occasion even manages"[68]. In order to be able to realize capital gains from their investments, private investors have a limited time horizon,[69] typically three to five years,[70] after which they intend to exit their investment based on a pre-specified exit strategy.

Buyouts can be segmented along two dimensions: the composition of the private investor group and the original shareholders' rationale for selling shares to private investors.[71]

First, the different buyout typologies according to the composition of the private investor group shall be discussed. The most frequent form of a buyout is the management buyout (MBO), in which incumbent management acquires a firm's equity alongside the private equity firm. More precisely, "an MBO is the purchase of the firm by a group of normally four to six senior managers who are already employed in the business, typically using their own funds plus external private equity and bank loans."[72] Occasionally, the private equity firm replaces management. In this so-called management buyin (MBI), replacement management will participate in the equity of the firm.[73]

If a significant number of employees invest in their company's equity alongside management and the private equity firm, this is the case of an employee buyout (EBO) or management and employee buyout (MEBO).[74]

An owner buyout (OBO) is characterized by an incomplete transfer of a company's equity to private investors. This enables prior owners of a company to sell part of their equity holdings and thereby diversify their personal wealth, while at the same time participating with their remaining equity holding in the company's future success.[75]

---

[65] See Shleifer/Vishny (1997), p. 766. The equity stake of the management team represents frequently a significant part of their personal wealth. See Koch (1997), p. 20.
[66] Shleifer/Vishny (1997), p. 766. See also Wright et al. (1994), p. 216 and Bruton et al. (2002), p. 709. Buyout transactions involving significant leverage are also termed Leveraged Buyout (LBO), with debt making up for up to 90% of the total deal value (see Schmid (1994), pp. 38f; Then Bergh (1998), p. 8).
[67] See Robbie et al. (1992), p. 445ff, Robbie/Wright (1996), pp. 1ff and Wright et al. (1994), pp. 215ff.
[68] Jensen (1989), p. 64.
[69] See Achleitner/Fingerle (2003), p. 3.
[70] See Rogers et al. (2002a), pp. 206ff, Rogers et al. (2002b), pp. 6ff and Rogers et al. (2002c) pp. 94ff.
[71] See Achleitner/Fingerle (2003), pp. 8ff.
[72] Howorth et al. (2004), p. 511.
[73] See Berger (1993), p. 13; Robbie/Wright (1996), p. 5; Howorth et al. (2004), p. 511.
[74] See Schwenkedel (1991), p. 12; Berger (1993), p. 14; Vest (1995), p. 17; Koch (1997), p. 26.
[75] See Hoffmann/Ramke (1992), pp. 29f; Becker (2000), p. 11.

15

An institutional buyout (IBO) occurs, when a private equity firm takes the initiative to acquire a company, without prior involvement of internal or external management.[76]

Concluding the segmentation of buyouts based on the composition of the private investor group, it is important to note that real world buyouts will not always fit in only one of the above-mentioned categories. For the purposes of this thesis, all of the above-mentioned buyout typologies – as well as possible sub-typologies – are taken into account.

Second, buyout typologies according to the original shareholders' rationale for selling shares shall be discussed.

Many family owned businesses face the problem of managerial and ownership succession. More often than not a successor is chosen from the ranks of the family, in order to continue leading the business according to family tradition. Whenever there is no family internal solution to managerial and ownership succession, several options arise: in the case of unclear ownership succession, the family could transfer their shares to a charity. In the case of unclear managerial succession, the family could either retain the shares of their business and hire external management or alternatively simply sell all or part of their shareholdings. When selling shares, a succession buyout may be an attractive option, as the family might retain part of their shareholdings while at the same time having the benefit of a private equity firm's expertise.[77]

Spin-off buyouts occur, if diversified corporations focus on their core businesses.[78] In this case, a non-core business may be bought out by incumbent management with the help of the muscle of a buyout specialist.

If a company is sold to a private equity fund because it is on the verge of bankruptcy or even in bankruptcy proceedings, this is the case of a turnaround buyout.[79]

A privatization buyout occurs if a state-owned company is sold to private buyout investors. Two completely different types of privatization buyouts have to be differentiated. On the one hand, there is the privatization of state-owned companies by free market economies. In this case, a privatization buyout is carried out in order to reduce public budget deficits.[80] On the other hand, state-owned firms may be privatized as part of a transition from communist regimes to free market economies.[81]

---

[76] See Haynes et al. (2002), p. 220.
[77] See Koch (1997), p. 32.
[78] For a detailed discussion of firms' core business see Zook/Allen (2001).
[79] See Jacoby (2000), pp. 42f. An excellent overview of turnaround investments is given by Kraft (2001), pp. 94ff.
[80] See Leibenstein (1966), pp. 412f.
[81] See Gros (1998), p. 116 for the case of Germany after reunification.

Achleitner and Fingerle also consider the going private buyout – where all outstanding shares of company listed on a stock exchange are bought out – as a separate buyout type according to the original shareholders' rationale for selling shares.[82]

For the purposes of this thesis all but one of the above-mentioned buyout types according to the original shareholders' rationale for selling shares are taken into account. Privatization buyouts as a result of the transition from communist regimes to free market economies are not included in this study, as the situation of such firms with respect to tangible and intangible assets as well as resources available will be very different from companies in free market economies.

2.2.3   Value Addition

In order to define value addition in the context of this thesis, it has to be clarified first, from whose perspective value addition will be analyzed, second, what the substance and third, what the individual levers of value addition are.[83]

The goal of any organization is to create value for its stakeholders which is subsequently distributed.[84] A variety of individuals or groups can influence an organization or are affected by its entrepreneurial success or failure. Those individuals or groups are called stakeholders.[85] Stakeholders of an organization include equity holders, management, employees, customers, competitors, suppliers, unions, states or countries and interest groups.[86] Since this thesis is intended to help private equity firms to be more successful in the post-investment phase of their investments, only the influence of private equity firms and the resulting value added or deducted for them will be taken into account.[87]

Value is created, if "payments" from a company to the stakeholder exceed "payments" from the stakeholder to the company. Payments can be both material and immaterial. Material payments are for example employee wages; immaterial payments on the other hand are for example power or status of managers.[88] Given that the success of private equity firms, defined above as the relevant stakeholder, and their investments is measured by material payments, only those will be taken into account. Private equity firms are therefore defined as creating value, if their cash inflows from dividends and portfolio company sale or liquidation proceeds

---

[82]   See Achleitner/Fingerle (2003), p. 10.
[83]   For the purposes of this thesis, the terms value addition and value creation will be used interchangeably.
[84]   See Jost (1998), p. 16.
[85]   See Freeman (1984), p. 25.
[86]   See Jost (1998), p. 17.
[87]   Value added to buyouts from bondholders' perspective has been analyzed by Kaplan (1988), pp. 85ff; Marais et al. (1989), pp. 155ff; Asquith/Wizman (1990), pp. 195ff. Kaplan (1988), pp. 82ff, Wright et al. (1992), p. 64 and Gräper (1993), pp. 139ff. examine value added to buyout from employees' perspective. Finally, value added to buyout from tax authorities' perspective has been studied by Kaplan (1988), pp. 48ff; Kaplan (1989), pp. 611ff; Jensen et al. (1989), pp. 727ff.
[88]   See Jost (1998), p. 16.

exceed their cash outflows from equity investment and transaction costs such as fees for consultants, lawyers, accountants as well as bank and equity arrangement fees and the opportunity cost of capital.

However, financial intermediaries such as private equity firms play no role in perfect capital markets: "when markets are perfect and complete, the allocation of resources is Pareto efficient and there is no scope for intermediaries to improve welfare. Moreover, the Modigliani-Miller theorem applied in this context asserts that financial structure does not matter: households can construct portfolios which offset any position taken by an intermediary and intermediation cannot create value."[89]

Such an extreme view is clearly contradicting what is observed in practice. Funds raised by private equity firms in Europe have grown in the last decade at a compounded annual growth rate in excess of 20% to a total of €27.5 billion in 2002. This means that there have to be frictions in capital markets that explain the existence of private equity firms as financial intermediaries. Theories of intermediation suggest "that it is frictions such as transaction costs and asymmetric information that are important in understanding intermediation."[90] Transaction costs are for example "fixed costs of asset evaluation [meaning] that intermediaries have an advantage over individuals because they allow such costs to be shared. Similarly, trading costs mean that intermediaries can more easily be diversified than individuals."[91] Private equity firms face marked transaction costs. As mentioned above the acquisition and sale of a portfolio company is associated with sizeable transaction costs such as fees for banks or equity arrangement fees. Private equity firms as financial intermediaries have an advantage over individuals as the fixed costs of asset acquisition and sale can be spread on a significantly larger amount of capital. With regard to asymmetric information it has been argued that an intermediary can acquire information which is not publicly available at a cost suggesting that "if there are some economies of scale, one might expect organizations to exist which gather and sell information about particular classes of assets."[92] Especially at the acquisition of a portfolio company private equity firms invest significant amounts of money in consultants, accounts and lawyers to acquire non-publicly available information on their target. Again,

---

[89] Allen/Santomero (1997), p. 1462. See also Fama (1980), pp. 39ff. "Perfect capital markets [are] characterized by: (1) a large number of fully-informed buyers and sellers, no one of whom has the power to influence market prices; (2) the absence of market frictions such as taxes, fees, information-acquisition or other transactions costs; (3) unanimity of opinion concerning the future value of asset prices, interest rates, and other relevant economic factors (this assumption is often called 'homogeneous expectations'); (4) perfectly competitive product and factor markets that are always in equilibrium; and (5) costless and instantaneous market access for all potential buyers and sellers" (Megginson (1996), p. 3). For a discussion of the main properties of perfect capital markets see also Breuer (1998), pp. 62ff.

[90] Allen/Santomero (1997), p. 1463. For a literature survey on the theory of financial intermediation relating to banking see Bhattacharya/Thakor (1993). In the field of insurance Dionne (1991) provides a literature survey.

[91] Allen/Santomero (1997), p. 1463. The role of transaction costs has been stressed by Gurley/Shaw (1960) and many subsequent authors.

[92] Leland/Pyle (1977), p. 383.

individual investors are better off if an intermediary allows sharing such fixed costs of information acquisition. Besides the acquisition of information that is not publicly available, intermediaries have also been claimed to overcome asymmetric information problems by delegated monitoring. "An intermediary (such as a bank) is delegated the task of costly monitoring of [...] contracts written with firms who borrow from it. It has a gross cost advantage in collecting this information because the alternative is either duplication of effort if each lender monitors directly, or a free-rider problem, in which case no lender monitors."[93] Private equity firms are not only monitoring their portfolio companies – they are also said to work side by side with the management team on adding value to a portfolio company. Summarizing, private equity firms can add value to a portfolio company also from a theoretical point of view as a result of transaction costs and information asymmetries giving private equity firms a cost advantage over individual investors.

In order to identify the individual levers of value addition available to private equity firms, in the following a simple model of portfolio company value creation shall be discussed. In order not to complicate the discussion, costs incurred by the private equity firm to acquire information (such as fees for consultants, accounts and lawyers) and transaction costs (such as bank and equity arrangements fees) will not be included in the model. Moreover, the monitoring and support costs incurred by private equity firms will not be modeled. Assuming that a portfolio company earns an operating and investment cash flow C_1 at the end of year 1 and is able to perpetually grow its operating and investment cash flow at the rate g, the all-equity value of the portfolio company is $PV(all-equity) = \dfrac{C_1}{r-g}$ assuming an all-equity opportunity cost of capital of r.[94] Assuming further that a private equity firm acquires a portfolio company in year t and sells it in year T, the all-equity net present value ($NPV(all\text{-}equity)$) created during this time is: $NPV(all-equity) = -\dfrac{C_t}{r_t-g_t} + \dfrac{C_T}{r_T-g_T} \cdot \dfrac{1}{(1+r_{dt})^{T-t}}$.[95] However, buyouts are usually financed with significant levels of debt. The overall net present value (NPV) created has therefore to take into account the present value of financing side effects ($PV(fse)$) resulting in:

$$NPV = -\frac{C_t}{r_t-g_t} + \frac{C_T}{r_T-g_T} \cdot \frac{1}{(1+r_{dt})^{T-t}} + PV(fse).$$[96] Value added by a private equity firm can therefore be attributed to an increase of portfolio company operating and investment cash flows (C), an increase in the expected growth rate of cash flows (g), as short a holding period

---

93   Diamond (1984), p. 393.
94   See Brealey/Myers (2000), p. 40f.
95   See Brealey/Myers (2000), p. 41f.
96   Given that capital markets have been found above to be less than perfect value can be created from financing side effects. The approach to analyze the value created by financial maneuvers separately from the value cre-

(*T-t*) as possible, a decrease in the all-equity opportunity cost of capital (*r*) or financing side effects. Private equity firms planning to add value to their portfolio company during the post-investment phase will focus primarily on increasing a portfolio company's operations and investment cash flows as well as the expected growth rate of cash flows.[97] An increase in a portfolio company's operations and investment cash flows as well as the expected growth rate can be achieved by working with portfolio company management to transform a business, thereby finding ways to increase a portfolio company's net sales and operating margin, decrease its working capital and sell non-required assets. All else equal, the post-investment value creation by the private equity firm will be the higher the shorter the holding period needed to implement operational changes in the portfolio company. Unfortunately, the all-equity opportunity cost of capital will usually be out of reach for private equity firms. The all-equity opportunity cost of capital is approximated by calculating the return earned by investing in other assets with the same riskiness that the portfolio company would exhibit if it was financed entirely with equity. Given that a private equity firm will usually not be able to influence the riskiness of other assets, the all-equity opportunity cost of equity will be out of reach as a value creation lever. Financing side effects will also be out of reach for private equity firms during the post-investment phase. Financing side effects can be extracted from – but are not limited to – interest tax shields and costs of financial distress.[98] However, the magnitude of the interest tax shield and the risk of financial distress associated with borrowing is determined in negotiations with banks and other lenders during the deal structuring phase.

Summarizing, value creation will be discussed in this thesis from the perspective of private equity firms and taking into account only material payments. Private equity firms are defined to add value, if the proceeds from dividends and portfolio company sale or liquidation proceeds exceed their cash outflows from equity investment, information acquisition costs such as fees for consultants, lawyers, accountants as well as transactions costs such as bank and equity arrangement fees and the opportunity cost of capital. The value created or destroyed in a buyout is influenced by changes in a portfolio company's operating and investment cash flows (*C*), a change in the expected growth rate of cash flows (*g*), the holding period (*T-t*), a change in the opportunity cost of capital (*r*) or the present value of financing side effects. During the post-investment phase, private equity firms may add value by working with management on growing portfolio company cash flows, increasing expected growth rates of cash flows and trying to do all this in as short a holding period as possible.

---

ated by the operations of a company is called adjusted present value (APV). See e.g. Luehrman (1997), pp. 145ff and Brealey/Myers (2000), p. 572.

[97] A considerable number of studies has been able to observe statistically significant increases in cash flows of portfolio companies while being owned by private equity firms (see Bull (1989); Smith (1990); Opler (1992)).

[98] See Luehrman (1997), pp. 145ff.

2.2.4   Post-Investment Phase

The post-investment phase can be defined most precisely dynamically, i.e. by separating it from precursor and successor phases in an overarching investment process. As discussed in chapter 2.1, the investment process of private equity firms can be divided up into seven different phases: raising of funds, deal generation, screening, approval and structuring, post-investment, exiting the investment and finally returning capital to investors. The post-investment phase therefore starts after all contracts regarding a certain deal are signed and finishes upon the exit of the portfolio company.

During the post-investment phase, private equity firm and management team work jointly on adding value to the portfolio company. As mentioned above, only the contributions of private equity firms to the development of portfolio companies will be analyzed in this thesis. Private equity firms' interaction with portfolio company management has been analyzed by prior research along the following four dimensions:

- Activities: private equity firms involve actively in their portfolio companies rather than being passive observers.[99]

- Organization: private equity professionals are frequently non-executive members of the portfolio company's board of directors. Only rarely, private equity professionals are part of the management team.[100]

- Information systems: private equity firms' involvement is based to a large degree on the management information provided by the portfolio company. Therefore private equity firms take an active role in tailoring portfolio companies' information systems to their needs. That said, information systems of portfolio companies are frequently a stumbling block in the relationship between private equity professionals and portfolio company management.[101]

- Resources: private equity professionals have a considerable skill base. However, the personnel base of private equity firms is very small: as an example, one of the largest private equity firms, Clayton Dubilier & Rice, managing a fund in excess of $3,5 billion, employs as little as 25 professionals. As a result, private equity firms have to supplement their management capacity by leveraging external resources such as man-

---

[99]   See MacMillan et al. (1989), pp. 27ff; Sapienza/Timmons (1989), pp. 245ff and Sapienza (1992), pp. 9ff; Landström (1990), pp. 345ff; Fredriksen et al. (1991), pp. 435ff and Fredriksen et al. (1997), pp. 503ff; Barney et al. (1996), pp. 257ff; Sapienza et al. (1996), pp. 439ff; Sweeting/Wong (1997), pp. 125ff; Fried et al. (1998), pp. 493ff; Schefczyk/Gerpott (1998), pp. 143ff and Schefczyk (2000), pp. 300ff; Brinkrolf (2002), pp. 139ff; Ruppen (2002), pp. 167ff; Reißig-Thust (2003), pp. 139ff; Busenitz et al. (2004), pp. 787ff.
[100]   See Rosenstein et al. (1993), pp. 99ff; Fried/Hisrich (1995), pp. 101ff; Schefczyk/Gerpott (1998), p. 158 and Schefczyk (2000), pp. 300ff; Reißig-Thust (2003), p. 204ff.
[101]   See Sapienza/Timmons (1989), pp. 245ff and Sapienza (1992), pp. 9ff; Barney et al. (1996), pp. 257ff; Schefczyk/Gerpott (1998), pp. 143ff and Schefczyk (2000), pp. 300ff; Ruppen (2002), pp. 160ff; KPMG/Manchester Business School (2002), pp. 3ff; Reißig-Thust (2003), pp. 197ff.

agement consultants, interim managers, industry experts, CEOs of other portfolio companies and executive search firms.[102]

2.3 Conclusion

This thesis belongs to the entrepreneurial finance stream of research in business administration. Research in this field can be structured along three dimensions: the perspective of the investor in private equity, the private equity firm and the recipient of private equity – the firm or the entrepreneur. This thesis analyzes the perspective of the private equity firm with respect to one step of the investment process: the post-investment phase. The post-investment phase is analyzed, however, only for investments that are part of the buyout financing stage.

The subject of this thesis is European private equity firms' post-investment value addition to buyouts, i.e. European private equity firms specializing in buyout investments will be taken into account with the exception of public private equity firms – they are not necessarily focusing on realizing capital gains on their investments. Moreover all forms of buyouts are included in this study despite privatization buyouts resulting from the transition of communist regimes to free market economies – the situation of firms from communist regimes will be significantly different from the situation of free market economy firms. Regarding value creation during the post-investment phase, private equity firms may add value by working with management on growing portfolio company cash flows, increasing expected growth rates of cash flows and trying to do all this in as short a holding period as possible. Value creation by private equity firms has been researched for the post-investment phase along the dimensions of private equity firm activities, organization of the relationship between private equity firm and portfolio company, information systems used and internal as well as external resources committed by private equity firms. All of the dimensions mentioned will be analyzed by this study.

---

[102] See Kraft (2001), pp. 256ff for private equity firms' usage of external resources and Burgel/Murray (2000), KPMG/Manchester Business School (2002), pp. 4ff, De Clercq/Sapienza (2002); Kaplan/Schoar (2003), pp. 13f for information on the skills of private equity professionals.

3 Framework for Structuring the Analysis of Post-Investment Value Addition to Buyouts

In this chapter, a suitable framework for analyzing post-investment value addition will be chosen. The process adopted works as follows. First, all frameworks used so far for the analysis of post-investment value addition will be evaluated with regard to their usefulness in structuring the problem in question. Post-investment value addition of private equity firms to their portfolio companies has been analyzed by researchers along the dimensions of private equity firm activities, organization of the relationship between private equity firm and portfolio company, information systems used and internal as well as external resources committed by private equity firms.[103] Second, a framework will be chosen that covers all of the above-mentioned dimensions of analysis. Third, the applicability of the framework will be discussed by matching its definition and assumptions with the specifics of the relationship between private equity firm and portfolio company.

3.1 Evaluation of Frameworks Used for the Analysis of Post-Investment Value Addition by Private Equity Firms

Analyzing studies on post-investment value addition by private equity firms, it is striking that most studies do not base their research on any form of analytical framework. The most popular frameworks for analyzing post-investment value addition by private equity firms belong to the new institutional economics[104] stream of research and the knowledge-based view. The neoclassical financing theory was mentioned by two studies as the major antagonist of new institutional economics. Rarely used was the corporate governance view, procedural justice theory and investment controlling. In the following, each of the frameworks mentioned will be briefly discussed with regard to its key assumptions, most important message and finally its suitability for structuring post-investment value addition by private equity firms.[105]

---

[103] See chapter 2.2.4.
[104] For an introduction see Coase (1984); Williamson (1985). The theories belonging to the "new institutional economics" stream are the property-rights, transaction cost and principal agent theory.
[105] The number of studies using certain frameworks as a basis for structuring research on post-investment value addition by private equity firms is shown in figure 3.

Theories used by studies on post-investment value addition

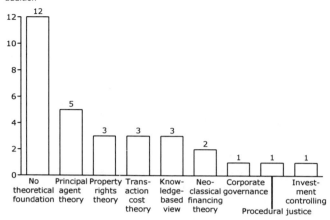

Figure 3: Number of studies using certain frameworks as a basis for researching post-investment value addition by private equity firms.[106]

3.1.1 Neoclassical Financing Theory

Neoclassical financing theory is a consequence of variations around one theme: perfect capital markets.[107] According to Schmidt three fundamental theories belong to this stream of research:[108] the Modigliani and Miller propositions, the capital asset pricing model and the efficient market hypothesis.

Modigliani and Miller state in their first proposition that "the market value of any firm is independent of its capital structure"[109]. From their first proposition it can be derived that "the expected yield of a share of stock is equal to the appropriate capitalization rate p_k [expected rate of return of any share in class k] for a pure equity stream in the class, plus a premium related to financial risk equal to the debt-to-equity ratio times the spread between p_k and r [rate of interest for sure streams]."[110] On the basis of proposition I and II, Modigliani and Miller derive a rule for the optimal investment policy of a company (proposition III): "the cut-

[106] This chart was composed based on the studies of MacMillan et al. (1989); Sapienza/Timmons (1989) and Sapienza (1992); Landström (1990); Fredriksen et al. (1991) and Fredriksen et al. (1997); Rosenstein et al. (1993); Fried/Hisrich (1995); Barney et al. (1996); Sapienza et al. (1996); Sweeting/Wong (1997); Fried et al. (1998); Schefczyk/Gerpott (1998) and Schefczyk (2000); Burgel/Murray (2000); Kraft (2001); Brinkrolf (2002); Ruppen (2002); KPMG/Manchester Business School (2002); De Clercq/Sapienza (2002); Kaplan/Schoar (2003); Reißig-Thust (2003); Busenitz et al. (2004). Several studies use more than one theoretical concept as basis of their studies.

[107] See Schmidt (1985), p. 423. For a discussion of the main properties of perfect capital markets see Breuer (1998), pp. 62ff.

[108] See Schmidt (1985), pp. 423ff.

[109] Modigliani/Miller (1958), p. 268.

off point for investment in the firm will in all cases be p_k and will be completely unaffected by the type of security used to finance the investment."[111] Optimal investment policies as outlined in proposition III help private equity firms when evaluating an investment proposal regarding a portfolio company. Once a private equity firm has made a decision to acquire a portfolio company, propositions I and II may help in structuring financing.[112] The evaluation of investment proposals and structuring financing is, however, part of the approval and structuring phase, which is not in the focus of this thesis. Modigliani and Miller's theories are therefore not appropriate for analyzing post-investment value addition to buyouts.

The capital asset pricing model "implies that the distribution of expected rates of return across all risky assets is a linear function of a single variable, namely, each asset's sensitivity to or covariance with the market portfolio, the famous beta, which becomes the natural measure of a security's risk"[113]. Similarly to portfolio selection theory, the capital asset pricing model is helpful for private equity firms primarily for portfolio construction purposes in the approval and structuring phase. The capital asset pricing model is therefore unsuitable for analyzing post-investment value addition to buyouts.

The efficient market hypothesis developed by Fama "presents both a statistical and a conceptual definition of an efficient capital market, where efficiency is defined in terms of the speed and completeness with which capital markets incorporate relevant information into security prices."[114] Fama distinguishes three degrees of market efficiency: First, in a weak form efficient market, current prices incorporate all relevant historical information. Second, in a semi-strong form efficient market, current prices reflect all relevant publicly available information. And third, in a strong form efficient market current prices reflect all relevant information – public and private.[115] The implication of the efficient market hypothesis is that market prices can be trusted, as competition among traders results in security prices that adequately reflect all relevant information. Although "this hypothesis has provided the theoretical underpinnings for the worldwide shift towards greater reliance on market-oriented economic policies and on

---

[110] Modigliani/Miller (1958), p. 271.
[111] See Modigliani/Miller (1958), p. 289.
[112] Modigliani and Miller derived their proposition I - which would make capital structure considerations pointless - under the assumption of no taxes. Deductibility of interest payments "can lead, as we showed in our 1963 article, to substantial gains from leveraging under some conditions, and gains of this tax-driven kind have undoubtedly figured both in the rise of corporate debt ratios generally in the 1980's and in some recent LBOs and voluntary restructurings in particular. But after netting out the offsetting tax costs of leveraged capital structures (such as those discussed in my paper 'debt and taxes' (1977) and its follow-up literature), tax savings alone cannot plausibly account for the observed LBO premiums" Miller (1991), p. 480.
[113] Miller (1999), pp. 97-98. The capital asset pricing model is attributed to Sharpe (1964); Lintner (1965); Mossin (1966).
[114] Megginson (1996), p. 13.
[115] See Fama (1970), pp. 383 with regard to the theoretical and statistical foundations and Fama (1991), pp. 1575ff for a survey of empirical studies testing these propositions.

capital market financing"[116], its usefulness to private equity firms seems to be limited and a potential application furthermore restricted to the approval and structuring as well as the exiting phase. The efficient market hypothesis is therefore not helpful for an analysis of the post-investment phase.

The realism of the assumptions of several of the above neoclassical financing theories has been subject to serious debate.[117] Given that, the main merit of neoclassical financing theories is their explanation of investment and financing decisions. Investment and financing decisions are, however, not in the focus of this study, as they belong to the approval and structuring phase of the private equity investment process. Neoclassical financing theory is therefore not suitable for structuring the analysis of post-investment value addition to buyouts.

3.1.2 Property Rights Theory

The property rights theory is a stream of research "characterized by a common emphasis on certain basic ideas concerning the interconnectedness of ownership rights, incentives, and economic behavior"[118]. Its assumptions about the human setting are:[119]

- Individuals are assumed to be rational individuals in the sense that they maximize their utility
- Individuals are assumed to be self-interested

Assumptions about the organizational setting are:

- Property rights define the right of an individual to deal with a good. Property rights can be divided up into four distinctive rights that may be held by different individuals: the right to use a good, the right to change form or substance of a good, the right to obtain income from a good and the right to sell a good[120]
- Property rights may either be held by a single individual or can be shared among several individuals[121]
- Transaction costs arise through the definition, exchange, policing or enforcement of property rights[122]

The property rights theory states that externalities may arise, if property rights are divided up among two or more individuals and property rights fail to account for harmful or beneficial effects between the parties or if there are difficulties in enforcing property rights. In this case,

---

[116] Megginson (1996), p. 15.
[117] See Schmidt (1985), pp. 424f for a discussion of the assumptions of the neoclassical financing theories in a private equity context.
[118] Furubotn/Pejovich (1972), p. 1137. For an introduction to the property rights theory see Coase (1937); Coase (1960); Alchian (1965); Demsetz (1967); Furubotn/Pejovich (1972).
[119] See Furubotn/Pejovich (1972), p. 1137.
[120] See Furubotn/Pejovich (1974), p. 4.
[121] See Demsetz (1967), pp. 347ff.
[122] See Demsetz (1964), pp. 11ff; Demsetz (1966), pp. 61ff.

an individual does not have to bear the entire social costs and benefits of his actions. As a result, positive or negative externalities may arise "which are neither compensated for on the market nor accumulated as costs for the individual in another manner"[123]. An optimal attribution of property rights therefore "requires a careful balancing of the marginal social costs and benefits from reducing externalities. Moreover, in making the cost-benefit calculations, due regard must be shown for the two-sidedness of the externality relation and for the initial structure of legal property rights."[124] More precisely, "from a property rights perspective, the most efficient property rights distribution is the one that minimizes the sum of transaction costs and the residual loss caused by negative external effects"[125]. Property rights theory therefore helps to answer how far an individual or the government should go with regard to the reduction of existing externalities.

With regard to post-investment value addition of private equity firms, property rights theory generates, due to its level of abstraction, some limited insight with regards to the level and organization of private equity firm involvement. The dimensions information systems as well as experience of private equity professionals and usage of external resources are not covered by the property rights theory. The property rights theory has, however, served as a methodological basis for developing the new institutional economics stream of research, or more precisely principal agent theory and transaction cost theory.[126]

3.1.3 Transaction Cost Theory

Transaction cost theory is closely related to property rights theory: it deals with the transfer of property rights between parties[127]. Transaction cost theory is different from property rights theory in so far that it focuses on explaining the transaction, not different kinds of property rights. Specific assumptions about the human setting are:

- Individuals are assumed to be rational in the sense that they optimize their utility.
- Individuals are assumed to behave opportunistically, i.e. showing "self-interest with guile"[128].
- Individuals are subject to bounded rationality, i.e. "individuals have neurophysiological and language limits which make them unable to store and process information without error and which also make it difficult for them, for example, to articulate their knowledge in ways that make it perfectly understandable to others"[129].

Specific assumptions about the organizational setting are:

---

[123]   Picot et al. (1997), p. 116.
[124]   Furubotn/Pejovich (1972), p. 1145.
[125]   Picot et al. (1997), p. 116.
[126]   See Schefczyk (2000), pp. 111-112.
[127]   For an introduction to transaction cost theory see the seminal work of Williamson (1975).
[128]   Williamson (1985), p. 47.
[129]   Mols (2000), p. 231; see also fundamentally Williamson (1975).

- The economic system is characterized by frictions or departures from perfection, giving rise to transaction costs.[130]
- Transactions may be governed by the market or integrated vertically by a firm so as to bring "in-house" the provision of a good or service.[131]

In order to determine whether the market or the firm should govern a transaction, the individual transaction has to be analyzed on the basis of three variables: frequency, uncertainty and asset specificity. These three variables determine, according to transaction cost theory, whether a transaction's costs will be lowest in the market or the firm.

The impact of transaction frequency on transaction costs is intuitive to understand. If a good or service is only rarely used, the cost of an investment related to this good or service will be too high to justify governing a transaction by the firm. Because transaction frequency seems to be so obvious, it is often excluded from detailed discussions of transaction cost theory. However, a high frequency of transactions is a necessary condition for coordinating a transaction by the firm.[132]

Uncertainty can be divided up into internal and external uncertainty.[133] External uncertainty is defined as the unpredictability of the external environment. Internal uncertainty arises, when an individual's performance cannot be determined by observing output measures. As a consequence of internal uncertainty, information asymmetries arise between transaction partners in the sense that one transaction partner has private information enabling him to take opportunistic actions. As countermeasures to opportunistic behavior, the performance of an individual may be measured on the basis of his inputs or trust may be developed between the transaction partners. Measuring inputs and the development of trust will lead to transaction costs being lowest in the firm.[134]

Asset specificity is generally regarded as the most important element in transaction cost theory.[135] Asset specificity refers to cases in which assets are only as valuable or much more valuable in the context of a specific transaction.[136] Six different kinds of asset specificity can be distinguished: site specificity, physical specificity, human assets specificity, brand name specificity and dedicated assets[137] as well as temporal specificity[138]. Assets specificity may give rise to strategic, opportunistic behavior: if a firm has invested in a transaction specific asset, its transaction partner may act opportunistically by paying a lower price than agreed for the good or service subject to transaction, given that the asset has no or much less value in the

[130] See Williamson (1985), p. 18.
[131] For a more detailed description see Williamson (1985), p. 52.
[132] See Mols (2000), p. 238.
[133] See Anderson/Gatignon (1986), pp. 1ff.
[134] See Ouchi (1979), pp. 833ff; Williamson (1985), pp. 211ff.
[135] See Alchian (1984), pp. 34ff.
[136] See Williamson (1979), p. 238.
[137] See Williamson (1991), pp. 269ff.
[138] See Masten et al. (1991), pp. 1ff.

context of another transaction. Therefore high asset specificity will result in transaction cost being lowest when governed by the firm.[139]

Summarizing, high frequency of transactions is a necessary condition for governing a transaction by the firm. Given high transaction frequency, the higher the internal uncertainty or asset specificity of a transaction, the higher the probability that transaction cost is lowest in firms.

Concluding, transaction cost theory helps to understand vertical integration or, more generally, problems that can be formulated in an internalization/externalization manner as a function of frequency, uncertainty and asset specificity of a transaction. Transaction cost theory may therefore help to understand the involvement of private equity firms as opposed to the usage of external resources as well as the organization of the relationship between private equity firm and portfolio company. However, there are no or only limited hints with regard to the dimensions performance of information systems and private equity professional experience.[140] Transaction cost theory covers therefore only three of the five dimensions of post-investment value addition of private equity firms to their portfolio companies.

3.1.4   Agency Theory

Agency theory is related to property rights theory in the sense that it deals with the transfer of property rights between parties and to transaction cost theory in the sense that it explains the transaction between two parties. However, agency theory focuses on a very specific kind of transfer of property rights: it models the relationship between a principal who delegates property rights to an agent. Agency theory can therefore be seen as the branch of property rights and transaction cost theory that is specialized on the delegation of property rights.[141]

Specifically, agency theory analyzes the relationship between a principal that has a task and an agent that is offered to execute the task. The process of interaction between principal and agent is well defined. A basic model will be presented in the following that will help to illustrate the ideas of agency theory: First, the principal offers a contract to the agent that specifies the job of the agent and the payments that the agent will get. Second, the potential agent decides whether to accept the contract. Third, if the agent decides to accept the contract, he works on the job as specified. Fourth, the agent either completes the job successfully or fails. Fifth, the agent receives the payment specified in the contract.[142]

In order to model the relationship between principal and agent, more specific assumptions have to be made. Specific assumptions about the human setting are:

---

[139]   See Picot et al. (1997), p. 109.
[140]   See Schefczyk (2000), p. 126.
[141]   See Schefczyk (2000), p. 113.
[142]   See Sappington (1991), p. 47; Jost (1998), p. 281. For an introduction to agency theory see Ross (1973); Jensen/Meckling (1976); Rees (1985).

- Principal and agent are assumed to be rational individuals in the sense that they maximize their respective utility while interacting with each other.
- Frequently the principal is assumed to be risk neutral whereas the agent is assumed to be risk averse.[143]
- Both principal and agent are assumed to be self-interested.[144]

Specific assumptions of agency theory about the organizational setting are:

- There is a goal conflict between the principal and the agent in the sense that the agent suffers from disutilities when choosing the actions preferred by the principal.[145]
- There is an information asymmetry between principal and agent in the sense that the agent has private information enabling him to take actions having negative externalities for the principal.[146]

Agency theory states that given the structure of interaction and the assumptions about the human and the organizational setting mentioned above, three agency conflicts arise. First, adverse selection "refers to the misrepresentation of ability by the agent"[147]. If the principal is unable to observe the true ability of an agent, he will offer a contract tailored towards an agent with average characteristics. As a result, only agents with average and below average abilities will accept the principal's offer. The principal in turn will then not employ any agent, resulting in a breakdown of markets.[148]

Second, moral hazard "refers to lack of effort on the part of the agent"[149]. The agent decides in this case to pursue a course of action being against the principal's interest. Due to the information asymmetries, the agent does not have to fear any sort of punishment: the agent can always excuse poor performance by referring to poor exogenous conditions.

The third type of agency conflict is differential risk preference. As stated above, agency theory assumes that the principal is risk neutral while the agent is risk averse. Even if most of the goals of principal and agent are aligned, principal and agent may prefer pursuing different actions due to differential risk preference.[150]

Agency theory has developed a number of solutions to agency conflicts. Signaling or screening can solve the adverse selection conflict. Signaling refers to a situation, where the agent is able to reveal his private information to the principal. Screening means that the principal can design a mechanism that induces the agent to reveal his private information. Both signaling

---

[143] A risk neutral person is assumed to be indifferent towards a guaranteed compensation or a lottery with the same expected value. A risk averse person on the other hand would prefer the guaranteed compensation to the lottery. See Eisenhardt (1989), p. 59; Jost (1998), p. 289.
[144] See Eisenhardt (1989), pp. 58f.
[145] See Spremann (1987), p. 6.
[146] For a detailed discussion of information asymmetries see Jost (1998), pp. 282f.
[147] Eisenhardt (1989), p. 61.
[148] See Akerlow (1970), pp. 488ff.
[149] Eisenhardt (1989), p. 61.
[150] Eisenhardt (1989), p. 58.

and screening solve the adverse selection conflict, as the true ability of an agent can be observed.[151]

The moral hazard conflict can be solved by behavior or outcome-based contracts. Behavior-based contracts may reduce moral hazard, if the principal is able to monitor his agent and thereby acquires information reducing asymmetries. As a matter of fact, monitoring is associated with a cost. Outcome-based contracts reward the agent on the basis of performance. Given that the performance of an agent is not entirely dependent on his inputs, but, as stated above, on exogenous effects, a risk is transferred to the agent. Unless the agent is risk neutral, a cost is associated with transferring risk to the agent. Both behavior and outcome based contracts are therefore means of solving the moral hazard conflict at a cost.[152]

The differential risk preference conflict may be solved by either reducing the risk aversion of the agent or by protecting the agent from the realization of exogenous effects. The risk aversion of the agent may be reduced, e.g. by delegating tasks and responsibilities to a team and measuring relative performance, which is independent from the impact of exogenous effects. Protecting the agent from the realization of exogenous effects is possible by, e.g. long-term contracts or deferred compensation.[153]

The agency conflicts and solution mechanisms mentioned above are associated with a cost. Jensen and Meckling define agency costs as the sum of bonding costs, monitoring costs and a residual loss. The cost of signals that the agent sends to the principal is defined as bonding cost. The cost of incentives and monitoring systems employed by the principal is defined as monitoring cost. A residual loss arises, if the marginal increase in welfare is lower at a certain point than the associated increase in bonding and monitoring costs associated with eliminating agency conflicts. The residual loss is therefore the loss resulting from those agency conflicts that could not be solved at a given level of bonding and monitoring costs incurred.[154]

Concluding, agency theory discusses the use of signaling, screening and monitoring activities, organizational setups and information systems to reduce opportunistic behavior in the forms of adverse selection, moral hazard and differential risk preference. Therefore, agency theory could give hints with regard to private equity firm activities, the organization of the relationship between private equity firm and portfolio company, and information system design. The dimensions experience of private equity firms and usage of external resource are, however, not covered by agency theory.

---

[151] Jost (1998), p. 240.
[152] See Ouchi (1977), pp. 95ff; Eisenhardt (1989), p. 61.
[153] See Jost (1999).
[154] See Jensen/Meckling (1976), p. 308.

3.1.5 Knowledge-Based View

Proponents of the knowledge-based view are among the most vocal critics of new institutional economics: "Our view differs radically from that of the firm as a bundle of contracts that serves to allocate efficiently property rights [...]. Rather, we suggest that organizations are social communities in which individual and social expertise is transformed into economically useful products and services [...]. Firms exist because they provide a social community of voluntaristic action structured by organizing principles that are not reduceable to individuals"[155].

Conner and Prahalad spell out one assumption with regard to the human setting of the knowledge-based view:[156] individuals are assumed to be boundedly rational, which means that individuals are "intendedly rational, but only limited so"[157], resulting in finite cognitive processing abilities. As a consequence of bounded rationality, tacit knowledge exists, "knowledge that can be acquired only through personal experience"[158]. Furthermore, heterogeneity with regard to the knowledge possessed by individuals arises, "because cognitive limitations prohibit one person [...] from absorbing the entire accumulated knowledge and skills of another"[159].[160]

Due the heterogeneity of knowledge possessed by individuals, the firms employing individuals are also heterogeneous with respect to their knowledge assets. Because of the existence of employees' tacit knowledge, it may be very costly for a competitor to imitate a product or service. As a result of the possession of heterogeneous and hard-to-imitate resources, firms benefit from a competitive advantage resulting in above normal returns.[161] Knowledge assets are not assumed, however, to be given. A given knowledge base would mean that "rents from acquiring superior resources [stem] from either luck or superior insight into the resource's true value"[162]. Dynamic capabilities, i.e. "the firm's ability to integrate, build, and reconfigure

---

[155] Kogut/Zander (1992), p. 384. For an introduction to the knowledge-based view see furthermore Nelson/Winter (1982); Foss (1993); Conner/Prahalad (1996); Teece et al. (1997).

[156] See Conner/Prahalad (1996), pp. 482ff. No specific assumptions about the organizational setting are made.

[157] Simon (1957), p. xxiv.

[158] Conner/Prahalad (1996), p. 482.

[159] Conner/Prahalad (1996), p. 482.

[160] Conner and Prahalad state that the knowledge-based view also holds when individuals are interacting which each other honestly, i.e. the assumption of opportunism of individuals is not required by the knowledge-based view. Conner and Prahalad argue that "even in the absence of opportunism, knowledge-based transaction costs can exist" (Conner/Prahalad (1996), p. 484). The rationale given for this claim is that "honesty does not rule out intense disagreement or haggling. Each party, acting truthfully, may have a different view of the factors (or their relative future importance) that should be taken into account in designing present and future courses of action based on the predictions of uncertain, present or future, exogenous or endogenous, realities. [...] Because of irreducible differences in perspectives, experience, or skills, even the tiniest contract period may still involve substantive disagreement and hence negotiation and friction between truthful parties" (Conner/Prahalad (1996), p. 484).

[161] See Barney (1991), pp. 99ff; Peteraf (1993), pp. 179ff.

[162] Foss/Foss (2000), p. 4.

internal and external [knowledge] to address rapidly changing environments"[163], help firms to enhance their knowledge base.

Concluding, the knowledge-based view helps to understand the impact of a firm's knowledge and dynamic capabilities on its performance. Portfolio companies having access to the knowledge and dynamic capabilities of private equity professionals and qualified external resources may therefore have an advantage over their competitors. Unfortunately, the means needed to integrate, build and reconfigure knowledge are not mentioned by the knowledge-based view: "little is actually said about the means of fostering superior capabilities. In our view this is due to the facts that, first, very little is said in the [knowledge-based view] about the nature of learning, and, second, very little is said about how the firm as an institution may promote (certain types of) learning relative to market organization"[164]. Therefore the knowledge-based view does not help to understand the usefulness of specific activities, organizational setups and information systems in building a portfolio company's knowledge and dynamic capabilities.

3.1.6 Corporate Governance View

The corporate governance view[165] discusses the relationship of a corporation with its major stakeholders.[166] At first sight the corporate governance view seems to be similar to agency theory, as it discusses the relationship between principals that delegate tasks to agents. However, rather than analyzing individual principal agent relationships, the corporate governance view examines a multi-stakeholder model of corporate governance.

---

[163] See Teece et al. (1997), p. 516.
[164] Foss/Foss (2000), p. 5.
[165] The discussion of the corporate governance view is based on Blair (1995). Ruppen (2002), pp. 24ff subsequently adapts Blair's model of a corporation to reflect the specifics of venture capital financed firms.
[166] No specific assumptions with regard to the human or organizational setting are made.

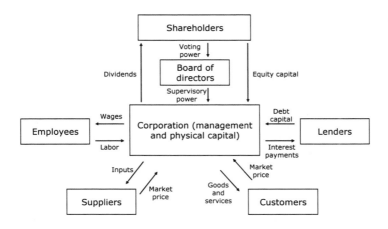

Figure 4: Corporate governance view of the corporation[167]

The corporate governance view is structured as follows. An entrepreneur or a management team runs the corporation. Management raises capital in order to acquire physical capital, pay for inputs from suppliers and employees' wages. Goods or services are sold to customers. Capital may be raised by borrowing debt capital from lenders or by issuing equity shares. Lenders give debt capital to a corporation in exchange for interest payments. Interest payments to lenders have priority over dividend payments to shareholders. However, the payments from the corporation to lenders are limited to interest payments plus the outstanding principal at the end of the lending period. Shareholders on the other hand give equity capital to a corporation in exchange for claims on the profits of a corporation. A corporation is profitable if the revenue from customer sales exceeds the payments to lenders, employees and suppliers. Shareholders are therefore said to be residual claimants. Due to their residual claim position, shareholders are expected to have the greatest motivation among major stakeholders to supervise the decisions a corporation makes. In addition to their motivation, shareholders also have the best ability to influence the decisions of a corporation: shareholders are entitled to elect the board of directors. The board of directors in turn has the power to hire and fire all of the top-level members of the management team and is responsible for monitoring and approving all important decisions and actions of a company.[168]

Concluding, the corporate governance view explains why shareholders are expected to involve actively in their investments. Moreover, the corporate governance view also specifies the organizational setting of the relationship between a firm and its stakeholders. Therefore

---

[167] See Blair (1995), p. 21.
[168] See Blair (1995), pp. 20ff.

the corporate governance view may be suitable to explain the dimensions activity and organization of post-investment value addition by private equity firms. However, the impact of shareholders' qualifications and knowledge on the corporation is not discussed by the governance view. Moreover, qualified external resources supporting the management of a corporation are not part of the corporate governance view. Finally, the corporate governance view does not mention systems used for the exchange of information between the corporation and its shareholders. The corporate governance view does not, therefore, help in getting a better understanding of the performance of information systems, the experience of private equity professionals and the usage of external resources to complement management team capacity and capability.

3.1.7 Procedural Justice Theory

Procedural justice theory builds on two assumptions regarding the human and the organizational setting. With regard to the human setting, procedural justice theory suggests that "fair treatment is central to people and a major determinant of their reactions to decisions"[169]. With regard to the organizational setting, procedural justice analyzes "individuals' reactions to decisions in which they are personally invested but that they cannot directly or fully control."[170]

Based on the above-mentioned assumptions, procedural justice comes to the conclusion that individuals value the process of decision making more highly than the actual outcome of a decision. More precisely, procedural justice theory "suggests that individuals value just procedures because they provide a means of indirect control over a decision when direct control is not possible [...]. Even when a particular decision has adverse outcomes for an individual, just procedures ensure the individual that, over time, he or she will receive what is due from the exchange relationship. In essence, just procedures allow individuals that their interests are being protected over the long run."[171]

Procedural justice theory has been developed by psychologists.[172] Therefore primarily affective reactions have been analyzed as a result of procedural justice: "procedural justice theorists have argued that fair procedures serve two purposes. One is to help protect individuals' interests; over the long run, fair procedures should result in individuals receiving what they are due. Consequently, the fairness of procedures is associated with positive attitudes toward a decision, such as satisfaction, agreement and commitment [...]. The second function of fair procedures is symbolic and helps to strengthen individuals' relationships with a group, leader, and organization. [...] Consequently, fair procedures are associated with positive attitudes

---

[169] Korsgaard et al. (1995), p. 63.
[170] Sapienza/Korsgaard (1996), p. 547.
[171] Sapienza/Korsgaard (1996), p. 547. For an introduction to procedural justice theory see also Lind/Tyler (1988); Thibaut/Walker (1975).
[172] The above-mentioned Lind, Tyler, Thibaut and Walker are all psychologists.

toward the group, leader, and organization, such as group harmony, trust in the leader, and organizational commitment."[173]

It is only recently that procedural justice has been used in the context of entrepreneurial finance proposing that procedural justice has a positive effect on venture performance: "if the parties view their relationship as being characterized by a high level of procedural fairness, this would suggest that they are willing to be adaptive in the near term with the adjustments having long-term payoffs in the form of positive venture outcomes. NVT members are likely to be more willing to cooperate with future VC requests and advice when they perceive that they are receiving fair treatment [...]. If a VC-NVT relationship were not procedurally fair, we suspect that it would be a rare NVT that would be willing to implement innovative adjustments requested by its VC. When VCs provide disagreeable pressure to NVTs, procedural justice theory suggests negative performance implications because adaptations and innovations are less likely to be made that would help the venture adjust to the changing market."[174]

Concluding, procedural justice theory explains the impact of just decision procedures on affective reactions and portfolio company performance. It helps therefore to understand "social processes [...] within interorganizational relationships"[175]. Procedural justice theory, however, does not offer hints with regard to private equity firm activities, information systems or the contributions of experienced private equity professionals and qualified external resources.

3.1.8 Investment Controlling

Investment controlling builds on one assumption regarding the organizational setting: it analyzes the oversight of portfolio companies by its shareholders or holding companies – excluding all other types of stakeholders. Investment controlling is characterized as the supervision that companies experience by its shareholders.[176] Investment controlling does not make any assumptions with regard to the human setting.

Building on the assumption with regard to the organizational setting, investment controlling analyzes first the activities of holding companies. Shareholders engaging in investment controlling are expected to implement standardized planning and control systems[177], to guide portfolio companies effectively and efficiently[178] and to participate in the coordination of portfolio company management's decisions with respect to predefined goals.[179] Second, in-

---

[173] Korsgaard et al. (1995), pp. 65-66.
[174] Busenitz et al. (2004), p. 795. The abbreviation VC refers to venture capitalists and the abbreviation NVTs to new venture teams.
[175] Busenitz et al. (2004), p. 804.
[176] Botta (1994), p. 30. For an introduction to investment controlling see Vogel (1998).
[177] Kleinschnittger (1993), p. 32.
[178] Seraphim/Herbst (1995), p. 23.
[179] Gebhardt (1995), p. 2225.

vestment controlling also discusses the organization of the interaction between holding and portfolio company. It is discussed as important antecedent to the degree of independency of the portfolio company, the implementation of holding company planning and control systems, the degree of holding company involvement in functional and operative processes as well as the portfolio company's culture.[180] Third, the importance of portfolio company information systems is underlined. Providing information relevant to decisions[181] and continuously updating holding company management in the decision process[182] is considered to be an important element of efficient investment controlling. Fourth, investment controlling also implicitly stresses the importance of experienced controlling professionals: investment controllers have to be able to adequately support portfolio company management to accomplish the targets set by the holding company.[183]

Concluding, investment controlling is a framework to structure the relationship between a holding company and a portfolio company taking into account investment controllers' activities, the organization of interaction, portfolio company information systems and the provision of experienced investment controllers. Unfortunately, investment controlling does not explicitly discuss the usage of external resources as a means to increase portfolio company performance. Investment controlling covers therefore all but one dimension of post-investment interaction between private equity professionals and portfolio company.

3.1.9 Summary Evaluation and Conclusion

The frameworks used so far for the analysis of post-investment value addition by private equity firms include neoclassical financing theory, theories belonging to new institutional economics, the knowledge-based view, the corporate governance view, procedural justice theory and investment controlling. Among the frameworks discussed so far, investment controlling seems to be the most comprehensive one, covering four out of the five dimensions of post-investment value addition (see table 2).

As a matter of fact it can be argued that a combination of different frameworks may result in the same or even better coverage of the dimensions of post-investment value addition. For example using the principal agent theory along with the knowledge-based view would cover all five dimensions of post-investment value addition. However, the goal is to identify a framework that covers – mutually exclusive and collectively exhaustive – all or at least most of the dimensions of post-investment value addition. Using one comprehensive framework rather than a combination of several frameworks will help structuring the arguments in this thesis in a better way. In this respect, investment controlling seems to be a good choice.

---

[180] Vogel (1998), p. 33.
[181] Seraphim/Herbst (1995), p. 24.
[182] Kleinschnittger (1993), p. 32.
[183] Schmidt (1989), p. 270.

Dimensions of post-investment value addition covered by theories	Activities	Organization	Information systems	Internal resources	External resources	Dimension covered
Neoclassical financing theory						0
Property rights theory	X	X				2
Transaction cost theory	X	X			X	3
Principal agent theory	X	X	X			3
Knowledge-based view				X	X	2
Corporate governance	X	X				2
Procedural justice		X				1
Investment Controlling	X	X	X	X		4

Table 2: Dimensions of post-investment value addition covered by theories used so far for the analysis of post-investment value addition by private equity firms

However, the number of dimensions covered by a framework is not necessarily an indicator of its quality. Unfortunately, investment controlling has not received a great deal of attention by researchers, it is primarily practitioners that have contributed to the field of investment controlling: "Begriff und Begriffsinhalt des Beteiligungscontrolling wurden bisher in der Literatur eher vernachlässigt. Während Beiträge aus der Wissenschaft nur vereinzelt zu verzeichnen sind, befassen sich Autoren aus der Unternehmenspraxis zunehmend mit dem Thema."[184] It seems therefore wise to rely on a mainstream controlling theory that has risen to a high level of completeness and precision as a result of continuous research coverage and discussion among the most reputable controlling theorists. One of the most highly regarded controlling theorists is Professor Péter Horváth, the controlling view of whom will be introduced in the following section.

3.2 The System-Based View of Controlling developed by Horváth as a Suitable Theoretical Concept

The system-based view of controlling developed by Horváth analyzes controlling as a subsystem of the leadership system of a firm.[185] The system-based view of controlling does not make specific assumptions regarding the human or organizational setting.

---

[184] Vogel (1998), p. 15.

[185] Horváth (2001), p. 151. Interestingly enough, no common view of controlling has emerged so far: "Die einschlägige Literatur ist durch eine Vielzahl sehr unterschiedlicher Definitionsansätze gekennzeichnet. Von einem einheitlichen Controllingverständnis [...] kann keine Rede sein" (see Weber (2002), p. 20). Rather than one view of controlling there are three streams of definitions that have established themselves over time (see Zenz (1999)). A first stream focuses on the provision of information as the core of controlling. Controlling is defined e.g. as management support by the provision of information (Hoffmann (1972), p. 85). A second stream defines controlling as the part of corporate management that is responsible for focusing firms on certain goals (Weber (2002), p. 23; see also Weber/Schäffer (2003), p. 1 for "Rationalitätssicherung der Führung" and Dyckhoff/Ahn (2001), p. 111 for "Sicherstellung der Effektivität und Effizienz der Führung als Kernfunktion des Controlling"). A third stream defines controlling to coordinate different subsystems of the leadership system of a company (see Horváth (1978), pp. 194ff). The latter view of controlling has received

Describing the system-based view of controlling, Horváth uses a very technical language. The most important terms will therefore be defined in order to facilitate a better understanding of Horváth's concepts:

- Systems are defined as a set of elements that are connected or can be connected to each other by a certain relationship[186].
- Systems can be put into a hierarchical relationship with each other. Systems consist of several subsystems. Any subsystem consists in turn of several system elements – which is that part of a system that a researcher does not which to break down any further.[187]
- For the purpose of his analysis, Horváth defines firms as systems. The firm as a system can be divided up into a leadership system and an operative system. The leadership system is defined as a system coordinating leadership processes (such as setting targets, planning, making decisions and controlling) that are intended to guide and arrange the actions of other persons.[188] The operative system is defined as a system coordinating the flow of goods, services and money.[189]

Horváth defines the controlling system as a subsystem of the firm's leadership system. The most important differences between the leadership system and the controlling system can be inferred from Horváth's definition of controlling: "Controlling besteht in der ergebniszielorientierten Koordination von Planung und Kontrolle sowie Informationsversorgung"[190]. The controlling system is limited to the coordination of planning and control as well as information systems, whereas the leadership system guides and arranges in addition also the personnel management system, the organizational system and the corporate vision.[191]

The controlling system can be broken down into four subsystems according to Horváth.[192] The first subsystem of controlling is controlling tasks comprising all activities needed for the realization of controlling goals. Controlling tasks can be differentiated with regard to the firms' goals in strategic and operative tasks, with regard to the activities pursued in tasks

---

so far most attention in the current discussion among controlling theorists: "Als drei wesentliche Begriffssichten lassen sich ein informationsbezogener, ein führungsphilosophiebezogener und ein koordinationsbezogener Ansatz unterscheiden, von denen letzterem in der aktuellen Diskussion die größte Aufmerksamkeit zukommt" (Weber (2002), p. 27). It is important to note, however, that each of the three views of controlling mentioned above – including the system-based view of controlling – has its inherent problems: "Alle drei Ansätze [...] weisen bei näherem Hinsehen Probleme auf. Diese betreffen entweder ihre mangelnde Originalität oder die Stringenz ihrer theoretischen Herleitung" (Weber (2002), p. 27).

[186] Horváth (2001), p. 98.
[187] Horváth (2001), p. 99.
[188] Horváth (2001), p. 114.
[189] Horváth (2001), p. 117.
[190] Horváth (2001), p. 150.
[191] See Weber/Schäffer (1999), pp. 14-16 and pp. 18-19.
[192] See Horváth (2001), pp. 151f.

building systems[193] and tasks coordinating systems[194] and finally with regard to the object of activities in planning and control tasks as well as tasks regarding the information system.[195]

The second subsystem of controlling is the controlling organization. The controlling organization comprises all structural and process aspects of controlling. Structural aspects of controlling deal with the positioning of the controlling function in a firm's hierarchy and the design of hierarchies within the controlling function. The positioning of the controlling function within a firm's hierarchy is determined by what position and competence controlling has relative to other functions and whether controlling tasks are pursued centrally or locally. Within the controlling function hierarchies are determined by the degree of delegation of tasks within a team of controllers and the possibility of individual controllers participating in decisions of the controlling function. Process[196] aspects of controlling try to answer how standardized controlling processes should be and whether processes should be divided up among different controllers.[197]

The third subsystem of controlling is the controlling instruments. Controlling instruments consist of immaterial and real tools helping a controlling organization to get its tasks done.[198] Immaterial instruments are methods and models. Real instrument is the information system, which is defined as a system that improves the amount or quality of information available or the flow of information.[199] An information system can be broken down along its process steps:[200] First, information needs have to be identified, where information need is defined as the type, amount or quality of information that a person needs in a given information context to fulfil a task in a given time and setting.[201] Second, once the information need is defined, the required pieces of information can be gathered. Third, different pieces of information are combined with the help of methods and models. Fourth, information is transmitted in the form of managerial reports.

---

[193] Tasks building systems are defined as the implementation or adaptation of computer based information systems (Horváth (2001), p. 131).

[194] Tasks coordinating systems are defined as planned involvement in – already implemented – planning and control as well as information systems and unplanned involvement in case of unforeseen disturbances (Horváth (2001), p. 143).

[195] See Horváth (2001), p. 152.

[196] Horvath does not define the term "process". For this thesis, the definition of the most well known proponents of process-based thinking, Hammer and Champy, shall be adopted. They define processes as "collection of activities that takes one or more kinds of input and creates an output that is of value to the customer" (Hammer/Champy (1993), p. 35). The customer, however, "is not necessarily a customer of the company. The customer may be inside the company, as it is, for instance, for the materials acquisition or purchasing process, which supplies materials to a company's manufacturing operations" (Hammer/Champy (1993), p. 39).

[197] See Horváth (2001), pp. 829ff.

[198] See Horváth (2001), p. 152.

[199] See Horváth (2001), p. 354.

[200] See Horváth (2001), pp. 354-355.

[201] Szyperski (1980), col. 904.

The fourth subsystem of controlling is the controller, the individual that actually makes tasks happen within a controlling organization. Horváth emphasizes that empirical research has been unable so far to specify the capabilities needed by a controller.[202]

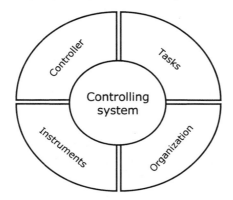

Figure 5: System-based view of controlling developed by Horváth[203]

Summarizing, the system-based view of controlling is a framework used to describe and analyze controlling systems based on the four controlling subsystems – tasks, organization, instruments and controller.[204] It seems to be a well-suited framework for analyzing post-investment value addition to buyouts, given that it seems to cover all relevant dimensions of post-investment value addition: activities, organization, information systems and resources committed. Different from investment controlling, the system-based view of controlling has been developed by one of the most highly regarded controlling theorists. Whether or not the system-based view of controlling is useful in analyzing post-investment value addition to buyouts will be discussed in more detail in the next chapter.

3.3 Discussion of the Application of the System-Based View of Controlling on the Relationship between Private Equity Firm and Portfolio Company

The discussion of the application of the system-based view of controlling on value addition of private equity firms to their portfolio companies will be carried out in two steps. It will be discussed first to what extent the post-investment value addition of private equity firms is similar to controlling as defined by Horváth. Based on the differences identified, the system-

---

[202] See Horváth (2001), pp. 879ff.
[203] Based on Horváth (2001), p. 152.
[204] Horváth (2001), p. 152.

based view of controlling will be adapted in order to reflect the particularities of post-investment value addition of private equity firms.

As shown above, Horváth defines controlling as a subsystem of the leadership system that coordinates planning, control and information systems focusing on certain goals. Private equity firms, however, work jointly with the management team on adding value to a portfolio company – not limiting themselves to planning, control and information systems as the object of their activities.[205] Private equity firms will therefore include all objects of the leadership system. Concluding, whereas Horváth defines controlling as a subsystem of the leadership system, private equity firms are an integral part of the leadership system of a firm.

The limitation of controlling to the coordination of planning, control and information systems is subject to discussion among controlling theorists. Schmidt, Küpper, Weber and Schäffer[206] are proponents of the idea that all elements of the leadership system have to be coordinated by the controlling function. Not coordinating the personnel management system, the organizational system or the corporate vision would lead to inefficiencies.[207] Concluding, Küpper, Schäffer, Schmidt, Weber and Zünd suggest applying controlling concepts more broadly.

In order to be applicable to the analysis of post-investment value addition to buyouts, the system-based view of controlling developed by Horváth has to be extended following the recommendations of the controlling theorists mentioned above: the analysis of private equity firm tasks will not be restricted to the objects planning, control and information systems. Instead, all activities of private equity firms with the goal of adding value to a portfolio company will be analyzed, i.e. activities of private equity firms that coordinate personnel management, the organizational system or the corporate vision are explicitly included.

One specification of the system-based view of controlling shall be made: according to the system-based view of controlling the controller is the person that makes tasks happen. In a private equity setup two groups that make controlling tasks happen have to be distinguished: private equity professionals and external resources. Due to their limited management capacity and capabilities, private equity firms leverage themselves through outside resources. [208] The analysis of the controller dimension will therefore focus on both the private equity professional and outside resources used.

Moreover the following limitations shall be made:

---

[205] See chapter 2.2.4.
[206] See Schmidt (1986); Küpper (1997), pp. 13-24; Weber (1995), p. 50; Weber/Schäffer (1999), pp. 14-16.
[207] For a detailed discussion see Hamprecht (1996), pp. 241ff; Weber/Weißenberger (1998), pp. 40ff; Weber/Schäffer (1999), p. 15.

- Following the system-based view of controlling, the organization dimension should comprise all structures and processes used by private equity firms to involve in their portfolio companies. In this thesis, however, only organization structures will be analyzed. Processes are not included due to the explicative research design of this thesis.[209]
- Instruments consist of theoretical (methods or models) and real tools (information systems) that help a private equity firm to get its tasks done. Due to the explicative research design of this study, theoretical instruments will not be part of this study.[210]

---

[208] See Smart et al. (2000), p. 24.

[209] Processes have been defined above as "collection of activities that takes one or more kinds of input and creates an output that is of value to the customer" (Hammer/Champy (1993), p. 35). Moreover it has been said that the system-based view of controlling focuses on standardization of processes and on dividing up processes among different actors. Researching processes would therefore imply aggregating activities to processes that can be mapped to a customer and furthermore determining which actors actually execute certain processes. Research at this level of detail can be done very well on a descriptive, case study basis. Due to its level of complexity, research into processes cannot, however, be included in an explicative, questionnaire-based study design.

[210] Theoretical instruments have been defined above as methods and models. Research into methods and models would be an important part of an instrumental research design. It does not fit, however, into the explicative study design chosen for this thesis. Therefore, theoretical instruments will not be discussed in this study.

4 Methodology of Data Analysis

In this chapter a suitable methodology of data analysis is chosen. First of all first-generation multivariate research techniques (e.g. multiple regression analysis, factor analysis, discriminant analysis or principal component analysis) are evaluated. Due to the limitations shared by first-generation techniques the discussion is restricted in the following to second-generation multivariate research techniques. Two second-generation techniques are discussed: variance- and covariance-based structural equation modeling. Structural equation modeling in general and variance-based approaches to structural equation modeling in particular are not common knowledge in entrepreneurship research. Therefore an introduction to structural equation modeling is given followed by a discussion of the differences between variance- and covariance-based approaches to structural equation modeling.

4.1 First-Generation Multivariate Research Techniques are Not Suitable

In the early 1970s the increasing availability of computers spurred a shift from univariate and bivariate approaches to research techniques allowing the simultaneous analysis of multiple variables. This "multivariate revolution"[211] saw the advent of research techniques such as multiple regression, multidimensional scaling, principal component, factor or cluster analysis.[212] All of the multivariate research techniques developed in that period are dubbed a "first generation of multivariate analysis" by Fornell, as each research technique shares at least one of the following four limitations.[213] First of all, most first-generation research techniques can analyze only observable variables. A variable is observable "if and only if its value can be obtained by means of a real-world sampling experiment"[214]. Second, nearly all first-generation research techniques assume that variables are measured without measurement error. Measurement error means that the "erhobene Merkmalsausprägung (Ist- oder Beobachtungswert) weicht von der wahren Merkmalsausprägung (Sollwert) ab"[215] and is attributable to several root causes: "measurement error results when respondents fill out surveys, but do not respond to specific questions, or provide inadequate answers to open-ended questions, or

---

[211] See Sheth (1971), p. 13.
[212] For a classification of research techniques belonging to the "multivariate revolution" in the 1970s see Kinnear/Taylor (1971), Sheth (1971) or Horne et al. (1973).
[213] See Fornell (1987), p. 411.
[214] McDonald (1996), p. 239.
[215] Rinne (1997), p. 20.

fail to follow instructions [...]. Measurement errors also arise from lack of control of the sequence in which the questions were asked, and various respondents' characteristics."[216] Third, first-generation research techniques assume simple model structures, analyzing "the impact of one or two variables in isolation"[217] rather than examining multiple criterion and predictor variables. Finally, several first-generation techniques are limited to exploratory applications, as "some or all of their estimators lack (known) properties necessary for statistical inference."[218] To provide examples, "traditional factor analysis handles unobservable variables but is not confirmatory; multiple regression can be applied in a (weak) confirmatory sense by testing the significance of estimated parameters and the regression equation, but it is limited to a single observable criterion variable; simultaneous equations and multivariate regression include several criterion variables, but (typically) ignore errors in measurement."[219]

As a matter of fact there are problems in business administration that can be analyzed, and correctly so, with the help of first-generation multivariate research techniques. In the case of research on private equity firms' post-investment value addition to portfolio companies, first-generation techniques have frequently been applied. This seems to be unsuitable, however, for the following reasons. First, all of the dimensions analyzed by prior studies – such as the involvement of private equity firms or the experience of private equity professionals – cannot be measured directly by anything that can be observed, but rather by multiple items covering different facets of a variable.[220] For example the experience of a private equity professional cannot be measured reasonably by only one question, such as the number of years spent in the private equity industry, as this would imply neglecting all other facets of experience, such as experience in the portfolio company's industry or profit and loss statement (P&L) responsibility.

Second, given that the responses to most of this study's survey items require the judgment of study participants, the survey instrument will be influenced to some degree by measurement error. For example asking for the involvement of a private equity firm in a specific task requires the private equity professional to judge whether the involvement was rather high or low.

---

[216] Cui (2003), p. 5. Jacoby differentiates three sources of measurement error: interviewer error, respondent error and instrument error (see Jacoby (1978), pp. 89-90). First, interviewer error refers to the fact that interviewers may – not even intentionally – influence the outcome of a study by their appearance or behavior (see Cannell/Kahn (1968); Katz (1942)). Second, respondent error refers to situations, when potential respondents cannot be reached, deny participating in the study, skip parts of a questionnaire or intentionally give incorrect answers (see Bortz/Döring (2002), pp. 248ff). Third, instrument error occurs, if the survey design or the wording of individual questions induces study respondents to commit errors (see Bortz/Döring (2002), pp. 253ff).

[217] Jacoby (1978), p. 91.

[218] Fornell (1987), p. 409.

[219] Fornell (1987), p. 411.

[220] Variables have therefore to be considered unobservable (see Dijkstra (1983), p. 67).

Third, the dimensions of post-investment interaction between private equity firm and portfolio company as well as the value added to a buyout require the design of a rather complex research model, studying "the impact of a variety of factors impinging in concert"[221]. That is, the relationship between a variety of criterion and predictor variables is analyzed. For example, each dimension of post-investment interaction will have to be measured by several observable variables implying the existence of multiple criterion and predictor variables.

Fourth, research on post-investment value addition to portfolio companies has left the initial exploratory stage of research and therefore requires the use of confirmatory research techniques with known properties for statistical inference. For example, the factors of private equity firms' involvement are well understood. It is unknown, however, what factors of private equity firm involvement have a significant impact on value added.

As a result of the above-mentioned limitations, first-generation multivariate research techniques such as regression analysis, factor analysis, discriminant analysis or principal component analysis are not suitable for analyzing post-investment value addition to buyouts.

4.2   Structural Equation Modeling Basics

In the 1980s a second generation of multivariate analysis emerged overcoming all four of the above-mentioned limitations of first-generation multivariate research techniques.[222] Second-generation techniques are able to construct unobservable variables measured by several indicators, model the measurement error of variables explicitly, are capable of analyzing multiple predictor and criterion variables simultaneously and can be used for confirmatory applications. Not surprisingly the application of second generation techniques has resulted in findings "that would not have been discovered by first-generation methods and that lead one to question the appropriateness of previous conclusions based on first-generation methods. [...] A drastic example is the reevaluation of the Westinghouse Head Start program on school achievement. The negative findings from applying traditional analysis of covariance to the data were used to justify the decision to phase out the summer programs for school children (Magidson and Sörbom 1980). When measurement considerations were incorporated in an explicit auxiliary theory about the measurement process, Magidson and Sörbom's covariance structure analysis found a weak but positive relationship between participation in the summer program and school achievement. Thus, by explicitly modeling both substantive theory and measurement theory, researchers have shown insignificant findings to be significant and nega-

---

[221]   Jacoby (1978), p. 91.

tive relations to be positive."[223] Second-generation research techniques therefore seem to be better suited to analyze post-investment value addition to buyouts. Out of the second-generation research techniques mentioned above, two are relevant for this thesis. Covariance- and variance-based approaches to structural equation modeling (SEM) are second-generation research techniques allowing the analysis of directional relationships between latent variables.[224] In the following paragraphs a brief introduction into SEM fundamentals will be given in order to facilitate a better understanding.

Structural equation models consist of two elements, the structural model (inner model) and the measurement model (outer model). The inner model determines the relationships between latent variables, where latent variables (constructs) are defined as abstract concepts that can be observed only indirectly through their effects on manifest variables. Two types of latent variables are distinguished. On the one hand there are exogenous latent variables, labeled with the Greek character ξ ("ksi"), that are independent variables in all equations. On the other hand there are endogenous latent variables, indicated by the Greek character η ("eta"), that are dependent variables in at least one equation. The relationship between latent variables is indicated by a one-headed arrow, representing a regression relationship.[225] Path coefficients indicating the strength of the regression relationship between latent variables are denoted by the Greek character γ ("gamma") for the regression of endogenous variables on exogenous variables or β ("beta") for the regression of endogenous variables on other endogenous variables. Structural equation models do almost never predict dependent variables perfectly. Therefore a structural error term is included, labeled with the Greek character ζ ("zeta"). The equation representing the structural model of figure 6 is then: $\eta = \gamma\xi + \zeta$.[226]

The outer model of a structural equation model determines the relationships between latent variables and their associated manifest variables. Manifest variables (also dubbed indicators, items, measures) consist of observed data from interviews or questionnaires. Although there is

---

[222] See Fornell (1987), pp. 409ff. Second-generation research techniques include canonical correlation, redundancy analysis, external single-set components analysis (ESSCA), partial least squares (PLS), covariance structure analysis, confirmatory nonmetric multidimensional scaling and latent structure analysis.

[223] See Fornell (1987), p. 410.

[224] See Fornell/Bookstein (1982), pp. 440ff. It is important to note that the benefits of SEM come at the cost of higher complexity: "a higher level of complexity [requires] greater knowledge about the conditions and assumptions for appropriate usage" (Chin (1998a), p. 7). Reviews of SEM usage are available in the fields of logistics (Garver/Mentzer (1999)), management information systems (Chin (1998a)), marketing (Steenkamp/van Trip (1991)), organizational behavior (Brannick (1995)) and strategy (Shook et al. (2004)).

[225] Two-headed arrows would represent a correlational relationship. The path coefficients indicating the strength of the correlation between two (exogenous) latent variables is denoted with the Greek character ϕ ("phi"). Given that the PLS design adopted later on allows only recursive relations among latent variables, the discussion of correlational relationships will not be deepened.

[226] See Fornell/Bookstein (1982), p. 441; Lohmöller (1984), p. 1-01; Diamantopoulos (1994), pp., 108ff; Chin (1998b), pp. 312ff. Latent and manifest variables are usually standardized to a mean of zero and unit variance so that the location parameter can be eliminated in calculations.

no fundamental difference between manifest variables, those associated with exogenous constructs are denoted x, whereas manifest variables associated with endogenous constructs are
labeled y. In SEM, every latent variable is connected to several manifest variables. In figure 6
latent variable η is modeled as a factor underlying its manifest variables. The strength of the
relationship between latent variable η and its manifest variables is measured by a simple regression (loading) coefficient indicated with the Greek character λ ("lambda"). Each manifest
variable is assumed to include some measurement error. Therefore a measurement error term
is included, denoted with the Greek character ε ("epsilon"). The two equations representing
the measurement model of the latent variable η are then: $y_1 = \lambda_{y1}\eta + \varepsilon_{y1}$ and $y_2 = \lambda_{y2}\eta + \varepsilon_{y2}$.

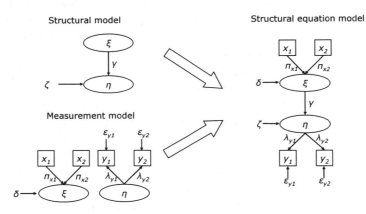

Figure 6: Structural equation model composition.

Latent variable ξ in figure 6 is assumed to be formed by its manifest variables. The strength of
the relationship between the manifest variables and latent variable ξ is measured by multiple
regression coefficients denoted with the Greek character π ("pi"). δ ("delta") is an error term
corresponding to the residuals from multiple regression. The equation representing the measurement model of latent variable ξ is then: $\xi = \pi_{x1}x_1 + \pi_{x2}x_2 + \delta$.[227]

As indicated above, there are two ways of modeling the relationship between latent and manifest variables.[228] On the one hand manifest variables can be modeled as indicators reflecting
an underlying factor. In this case, the indicators depend on the latent variable – the direction
of causality is from the construct to the indicators (see indicators of latent variable η). Mirror-
ing the same underlying construct, each indicator of this type has to be correlated positively

[227] The nomenclature follows Chin (1998b), pp. 312ff.
[228] The discussion of alternative measurement model specifications is deepened here, as measurement model
misspecification can result in seriously flawed SEM results and has moreover been shown to be an error
committed frequently even in top journal publications (see Jarvis et al. (2003), p. 207).

with its construct. Standardizing both indicators and latent variable to a mean of zero and a standard deviation of one, it can be shown that the correlation of two indicators of this type is given by the product of the indicators' correlation coefficients with the underlying construct. Considering the correlation of y_1 and y_2 in figure 6: $Corr$ $(y_1, y_2) = \lambda_{y1}\lambda_{y2}$.[229] This type of indicator is referred to as a reflective indicator.[230] For example "the responses to a series of items on a math test should reflect a student's quantitative ability"[231]. That is, the response to each measure of a math test is a consequence of a person's quantitative ability. Students with high quantitative abilities will do equally well on different items of a math test, implying that the indicators of a math test will be positively correlated.

On the other hand, indicators may be modeled to give rise to latent variables. In this case, the indicators cause the latent variable – the direction of causality is from the indicators to the construct (see indicators of latent variable ξ in figure 6). Giving rise to latent variables, one cannot know the correlation between this type of indicators – there may be positive, negative or zero correlations.[232] This type of indicator is referred to as a formative indicator.[233] For example "job loss, divorce, recent bodily injury, and death in family could be four causal indictors"[234] of the latent variable life stress. That is, job loss, divorce, injury and death in family are determinants of life stress rather than a consequence implying that the indicators of the latent variable life stress need not be correlated.[235]

4.3   Variance- and Covariance-Based Approaches to Structural Equation Modeling

Structural equation models can be estimated by two different approaches – covariance-based and variance-based. In the following paragraphs, both research techniques will be briefly introduced and discussed, weighing up their advantages and drawbacks in order to finally choose a technique for this doctoral dissertation.

---

[229] See Bollen/Lennox (1991), p. 307 for a mathematical derivation assuming that both construct and indicators are standardized variables.
[230] See Jarvis et al. (2003).
[231] Bollen/Ting (2000), p. 3.
[232] For a mathematical derivation see Bollen/Lennox (1991), p. 307.
[233] See Bollen/Lennox (1991), p. 306.
[234] Bollen/Lennox (1991), p. 306.
[235] Another, very colorful example of formative indicators "would be the amount of beer, wine, and hard liquor consumed as indicators of mental inebriation. Potential reflective measures might be blood alcohol level, driving ability, MRI brain scan, and performance on mental calculations. If truly reflective, an improvement in the blood alcohol level measure for an individual would also imply an improvement in the MRI activity and other measures since they are all meant to tap into the same concept or phenomenon. Conversely, for the formative measures, an increase in beer consumption does not imply similar increases in wine or hard liquor consumption." (Chin (1998a), p. 9).

Jöreskog, Keesling and Wiley originally designed covariance-based approaches for SEM.[236] The widespread usage of covariance-based approaches – "in fact, to many social science researchers, the covariance-based procedure is tautologically synonymous with the term SEM"[237] – is to a large part due to the availability of easy-to-use software packages such as AMOS or EQS. Covariance-based SEM typically makes use of a maximum likelihood function that "attempts to minimize the difference between the sample covariances and those predicted by the theoretical model [...]. The parameters estimated by this procedure attempt to reproduce the covariance matrix of the observed measures."[238] Using matrix algebra, the matrix of model parameters Φ is determined in a way that the covariance matrix predicted by the theoretical model Σ (Φ) is as similar as possible to the sample covariance matrix S. This is done by minimizing the discrepancy function $F(S,\Sigma)$, which is zero when the theoretical and the sample covariance matrices are identical ($S=\Sigma$) and otherwise positive, increasing as the difference between S and Σ increases.[239] The most commonly used discrepancy function is the normal theory maximum likelihood function. With p measured indicators, the function is defined as $F_{ML} = \ln|\Sigma| - \ln|S| + Tr(S\Sigma^{-1}) - p$,[240] where $\ln|\Sigma|$ is the natural logarithm of the determinant of the model covariance matrix, $\ln|S|$ is the natural logarithm of the determinant of the sample covariance matrix and $Tr(S\Sigma^{-1})$ is the trace (sum of the elements of a matrix diagonal) of the product of sample covariance matrix and inverted model covariance matrix.

Despite the advantages associated with a second-generation multivariate research technique in general,[241] covariance-based approaches have four major statistical problems.[242] First, the maximum likelihood procedure, which is the most popular estimation procedure in covariance-based SEM, assumes that manifest variables have a multi-normal distribution and interval scaling.[243] This assumption will be, however, "very unrealistic in most economic applications"[244]. Of course it may be argued that the maximum likelihood procedure is not liable to violations of this assumption.[245] Even if the maximum likelihood procedure is not susceptible to violations, the χ^2 ("chi-square") measure used to assess model fit of covariance-based structural equation models is "very sensitive to departures from multivariate normality of the observed variables"[246].

---

[236] See Jöreskog (1970); Keesling (1972); Wiley (1973).
[237] Chin (1998b), p. 295.
[238] Chin (1998b), p. 297.
[239] MacCallum et al. (1996), pp. 130ff.
[240] See Hänlein/Kaplan (forthcoming), p. 19.
[241] See chapter 4.2.
[242] See Hänlein (forthcoming), pp. 72ff.
[243] See Jöreskog (1967), pp. 443ff; Fornell/Bookstein (1982), p. 440.
[244] Jöreskog (1973), p. 94.
[245] See Diamantopoulos (1994), p. 116.
[246] Jöreskog/Sorbom (1982), p. 408.

Second, the χ^2 measure has, besides the above-mentioned assumption, an additional problem that makes its use highly questionable. The χ^2 test is highly sensitive to sample size:[247] "Because the chi square test is directly proportional to sample size, virtually any model is likely to be rejected, if the sample size is large enough"[248].

Third, covariance-based SEM is not suitable for analyzing small samples. When analyzing small samples, it is likely that two estimation problems occur: nonconvergence and improper solutions.[249] Nonconvergence refers to the fact that the iterative maximum likelihood procedure does not converge within a reasonable number of iterations. Improper solutions refer to situations, where variance estimates have negative values (also referred to as Heywood cases) or where correlation coefficients have a value greater than 1.[250] Both nonconvergence and improper solutions have been shown to decrease with increasing sample size.[251] As a result of estimation problems in presence of small samples, several rules of thumb for minimum sample size requirements by covariance-based SEM approaches have been suggested. In general sample sizes of less than 100 are not acceptable for covariance-based SEM – sample sizes of more than 200 are recommended. [252]

Fourth, latent variables constructed by formative indicators may be embedded into covariance-based structural equation models only with restrictions. Several problems arise when formative indicators are used in covariance-based structural equation models. Specifically identification problems, occurrence of implied covariances of zero among some indicators and the existence of equivalent models are problems associated with the use of formative indicators. All three of the problems can be managed. However, the resolution of the problems mentioned requires "altering the original model in terms of its substantive meaning or parsimony, or both"[253].

Concluding, covariance-based structural equation models – while offering the advantages of a SEM technique in general – have four major statistical problems: the assumption of multinormality of measures, a significant sample size sensitivity of the χ^2 test, minimum sample size requirements and difficulties associated with the use of formative indicators.

Herman Wold developed an alternative, variance-based SEM technique. Although Herman Wold had designed two iterative procedures using a least squares estimation approach as early

---

[247]   See Jöreskog (1969), pp. 183ff.
[248]   Bagozzi (1981a), p. 380.
[249]   See Boomsma/Hoogland (2001), pp. 139ff.
[250]   See Dillon W. R. et al. (1987), pp. 126ff.
[251]   See Boomsma (1983); Boomsma (1985).
[252]   See Marsh et al. (1998), p. 187 and the literature cited therein.
[253]   MacCallum/Browne (1993), p. 540.

as 1966,[254] its application to latent variable path modeling came to Wold's mind with the advent of the covariance-based SEM software package LISREL in the early 1970s: "It struck me that it might be possible to estimate models with the same arrow scheme by an appropriate generalization of my [least squares] LS algorithms for principal components and canonical correlations. The extension involved two crucial steps, namely from two to three LVs and corresponding blocks of indicators, and from one to two inner relations. Once these steps were taken, the road to an iterative LS algorithm of general scope for estimation of path models with latent variables observed by multiple indicators was straightforward."[255] The basic partial least squares (PLS) design was then finished in 1977[256] and subsequently extended by Lohmöller with regard to various inner weighting schemes[257] and Hui with regard to non-recursive relations[258].

The PLS estimation procedure differs from covariance-based approaches with regard to the optimization objective. Whereas covariance-based approaches minimize residual covariance, the PLS estimation procedure minimizes residual variance. More precisely, the PLS estimation algorithm works as shown in figure 7. In step one, weight coefficients ω ("omega") are determined that allow the aggregation of manifest variable scores to latent variable estimates. Given that weights cannot be estimated in the first iteration – latent variable scores for performing a regression analysis are not available yet – PLS uses "arbitrary values for the weights to initiate the iteration"[259].

In step two, latent variable case values are estimated by summing the manifest variables in each block weighted by their respective weight coefficient ω obtained in step one.[260] Thus the latent variable scores are linear combinations of their observed indicators.

---

[254] See Wold (1966).
[255] Wold (1982a), p. 200.
[256] See Wold (1982b).
[257] See Lohmöller (1984); Lohmöller (1989).
[258] See Hui (1982).
[259] Fornell/Cha (1994), p. 64.
[260] The weight coefficients obtained in step one are rescaled in step two so that the latent variable scores obtained have unit variance.

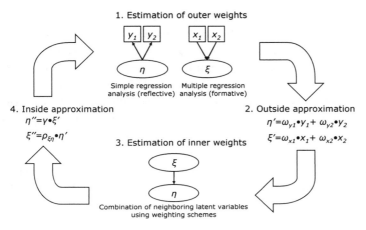

Figure 7: PLS algorithm[261]

In step three, the weight coefficients γ are obtained for the relations between latent variables, so that $Var[\zeta]$ is minimized for all endogenous latent variables. Three schemes for obtaining the weight coefficients γ are distinguished: centroid weighting, factor weighting and path weighting. First, the centroid weighting scheme sets weight coefficients either equal to +1 or −1 depending on the sign of the correlation between two latent variables. Second, the factor weighting scheme uses the correlation coefficient between two latent variables as weight. Finally, the path-weighting scheme determines weight coefficients depending on whether latent variables are antecedents or consequents of a certain "focal" latent variable. "To do this, all independent latent variables impacting the target latent variable are weighted by the multiple regression coefficients whereas all dependent LVs are weighted by the correlation coefficients".[262] Due to the limited differences in results obtained by the different weighting schemes,[263] the choice of a certain weighting scheme is almost arbitrary. Usually, the path weighting scheme is chosen, as it is "the only procedure […] that takes into account the directionality of the structural model"[264].

In step four, a new set of latent variable scores is calculated by aggregating latent variable scores obtained in step two with the help of the weights calculated in step three. More precisely, the score of a certain latent variable is obtained as a weighted aggregate of the latent variables directly connected to it in the path diagram.

---

[261] Adapted from Hänlein (forthcoming), p. 76. The weights used in step two are a rescaled version of the provisional weights obtained in step one so that latent variable scores have unit variance. The inside approximation shown makes use of the path weighting scheme.
[262] Chin (1998b), p. 305.
[263] See Noonan/Wold (1982), pp. 75ff.
[264] Chin (1998b), p. 305.

The PLS algorithm then returns to step one and determines new coefficients for each manifest variable. Rather than choosing arbitrary coefficients, regressions between manifest and latent variables are performed to determine coefficients. In the case of formative indicators, a multiple regression of the latent variable estimate on its indicators is performed minimizing $Var[\delta]$. In the case of reflective indicators, a simple regression of each indicator on the respective latent variable estimate is performed minimizing $Var[\xi]$. The simple regression (loading) coefficients λ and multiple regression coefficients π are subsequently used as weights ω ("omega") for aggregating manifest variables (step two).[265] The PLS algorithm then repeats steps one to four until the weights obtained do not change any more.

After convergence of the PLS algorithm,[266] weights and loading coefficients are calculated for the outer model, path coefficients and correlations for the inner model, and R-square coefficients for all endogenous latent variables.[267]

Going back to the statistical problems of covariance-based approaches, PLS is not susceptible to any of the four statistical problems mentioned. First, whereas covariance-based approaches require multi-normal distribution and interval scaling of manifest variables, "PLS estimation involves no assumptions about the population or scale of measurement"[268]. Therefore PLS is well suited for situations in which the distribution of manifest or latent variables is not well understood.

Second, the fit of PLS models is assessed using the coefficient of determination R^2 rather than the χ^2 test employed by covariance-based approaches.[269] The coefficient of determination is not biased by the sample size.[270]

---

[265] For reflective indicators, the simple regression coefficients (loadings) are used as weights for aggregating manifest variable scores to a latent variable score. "It is well-known that when using the loadings as weights for the LV, and doing this repeatedly (without inserting other steps as the inside approximation), than the LV will become the first principal component. (This algorithm for principal component analysis is called the power method, or vector iteration method, or von Mises method)" (Lohmöller (1984), p. 2-03).

[266] "For one and two block models, the iterative algorithms of PLS are almost always convergent. For multi-block models, however, convergence has not been proved, but practice suggests that non-convergence is rare" (Fornell/Cha (1994), p. 63.

[267] For a detailed description of the PLS algorithm see Lohmöller (1989), pp. 28ff; Fornell/Cha (1994), pp. 62ff; Chin (1998b), pp. 308ff.

[268] Fornell/Bookstein (1982), p. 443; Chin (1998b), p. 295. The only distributional requirement of PLS is the so-called predictor specification: it is assumed that each dependent variable is a (preferably) linear function of its independent variables and that there is no linear relationship between independent variables and the residual (see Lohmöller (1989), pp. 63ff). This can be considered as fulfilled in most cases (see Cassel et al. (1999); Naik/Tsai (2000)). Concluding, predictor specification "avoids the assumptions that the observations are jointly ruled by a specified multivariate distribution, and that the observations are independently distributed" (Fornell/Cha (1994), p. 55).

[269] See Kvalseth (1985), pp. 279ff for an introduction to the coefficient of determination R².

[270] See Chin (1998b), p. 316.

54

Third, whereas covariance-based approaches require considerable sample sizes for the maximum likelihood algorithm to converge,[271] PLS works even with very small sample sizes[272] in relation to the number of indicators or latent variables estimated. PLS is therefore well suited for analyzing complex structural equation models: "in large, complex models with latent variables PLS is virtually without competition"[273]. This is a result of the PLS estimation procedure that involves only a part of a structural equation model in each step of the analysis. The minimum sample size can be approximated with the following heuristic: "In general, one simply has [...] to find the largest of two possibilities: (a) the block with the largest number of formative indicators (i.e., largest measurement equation) or (b) the dependent [latent variable] LV with the largest number of independent LVs impacting it (i.e. largest structural equation)."[274] If one used a regression heuristic of 5 cases per parameter,[275] the sample size requirement would be 5 times either (a) or (b), whichever is larger.

Fourth, PLS can make use of both reflective and formative indicators of latent variables, whereas covariance-based approaches are restricted to the use of reflective indicators only.[276]

PLS is, however, not superior to covariance-based techniques in every respect: "it would be extremely misleading to view PLS only as an alternative to LISREL with less stringent assumptions."[277] PLS has the drawback that parameter estimates are biased with respect to the underlying, true parameters. This is due to the fact that latent variable scores are estimated as weighted aggregates of their corresponding indicators, which are always measured with a degree of noise or so-called measurement error. As a result, "the estimates of loadings and structural coefficients for the latent variable relationships are biased, being overestimated and underestimated, respectively"[278].

Parameter estimates obtained with covariance-based approaches on the other hand "are always consistent with respect to the model postulated, no matter how poor the indicators and the data are."[279] This is due to the fact that covariance-based algorithms do not estimate latent variable scores anywhere in the estimation process.

The bias of PLS parameter estimates relative to maximum likelihood (ML) estimates can be calculated for structural equation models with one and two latent variables:[280] It decreases as

---

[271] See above.
[272] Wold provides an extreme example of the low sample size requirements of PLS by estimating two latent constructs with a total of 27 variables with a data set of only ten cases (see Wold (1989)).
[273] Wold (1985), p. 590. This view is shared by Fornell/Bookstein (1982) and Fornell et al. (1990).
[274] Chin (1998b), p. 311.
[275] Bentler and Chou give a heuristic of five cases per parameter estimated (Bentler/Chou (1988), p. 172).
[276] See Chin (1998b), pp. 295ff.
[277] Hänlein (forthcoming), p. 79.
[278] Fornell/Cha (1994), p. 66.
[279] Lohmöller (1989), p. 215.
[280] See Lohmöller (1989), pp. 204ff. Bias formulas for estimating the amount of bias in structural equation models with more than two latent variables have not been provided so far.

the number of observations in the sample increases and as the number of indicators increases. The "PLS estimation tends toward the true population parameter as the number of indicators and sample size increase."[281] This behavior of PLS parameter estimates is called consistency at large.

A specific SEM technique should not only be chosen based on the advantages and drawbacks mentioned above. In the choice of a SEM technique, a researcher has to respect the different optimization philosophies minimizing residual variance and residual covariance, respectively. This "philosophy" discussion can be boiled down to the question, how much confidence one has in the correctness of the underlying model. If, based on strong theoretical and empirical evidence, one believes that the structural equation model is correct and that the indicators for each latent variable have no other shared factors, a covariance-based approach may be adopted. Assuming that model and indicators are correct, covariance-based approaches will choose parameters minimizing the difference between sample covariance and the covariance predicted. Covariance-based approaches are therefore parameter-oriented, giving optimal parameter accuracy. If, on the other hand, the structural equation model has so far not been tested or new latent variable measures are introduced, the PLS method should be chosen to obtain optimal predictions for dependent variables. That means "that there is a choice between parameter accuracy and prediction accuracy. We cannot have both, except for the special case when LISREL and PLS produce the same parameter estimates."[282]

For this thesis, the variance-based PLS approach for SEM will be adopted for the following reasons. First, returning to the above philosophy discussion, the research field of entrepreneurial finance is relatively new. As a result, relatively few structural models and latent variable measures have been tested. PLS is therefore the recommendable approach. Second, the indicators used in this study turn out to include both formative and reflective measures, which can hardly be modeled with covariance-based techniques due to identification problems. Third, the sample size of 101 portfolio companies is significantly below the recommended sample size of 200 for covariance-based SEM. Fourth, the measures used include nominal indicators, which conflicts with the assumptions of multi-normality and interval-scaling of covariance-based techniques.

---

[281] Chin et al. (1996), p. 31.
[282] Fornell/Cha (1994), p. 74.

5 Derivation of Hypotheses and Design of the Survey Instrument

In the previous chapter variance-based SEM – PLS to be precise – was chosen as methodology of data analysis. As shown above, a structural equation model consists of two elements, the structural model – determining the relationship between latent variables – and the measurement model – determining the relationship between latent variables and their associated manifest variables. This chapter will first specify the structural model by linking latent variables with a set of hypotheses. It is important to note that the hypotheses derived are small in number and relatively abstract when compared to research relying on first-generation techniques. This is due to the fact that hypotheses link a small number of abstract latent variables rather than a large number of manifest variables. The relationship between latent variables and their associated manifest variables – the measurement model – is discussed separately in a second part. The separate discussion of structural model and measurement model is due to the fact that relationships among latent variables can reasonably only be analyzed if each latent variable is measured appropriately. Both structural model and measurement model will be based on existing studies on post-investment value addition by private equity firms. The system-based view of controlling serves thereby as a framework to logically organize the dimensions of post-investment value addition.

5.1 Derivation of Hypotheses

5.1.1 Activities of Private Equity Firms

As discussed in chapter 3.3, the analysis of private equity firm activities will not be restricted to planning, control and information system activities. Extending the system-based view of controlling, all activities of private equity firms, which have the goal of adding value to a portfolio company, will be analyzed.

Private equity firms "play roles over and beyond those of traditional financial intermediaries"[283]. Traditional financial intermediaries such as banks frequently restrict themselves to giving capital to a firm and monitoring it subsequently. Private equity firms provide in addi-

---

[283] Hellmann/Puri (2002), p. 169.

tion managerial assistance to the management of their portfolio company.[284] Although most private equity firms offer some sort of managerial assistance to their portfolio companies, the focus and the magnitude of their activities can differ considerably. Empirical evidence suggests that private equity firms are most involved in financial and personnel management issues, where involvement is not necessarily continual, overly time consuming or requiring specialist know-how beyond the financial engineering skills readily available in any private equity firm. They are less involved in management team selection and operations, where involvement has to be on a continual basis, takes time or requires specialist skills such as work experience in the portfolio company's industry or P&L experience. Private equity firms with a broad spectrum and overall high level of involvement are called hands-on, whereas private equity firms with a narrow spectrum of activities focusing on financial or personnel management issues and a limited level of involvement are considered hands-off.[285]

Researchers have hypothesized that hands-on involvement of private equity firms will add value to portfolio companies.[286] Due to their management expertise, private equity firms may on the one hand help portfolio company management in making better business decisions. On the other hand hands-on involvement of private equity firms may keep portfolio company management from making wrong decisions. As shown in table 3, the majority of empirical studies conducted so far have been able to confirm the hypothesis, for various countries and financing stages. However, a non-negligible number of studies have on the other hand been unable to find any relationship and one study even found evidence for a negative relationship between private equity firm involvement and value added to portfolio companies.[287]

The difficulty of researchers to find evidence for the positive impact of private equity firm involvement on the performance of portfolio companies can be attributed to two causes. First, almost all of the studies shown in table 3 include portfolio companies of more than one financing stage. However, hands-on involvement is characterized by different activities in different financing stages.[288] Mixing portfolio companies in different financing stages into one sample may therefore conceal a positive relationship between hands-on involvement and value added to the portfolio company. Second, all but one of the studies shown in table 3

---

[284] See Fenn et al. (1997), pp. 54ff. Providing both capital and managerial assistance differentiates private equity firms also from management consultants. Management consultants provide managerial assistance, however, only rarely invest in their clients.

[285] See Harrison/Mason (1992), p. 389. Similar empirical findings on the activities of private equity firms are provided by MacMillan et al. (1989), p. 32; Gorman/Sahlman (1989), p. 237; Landström (1990), p. 357; Ehrlich et al. (1994), p. 75; Elango et al. (1995), p. 165; Morris et al. (2000), p. 73; Kraft (2001), p. 242; Schefczyk/Gerpott (2001), p. 301; Brinkrolf (2002), p. 141; Ruppen (2002), p. 191; Reißig-Thust (2003), p. 263.

[286] See all of the studies listed in table 5.

[287] See table 3.

[288] Schefczyk (2000), pp. 305-306 shows that activities of private equity firms investing in early or late stage portfolio companies are significantly different.

make use of first-generation multivariate research methods such as factor analysis, cluster analysis or regression analysis – techniques that are limited to the analysis of observable variables. The involvement of private equity firms is, however, not observable. It is rather a latent variable measurable through an array of individual activities. In this context the use of first-generation techniques is methodologically flawed. Using a methodologically flawed research technique may have obscured the relationship between involvement and value added to portfolio companies.

Author	Sample	Methodology	Impact of hands-on private equity firm involvement on value added
MacMillan et al. (1989)	62 US seed, start-up and expansion stage portfolio companies (pfc.) in high tech, health care and specialty retailing sectors	Factor, cluster and regression analysis	O
Sapienza/Timmons (1989) and Sapienza (1992)	51 US pfc. (all financing stages) in high-tech, service and low-tech sectors	Regression analysis	+
Landström (1990)	162 Swedish seed, start-up and expansion stage pfc.	Cluster analysis	+
Fredriksen et al. (1991) and Fredriksen et al. (1997)	59 Swedish seed, start-up and expansion stage pfc.	Factor, cluster and regression analysis	O
Barney et al. (1996)	205 US start-up and expansion stage pfc.	Factor and regression analysis	O
Sapienza et al. (1996)	65 US and 156 European (British, French and Dutch) pfc. (all financing stages)	Regression analysis	+
Sweeting/Wong (1997)	7 UK start-up, expansion and buyout stage pfc.	Case studies	O
Fried et al. (1998)	10 publicly held US biotech firms and 68 US seed, start-up and expansion stage pfc.	Descriptive statistics	+
Schefczyk/Gerpott (1998) and Schefczyk (2000)	103 German pfc. (all financing stages)	Correlation and causal analysis	+
Brinkrolf (2002)	59 German seed and start-up stage pfc.	Correlation analysis	-
Ruppen (2002)	119 Swiss, German, British and US expansion stage pfc.	Descriptive statistics	+
Reißig-Thust (2003)	114 German pfc. (all financing stages)	Correlation analysis	+
Busenitz et al. (2004)	183 US start-up and expansion stage pfc.	Correlation and regression analysis	O

Table 3: Impact of post-investment involvement on value added to portfolio company (+: positive relationship; O: no relationship; -: negative relationship)

Concluding, researchers have hypothesized that private equity firms may add value to portfolio companies through hands-on involvement. So far, the majority of empirical studies have been able to detect the relationship between hands-on involvement and value added. However, a non-negligible number of studies were unable to detect the relationship, presumably due to the analysis of portfolio companies in different financing stages and the use of first-generation research techniques. Given that this thesis analyzes portfolio companies in the buyout financing stage only and is making use of the second-generation multivariate research technique partial least squares, the following hypothesis is expected to be verified:

H 1: *Hands-on involvement of private equity firms has a positive impact on the value added to a buyout.*

5.1.2 Organization of Involvement

Following the system-based view of controlling, the organizational structure of interaction between private equity firms and their portfolio companies shall be analyzed in the following.

The interaction between private equity firms and their portfolio companies can be organized either in a rather informal or somewhat formal way.[289] Formal ways of organizing the interaction between private equity firm and portfolio company are board representation[290] or membership in the management team (in two-tier board systems) or the group of executive directors (in one-tier board systems)[291]. Empirical studies have shown that board representation is a common form of interaction between private equity firms and their portfolio companies,[292] whereas membership in the management team is relatively rare due to the time commitment implied and the industry expertise and company-specific knowledge needed.[293] Informal settings imply that private equity firms advise their management team on business decisions to be taken without threatening with formal action in the board of directors or the management team. Says a venture capitalist cited by Fried and Hisrich: "It's really the personal relationship that you develop with the guy running the company and his team and the other directors. [You have influence] if they conclude that you are an interesting person committed to the success of the company, that you're going to work hard at it, that you're not going to try to run it, that you're going to be very open, and that you think clearly and communicate clearly and are just

---

[289] See Fried/Hisrich (1995), pp. 106ff.

[290] For a – although somewhat outdated – review and synthesis of the literature on the board of directors see Zahra/Pearce (1989). An overview and comparison of board systems in European countries can be found in Gregory/Simmelkjaer (2001), pp. 43ff.

[291] For an overview and comparison of managerial bodies in Europe see Gregory/Simmelkjaer (2001), pp. 43ff.

[292] Reißig-Thust (2003), p. 205 found that German private equity firms are represented on the board of directors in 80% of all portfolio companies studied.

[293] Reißig-Thust (2003), p. 205 finds that private equity firms had taken management tasks in only 7% of the portfolio companies studied.

a valuable person to have around."[294] Empirical evidence suggests that private equity firms are increasingly using informal forms of organization.[295]

Informal organization of the relationship with the portfolio company is believed to drive value added. On the one hand side overly formal interaction is believed to impact negatively on value added to a portfolio company: an overly formal organization may give rise to resentment by portfolio company management or even open confrontation. Informal ways of interaction on the other hand are believed to add value to portfolio companies as they are more effective in convincing portfolio company management of the course of action to be taken. Says a private equity professional quoted by Fried and Hisrich: "What gives me the most influence is if the entrepreneur accepts me as a partner in this venture, and he respects my opinion, my industry knowledge, to the point where he seeks out my advice. If I can position myself that way, I can work very effectively with someone"[296]. The benefits of an informal organization of the relationship between private equity firm and portfolio company have been largely confirmed by empirical studies conducted so far, identifying informal ways of interaction with a portfolio company as the most effective organizational setting for influencing managers.[297]

H 2: Informal organization of the relationship between private equity firm and portfolio company has a positive impact on value added.

Author	Sample	Methodology	Impact of informal organization on value added
Fried/Hisrich (1995)	14 US seed, start-up and expansion stage pfc.	Case studies	+
Schefczyk/Gerpott (1998) and Schefczyk (2000)	103 German pfc. (all financing stages)	Correlation and causal analysis	+
Reißig-Thust (2003)	114 German pfc. (all financing stages)	Correlation analysis	O

Table 4: Impact of informal organization of the relationship between private equity firm and portfolio company on value added. (+: positive relationship; O: no relationship; -: negative relationship)

5.1.3 Information Systems

Information systems are an important input to post-investment value addition by private equity firms. Private equity firms have access to a number of information systems: the portfolio company's information system, the information systems of external resources such as man-

---

[294] Fried/Hisrich (1995), p. 106.
[295] Schefczyk/Gerpott (1998), p. 151 found that private equity firms were using informal settings for interaction in 42% of all portfolio companies studied. Several years later Reißig-Thust (2003), p. 205 found that private equity firms advise their portfolio companies in informal settings in already 79% of all cases.
[296] Fried/Hisrich (1995), p. 107.

agement consultants, industry experts or executive search firms, and finally their own proprietary information system. Empirical studies conducted so far found that the portfolio company's information system is most important for private equity firm intelligence: due to the size and complexity of portfolio companies in the buyout stage, private equity firms' proprietary information systems, maintained by a handful of professionals, are only of limited profoundness. The information systems of external resources are profound, however, too expensive for continuous use and relevant only for narrowly circumcised topics. Therefore this section will focus on the performance of portfolio company information systems.[298]

Having effective portfolio company information systems is associated with two benefits for private equity firms. Well-informed private equity firms can identify developing issues faster.[299] Moreover, private equity firms with effective information systems are able to make their decisions on a solid data base and are therefore more likely to make the right decisions adding value to the portfolio company.[300] The performance of portfolio company information systems is therefore expected to have a positive impact on value added.

H 3: The performance of portfolio company information systems has a positive impact on value added.

A portfolio company's information system can be analyzed along its process steps, just as any other information system: identification of information needs, gathering of information, combination of different pieces of information with the help of methods and models and finally transmission in form of managerial reports.[301] For private equity firms using a portfolio company's information system, the process works as follows: First, private equity firms define their information needs. Then, portfolio company executives or employees coordinate the gathering and combination of different pieces of information within their organization.[302] Finally, portfolio company executives or employees transmit information to the private equity firm. Given that this thesis focuses on post-investment value addition by private equity firms, only the definition of information needs by private equity firms and the transmission of information to the private equity firm will be analyzed.

---

[297] See table 4.
[298] See Nagtegaal (1999), pp. 193ff.
[299] See KPMG/Manchester Business School (2002), p. 4.
[300] See KPMG/Manchester Business School (2002), p. 4.
[301] See chapter 3.2.
[302] Private equity firms will not always ask a portfolio company executive to coordinate information gathering and combination. As one interviewed private equity professional put it: "if I need a certain piece of information, I will not always call the CFO and detract him from normal work. At times, I will rather call a knowledgeable finance professional of the portfolio company and ask him directly for the data."

Definition of information needs and transmission of information from portfolio companies to private equity firms is analyzed by researchers along three dimensions:[303] completeness and intensity of reporting, frequency of interaction and quality of information.

The basis for any information system set up between a portfolio company and a private equity firm is a formalized, written reporting. Reißig-Thust argues that complete and intense formal reporting helps private equity firms to identify deviations of the portfolio company from the business plan, which in turn allows private equity firms to intervene in time and take counter-measures. Reißig-Thust proposes therefore that private equity firms implementing a comprehensive and intense formal reporting benefit from elevated investment success. Testing the hypothesis at 113 German portfolio companies of private equity firms, Reißig-Thust is, however, not able to confirm this hypothesis.[304]

Although Reißig-Thust does not offer an explanation for this finding, Henry Mintzberg discovered as early as 1972 that executives dislike written reports as a source of information. Executives require information that has to be current to the degree that "gossip, hearsay, and speculation constitute a large part of the manager's information diet"[305] – formal reporting, however, always provides information with a time lag determined by the reporting frequency. Moreover, Mintzberg found that executives prefer information that triggers actions rather than digging through report data.[306]

H 3a: Completeness and intensity of portfolio company reporting have no impact on the perceived performance of information systems.

Besides formalized, written reporting, private equity firms exchange information with their portfolio company through telephone and personal interaction. Frequent interaction between private equity firm and portfolio company has been shown to generate trust.[307] Given a trustful relationship, portfolio company management will be more likely to communicate also unpleasant news. Moreover frequent interaction will give private equity professionals a deeper understanding of the portfolio company's business and industry.[308] Then frequent interaction

---

[303] Sapienza/Timmons (1989), Sapienza et al. (1996), Schefczyk (2000), pp. 300ff and Ruppen (2002), pp. 160ff focus on the analysis of the frequency of interaction. KPMG/Manchester Business School (2002), pp. 2ff emphasize the importance of quality of information transmitted by portfolio companies. Reißig-Thust (2003), pp. 207ff and pp. 229ff analyzes the completeness and intensity of reporting on the basis of the work of Ehrlich et al. (1994), pp. 72ff. Apart from reporting systems, Reißig-Thust includes also the frequency of interaction in her analysis.

[304] See Reißig-Thust (2003), p. 126 and p. 235. The findings of Reißig-Thust are consistent with previous research on reporting practices in small enterprises: studies have unanimously found that the completeness and intensity of reporting has no impact on the performance of small firms (see Ray/Hutchinson (1983); Thomas/Evanson (1987), pp. 555ff; McMahon/Davies (1994), pp. 14ff).

[305] See Mintzberg (1972), p. 95.

[306] See Mintzberg (1972), pp. 92ff.

[307] See Welpe (2002), p. 21.

[308] See De Clercq/Sapienza (2002).

makes the information transmitted more current. Frequent interaction is therefore likely to have a positive impact on the perceived performance of information systems.[309]

H 3b: Frequency of interaction between private equity firm and portfolio company has a positive impact on the perceived performance of information systems.

High frequency of interaction will not be helpful, however, if information of poor quality is transmitted. Poor quality information, i.e. information not "fit for use by the information customer"[310], will give private equity firms a hard time deducing action implications: private equity firms will have to put in a significant amount of time to verify and analyze poor quality information. High quality of portfolio company information is therefore proposed to have a significant impact on the perceived performance of information systems.

H 3c: Quality of portfolio company information has a positive impact on the perceived performance of information systems.

5.1.4 Actors

The fourth dimension of the system-based view of controlling is the actor. Due to their limited resources, private equity firms have to leverage themselves through a number of external resources and are therefore not the only actors.[311] The analysis of actors will therefore focus on both the private equity professional and external resources used to complement management capacity and capabilities.

5.1.4.1 Private Equity Professionals

Flat hierarchies are typical for private equity firms. Three hierarchy levels are distinguished: partner, investment manager and analyst. During the post-investment phase, typically one specific partner is responsible for guiding a portfolio company. At times, especially for investments requiring intensive monitoring and support, the private equity partner may delegate tasks to an investment manager. An analyst will support both investment manager and partner with analyses. The private equity professional, whose experience is relevant for the post-investment phase, is therefore the partner responsible for a portfolio company.

Private equity partners have been shown to be highly experienced individuals on average, although there is some variation. In a survey of 148 US private equity partners, Smart, Payne and Yuzaki found that 42% had been in the private equity industry for more than eleven

---

[309] Empirical studies conducted so far have not analyzed the impact of frequency of interaction on perceived performance of information systems. However several empirical studies have been able to show that high interaction frequency is associated with increased private equity firm efficiency (see Sapienza/Timmons (1989); Sapienza et al. (1996)) and increased portfolio company performance (see Ruppen (2002), p. 164; for counter-evidence see Schefczyk (2000), p. 308; Reißig-Thust (2003), p. 235).

[310] Huang et al. (1998), p. 43.

[311] See Smart et al. (2000), p. 24.

years, 40% between four and eleven years and 18% had less than four years private equity experience. In addition to private equity experience, partners were found to have significant business experience prior to entering the private equity industry. 81% had more than three years of prior business experience and 42% had more than ten years. Although some private equity partners gathered their business experience in professional services industries such as consulting, 68% of the partners surveyed had operating experience.[312]

Differences in experience among private equity partners are believed to have an impact on the performance of portfolio companies.

Past research in judgment and decision-making has shown different effects of increased experience on decision quality. On the one hand there is evidence that more experienced individuals tend to develop more efficient decision processes. For example increased experience helps an individual to focus on the key dimensions of a problem and ignore extraneous variables.[313] On the other hand increasing experience may not always result in better decisions. For example increasing experience may induce an individual to suffer from overconfidence, overestimating the likelihood of certain events.[314] It is unclear therefore from past research in judgment and decision-making whether or not more experience will result in better decision making.

Not surprisingly, studies on the impact of private equity professional experience on the performance of a private equity fund or an individual investment show mixed results. Burgel and Murray found in their dataset of 134 UK private equity funds a marginally significant correlation between experience and fund performance. The validity of Burgel and Murray's findings are doubtful, however, as experience has been operationalized in a very simple, potentially too simple way. Burgel and Murray measured experience on the basis of whether private equity firms had raised their first-time versus a follow-up fund. This measure of experience may determine at best the average private equity experience of fund professionals, neglecting any other experience. Moreover, professionals of first-time versus follow-up funds may not even be characterized by differing experience, given that only highly experienced individuals are able to raise a fund.[315]

Similarly, Kaplan and Schoar found a positive and significant correlation between experience – measured as the sequence number of a fund – and fund performance in their analysis of 746 US private equity funds. Again, the validity of Kaplan and Schoar's findings is doubtful due to their over-simplistic measurement of experience.[316]

---

[312] See Smart et al. (2000), pp. 11ff.
[313] See Chase/Simon (1973), pp. 55ff; Choo/Trotman (1991), pp. 464ff; Weber (1980), pp. 214ff. An extensive overview of efficiency gains as a result of more experience is given by Shepherd et al. (2003), p. 383.
[314] See Oskamp (1982), pp. 287ff; Mahajan (1992), pp. 329ff; Zacharakis/Shepherd (2001). An overview of detrimental effects of increasing experience is given by Shepherd et al. (2003), pp. 383f.
[315] See Burgel/Murray (2000).
[316] See Kaplan/Schoar (2003), pp. 13f.

De Clercq and Sapienza on the other hand were not able to confirm a positive relationship between experience and portfolio company performance in their sample of 263 randomly selected portfolio companies. The validity of De Clercq and Sapienza's findings is questionable, however, as well. Experience was measured as the average private equity experience held by all of a firm's partners. Other measures of experience, such as operative experience or professional services experience of private equity partners were neglected.[317]

Given that confirmatory studies on the relationship between experience and performance show methodological deficiencies, this thesis will follow the findings of an exploratory survey among 24 UK private equity executives reflecting industry beliefs: private equity executives interviewed by KPMG and Manchester Business School regarded the skill base of a private equity firm as a crucial success factor. [318]

H 4: Experience of private equity professionals has a positive impact on value added to the portfolio company.

With regard to the skills needed KPMG and Manchester Business School emphasize that private equity firms are currently relying too heavily on a finance-based skill set, whereas – especially for post-investment involvement – non-financial, industry expertise would be needed. Says a private equity partner cited by KPMG and Manchester Business School: "The skill base was ex-investment but is increasingly ex-business. We are actively trying to change the skill base in that direction."[319]

5.1.4.2 External Resources

External resources are used by private equity firms to complement their own management capacity and capabilities. Kraft found in his study of 44 US private equity firms focusing on turnaround investments that industry experts were the most heavily used outside resource followed by management consultants and interim managers.

Industry experts are frequently recruited among management team members of former buyouts. Instead of playing golf day by day, as one of the private equity professionals interviewed put it, management teams of previous buyouts may be interested in taking the challenge of adding value to a portfolio company. Particularly in cases in which private equity professionals do not know a portfolio company's industry very well, industry experts may help to build up industry specific know-how.

Management consultants may be used post-investment for two purposes. Management consultants may be used directly after the acquisition of a portfolio company to identify and prioritize sources of value creation developing key strategic milestones, a quick-hit operational plan and business development opportunities. Management consultants may also be used to coordinate company improvement efforts designed at acquisition, elaborating growth strate-

---

[317] See De Clercq/Sapienza (2002).
[318] KPMG/Manchester Business School (2002), pp. 4ff.
[319] KPMG/Manchester Business School (2002), p. 8.

gies, managing add-on acquisitions, reducing costs and assets or designing customer retention programs.[320]

Whereas management consultants are usually focusing on supporting portfolio company management, interim managers are different in so far as they replace some or all members of a management team.[321]

Besides industry experts, management consultants and interim managers, private equity firms interviewed for the purposes of this study also claimed to use executive search firms and CEOs of other portfolio companies on a regular basis. Executive search firms are used to find suitable candidates for portfolio company management positions. Some private equity firms also claimed to bring together the CEOs of their portfolio companies on a regular basis in order to let them exchange their experience.

The impact of external resource usage on the performance of private equity funds or individual portfolio companies has so far only been analyzed by one study. In his analysis of 44 turnaround funds, Kraft concludes that low, medium and high-performing private equity funds do not show differences in the usage of external resources. The validity of Kraft's findings is, however, questionable given that Kraft does not use any statistical test giving an indication of significance levels. Moreover Kraft's findings are contradicted by private equity firms' behavior. Private equity firms do make significant use of external resources.[322] Given the focus of private equity firms on financial results, external resources would have to add value to an investment – otherwise private equity firms would quickly stop using them. Says Bill Price (managing partner of Texas Pacific Group, one of the largest private equity funds worldwide): "The bottom line is equity investing in our business, so we don't give it away lightly. But, in some cases, consultants […] add enough value so it is appropriate."[323] Complementing private equity firms' management capacity and capabilities, external resources are therefore expected to add value to a portfolio company.[324]

H 5:   *Usage of external resources is positively associated with value added to the portfolio company.*

5.1.5 Summary of Hypotheses and Research Model

The endogenous variable of this study's research model is "value added to buyout". Four exogenous and one endogenous variables are expected to have an impact on the "value added to buyout". Specifically, private equity firms are expected to add value to buyouts by:

---

[320] See Bain&Company (2003), p. 5.
[321] See Kraft (2001), p. 256.
[322] See Kraft (2001), p. 258.
[323] Valdmanis (1998).
[324] This expectation is consistent with previous research on external resource usage by small and medium sized enterprises. Robson/Bennett (2000), pp. 202ff find statistical significant relationships between the use of external business advice in the fields of business strategy or staff recruitment and employee and turnover growth.

- Hands-on involvement
- Informal organization of the relationship between private equity firm and the portfolio company
- Construction of high performing portfolio company information systems
- Provision of experienced private equity professionals
- Usage of external resources

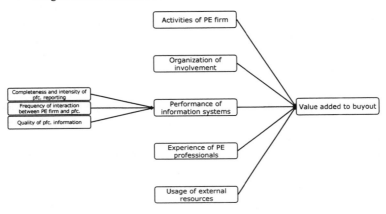

Figure 8: Research model.

The second endogenous variable "performance of information systems" is in turn expected to be influenced by the latent variables "completeness and intensity of portfolio company reporting", "frequency of interaction between private equity firm and portfolio company" and the "quality of portfolio company information". High performing portfolio company information systems are expected in the case of:

- High frequency of interaction between private equity firm and portfolio company
- High quality of portfolio company information

Complete and intense portfolio company reporting is expected to have no impact on the performance of information systems.

5.2 Design of the Survey Instrument

In the previous chapter variance-based SEM in the form of PLS was chosen as method for data analysis. Choosing a SEM technique for data analysis requires the operationalization of latent variables by suitable indicators. The purpose of this chapter will therefore be to design a survey instrument measuring all nine latent variables included in the above research model.

5.2.1 Fundamental Considerations

Three fundamental considerations have to be taken into account with respect to the operationalization of this study's latent variables. First of all, a tradeoff has to be made between the breadth of the research model and the depth of latent variable measures.[325] Due to the limited amount of time that a survey participant will invest in answering a questionnaire, only a limited number of questions can be included in a survey instrument. This limited number of questions can, on the one hand, be used to analyze a relatively simple research model with in-depth latent variable measures. For example Reinartz et al. analyzed the impact of customer relationship management (CRM) implementation on performance – a comparatively simple research model.[326] The CRM implementation variable was operationalized in-depth, however, using more than 40 items. On the other hand, a limited number of questions can be used to analyze a rather complex research model with straightforward latent variable measures. This strategy was adopted for the current study. The relationship among nine latent variables is analyzed with the help of one to 22 items per latent variable.

Second, (interval scaled) items can be measured either directly or by rating scales with predefined response alternatives. For example the age of a person can be measured either by a rating scale with predefined age categories (e.g. 20–24 years) or by asking directly for the precise age of a person. In this study all items were measured by rating scales. The decision to use rating scales, even if a variable could have been measured directly, was taken to avoid the problem of missing values and to decrease the time needed to fill in the questionnaire. For example a study participant may not know the precise age of the partner responsible for the portfolio company. Using rating scales, the study participant may, however, be able to indicate the partner's age within the given age categories. Asking for the precise age of the partner will require the study participant to look it up in his records, thereby increasing the time needed to answer the questionnaire. Alternatively the study participant might simply skip the question regarding a partner's age and go on to the next question leaving a missing value.

Third, the optimal number of response alternatives for a rating scale is subject to discussion. On the one hand rating scales with only two or three response alternatives "are generally inadequate in that they are incapable of transmitting very much information and they tend to frustrate and stifle respondents."[327] On the other hand "the marginal returns from using more than nine response alternatives are minimal and efforts for improving the measurement instrument should be directed toward more productive areas."[328] Therefore the optimum is somewhere between four and nine response alternatives for a scale. Moreover, an odd number of response alternatives is justified, whenever the study participant can legitimately claim a

---

[325] See Hänlein (forthcoming), p. 33.
[326] See Reinartz et al. (2003).
[327] Cox (1980), p. 420.
[328] Cox (1980), p. 420.

neutral position. An even number of response alternatives is preferable, when the study participant should be forced to take a supportive or dismissive position.[329] Regarding the items of this survey, the study participant can reasonably take a neutral position. For example the performance of a portfolio company can be just as foreseen in the business plan – implying that the study participant takes a neutral position between the two extremes – worse and better than business plan.[330] The optimum number of response alternatives for a rating scale for this study is therefore either five, seven or nine. The choice among those three alternatives is almost arbitrary. For reasons of consistency with other research projects in this field of research,[331] a number of seven response alternatives was chosen.

In the following section, each of the research model's nine latent variables – as well as the items used for measurement – will be discussed in more detail.

5.2.2 Activities of Private Equity Firms

The activities of private equity firms were operationalized in this study by a total of 22 individual activity measures in the fields of business development/partnerships, operations, management recruiting, management coaching, finance and controlling. Each activity was measured by a rating scale with seven response alternatives. The seven response alternatives were calibrated by an unlabeled semantic differential:[332] "low involvement" – "high involvement".

The most influential operationalization of private equity firm activities is from MacMillan et al., which has been adopted by almost all studies analyzing the impact of post-investment involvement on value added to a portfolio company.[333] Two studies that did not adopt MacMillan et al.'s operationalization were conducted by Sweeting and Wong as well as Fried et al.[334] Sweeting and Wong were unable to adopt the operationalization of MacMillan et al., as they made use of a case study methodology rather than a questionnaire-based survey design. Fried et al. did not use the operationalization of Macmillan et al. due to their focus on board involvement in strategy issues. Fried et al. therefore chose an operationalization of board in-

---

[329] See Cox (1980), pp. 407ff.
[330] See Schefczyk (2000), p. 165.
[331] See e.g. Brettel (forthcoming); Reißig-Thust (2003).
[332] The semantic differential, developed by Osgood et al. (1957), usually takes the form of a 5- or 7-point bipolar scale. Three forms of the semantic differential can be distinguished with respect to the labeling of points on the scale: the unlabeled semantic differential labels only the two extreme points of the rating scale; the numerical semantic differential puts in addition to that a number next to every response alternative; the labeled semantic differential labels not only the extreme points, but every single point in the rating scale (see Garland (1990), pp. 19ff). The unlabeled semantic differential chosen here is regarded as the best alternative in cases in which the abstract thinking of study participants is required (see Garland (1990), pp. 19ff).
[333] The survey instrument of MacMillan et al. (1989) has been replicated in identical or slightly adapted form by Sapienza/Timmons (1989) and Sapienza (1992), Landström (1990), Fredriksen et al. (1991) and Fredriksen et al. (1997), Barney et al. (1996), Sapienza et al. (1996), Schefczyk/Gerpott (1998) and Schefczyk (2000), Brinkrolf (2002), Ruppen (2002) and Reißig-Thust (2003).
[334] See Sweeting/Wong (1997), pp. 125ff; Fried et al. (1998), pp. 493ff.

70

volvement in the formation and evaluation of strategy originally developed by Judge and Zeithaml.[335] Given that this study uses a questionnaire-based survey design, the study of Sweeting and Wong is not useful for an operationalization of private equity firm activities. Moreover the focus of Fried et al. on private equity firms' involvement in strategy formation and evaluation is too narrow for the current study that intends to analyze the entire spectrum of activities directed at portfolio companies. The operationalization of MacMillan et al. was therefore chosen to form the basis of this study's operationalization of private equity firm activities.

In their seminal study, MacMillan et al. measured the involvement of private equity firms in their portfolio companies with a total of twenty activities. With the help of factor analysis, MacMillan et al. found that fifteen variables attributable to the four factors "development and operations", "management selection", "personnel management" and "financial" explained most of the variance of private equity firm activities.[336] The basis of the current study's activity construct is formed by a slightly adapted list of Macmillan et al.'s activities. The factor "development and operations" was made up of the activities "formulating marketing plans", "testing or evaluating marketing plans", "soliciting customers or distributors", "selecting vendors and equipment", "developing production or service techniques" and "developing actual product or service" in MacMillan et al.'s survey instrument. Two activities, namely "developing actual product or service" and "developing production and service techniques", were dropped with regard to this study's survey instrument, as pre-testers unanimously deemed them irrelevant for buyout investments.[337] Moreover two activities, namely "focusing or consolidating operations" and "optimizing working capital", were included to get a complete picture of private equity firms' activities in the field of operations. The factor "management selection" was made up of the activities "searching for candidates of management team", "interviewing and selecting management team" and "negotiating employment terms with candidates". The list of activities measuring private equity firm involvement in the selection of a management team covers all major process steps and was therefore used unchanged for this study's survey instrument. The factor "personnel management" consisted of three activities, namely "serving as a sounding board to entrepreneur team", "motivating personnel" and "managing crises and problems". Again, the three activities proved to represent personnel management activities of private equity firms well and were therefore included unchanged as measures of this study's activity construct. Finally, the factor "financial" was composed by the activities "obtaining alternative sources of debt financing", "obtaining alternative sources of equity financing" and "monitoring financial performance". In order get a complete picture

---

[335] See Judge/Zeithaml (1992), pp. 766ff.
[336] See MacMillan et al. (1989), p. 33.
[337] With respect to the two activities dropped, MacMillan et al. seem to focus overly on portfolio companies in the seed and start-up financing stage.

of private equity firms' activities in the field of finance, two activities, namely "selling non-required assets" and "finding the right mix between debt and equity as well as short and long-term financing" were included.[338]

The above list of activities based on the survey of MacMillan et al. does not include measures in the fields of business development/partnerships or controlling. Nevertheless, Reißig-Thust has shown in her study of 114 portfolio companies of 49 German private equity firms that controlling has a positive and highly significant impact on the performance of a portfolio company.[339] Therefore three measures of the involvement of private equity firms in portfolio company's controlling systems were included: "designing management team performance measures and setting targets", "optimizing reporting systems" and "linking incentives to performance measures".[340] Moreover, participation of private equity firms in business development and the construction of partnerships has been expected to contribute to portfolio company success,[341] although the study of Reißig-Thust was unable to prove that relationship.[342] Three measures of business development/partnerships were thus included in the survey instrument: "defining acquisition and divestment program", "identifying and organizing partnerships and alliances" and "directing business plans".[343]

Concluding, this study takes the survey instrument of MacMillan et al. as a basis, developing it further by including measures in the fields of operations, finance, business development/partnerships and controlling. The result is a total of 22 activities measuring all aspects of private equity firms' post-investment activities in the fields of business development/partnerships, operations, management recruiting, management coaching, finance and controlling.

5.2.3   Organization of Involvement

The "organization of involvement" was operationalized in this study by three nominal variables, measuring whether or not a private equity firm had been carrying out consulting tasks, was a member of the board of directors/supervisory board or had been carrying out management tasks.

---

[338]   See (MacMillan et al. (1989), p. 33.
[339]   See Reißig-Thust (2003), p. 202.
[340]   Due to the insufficient operationalization of controlling as a single item measure by Reißig-Thust, the three measures mentioned have been constructed on the basis of expert interviews with private equity professionals.
[341]   See Rogers et al. (2002c), pp. 94ff.
[342]   See Reißig-Thust (2003), p. 202.
[343]   Due to the insufficient operationalization of business development/partnerships as a single item measure by Reißig-Thust, the three measures mentioned have been constructed on the basis of expert interviews with private equity professionals.

As discussed in chapter 5.1.2, the interaction between private equity firms and their portfolio companies can be organized in a rather formal way through board or management team interaction or in a fairly informal way advising portfolio company management on business decisions to be taken without resorting to formal power. "Organization of involvement" has been operationalized so far only once: Schefczyk used the indicators "asking for operative information", "carrying out consulting tasks", "participation of your firm in the board of directors/supervisory board" and "carrying out management tasks".[344] Whereas the indicator "carrying out consulting tasks" is indicative of a rather informal organization of the relationship between private equity firm and portfolio company, the indicators "participation of your firm in the board of directors/supervisory board" and especially "carrying out management tasks" are suggestive of a relatively formal setup of interaction between private equity firm and portfolio company. The usefulness of the indicator "asking for operative information" is, however, completely unclear – there is neither a connection to organization nor an indication of formal versus informal interaction. In this study the construct "organization of involvement" was therefore operationalized with the first three items mentioned – "carrying out consulting tasks", "participation of your firm in the board of directors/supervisory board" and finally "carrying out management tasks". The three alternative forms of interaction were operationalized as nominal variables – a scaling also chosen by Schefczyk and Reißig-Thust.[345]

Concluding, this study takes the survey instrument of Schefczyk as a basis, focusing the construct "organization of involvement" by dropping one indicator. The result is a list of three nominal indicators measuring whether a private equity firm adopts a formal or rather informal way when interacting with a portfolio company.

5.2.4 Information Systems

Portfolio company information systems were mapped in this study by four constructs: "completeness and intensity of portfolio company reporting", "frequency of interaction between private equity firm and portfolio company" and the "quality of portfolio company information" are supposed to have a positive impact on the "perceived performance of (portfolio company) information systems", which in turn is expected to have a positive impact on "value added to buyout". The four information system constructs were operationalized in this study as follows.

---

[344] Schefczyk (2000), p. 418. More precisely, Schefczyk/Gerpott (1998), pp. 145f differentiates "Mitarbeit von VCG in PU-Gremien (Beirat, Aufsichtsrat, Gesellschafterausschuss o.ä.) als Beratung im weiteren Sinne", "temporäre Übernahme von operativen Linienaufgaben in einem PU durch einen VCG-Vertreter" and "in einem interaktiven Prozess im Arbeitsalltag realisierten, professionellen, ganzheitlichen und temporär begrenzten Unterstützung durch VCG-Mitarbeiter bei der Lösung betriebswirtschaftlicher Probleme der PU [...], die als Beratung im engeren bzw. klassischen Sinn darauf ausgerichtet ist, Entscheidungen und Verhaltensweisen des PU zu beeinflussen." The operationalization of Schefczyk has been replicated in slightly adapted form by Reißig-Thust (2003), p. 205.

[345] See Schefczyk (2000), p. 300; Reißig-Thust (2003), p. 206.

The construct "completeness and intensity of portfolio company reporting" was operational-ized in this study by the items "revenue", "balance sheet and P&L", "cash flows", "interim qualitative reports on business situation", "reports on planned investments" and "reports on R&D or other projects". The construct has been designed on the basis of the survey instru-ments of Brettel and Reißig-Thust.[346] Starting from their operationalization, two changes were made. First, the item "budget compliance" was dropped, as financial reports of established companies will usually include budget, actual and forecast data. The information on whether a company complies with budget or not will therefore be contained in the P&L, balance sheet and cash flow data supplied. Moreover, the item "other company-specific success ratios" was dropped due to its ambiguity: different private equity professionals will have different con-ceptions of suitable success ratios – therefore data supplied with regard to this item cannot be compared across different private equity firms or even different private equity professionals of the same private equity firm. Each of the six remaining items was then measured by a rat-ing scale with seven response alternatives. Following Brettel and Reißig-Thust, the seven re-sponse alternatives were labeled: "never", "on request", "yearly", "half-yearly", "quarterly", "monthly" and "weekly".[347]

The construct "frequency of interaction" was operationalized by the three items "written con-tacts", "telephone calls, video conferences" and "personal meetings with management". The operationalization is based on the survey instruments of Sapienza, Schefczyk, Brettel, and Reißig-Thust,[348] which have been adapted in two respects. First, written and telephone con-tacts, while measured jointly in the above studies, were measured separately in this study: written and telephone contacts are not necessarily identical in terms of the information con-veyed.[349] Second, the item telephone contacts has been expanded to include video confer-ences as a state-of-the-art communication technique. Each of the three items of the construct "frequency of interaction" was measured by a rating scale with seven response alternatives. Following Brettel and Reißig-Thust, the seven response alternatives were labeled as follows: "never", "yearly", "half-yearly", "quarterly", "monthly", "weekly" and "daily".[350]

The construct "quality of portfolio company information" was operationalized by the vari-ables "timeliness", "appropriateness/suitability for your information needs" and "reliability".

---

[346] See Brettel (forthcoming), p. 257; Reißig-Thust (2003), p. 198.
[347] See Brettel (forthcoming), p. 257; Reißig-Thust (2003), p. 198. Labeling the response alternatives with re-gard to items of the construct completeness and intensity of portfolio company reporting is reasonable, as the respective frequencies can easily be given by study participants. Doubt about the comprehension of individ-ual response alternatives is thereby eliminated to the greatest possible extent (see Garland (1990), pp. 19ff).
[348] See Sapienza (1992), p. 25; Schefczyk (2000), p. 300; Reißig-Thust (2003), pp. 207f; Brettel (forthcoming), pp. 258f.
[349] See Mintzberg (1972), pp. 92ff.
[350] See Brettel (forthcoming), p. 259 and Reißig-Thust (2003), p. 207.

74

This operationalization follows the study of KPMG and Manchester Business School.[351] It was chosen among the available information quality operationalizations[352] due to its focus on the private equity industry. Each item was measured by a rating scale with seven response alternatives. The seven response alternatives were calibrated by an unlabeled semantic differential: "poor" – "good".[353]

The construct "performance of portfolio company information systems" is a second-order molar factor, i.e. a higher order latent variable that is modeled as being causally impacted by a number of first order latent variables.[354] "However, to postulate the existence of a second order factor that sits in a vacuum holds little value"[355] and besides that cannot be modeled with PLS. Therefore the second-order latent variable "performance of information systems" had to be operationalized by a measurable item. This was done with a general question reflecting the perceived performance of portfolio company information systems: "overall, do you feel that your portfolio company kept you well informed". The item was measured by a rating scale with seven response alternatives. The meaning of the seven response alternatives was specified with an unlabeled semantic differential: "not at all" – "absolutely".[356]

5.2.5 Experience of Private Equity Professionals

The latent variable "experience of private equity professionals" was operationalized with the items "work experience in professional services", "private equity experience", "P&L responsibility" and "work experience in the portfolio company's industry". The four items were measured by a scale with seven response alternatives, labeled as follows: "0–6 months", "6–12 months", "1–2 years", "2–4 years", "4–8 years", "8–16 years" and "more than 16 years".

As discussed above, the operationalization of experience in prior studies on the relationship between private equity professional experience and the impact on value added to portfolio companies has been simple: the indicators used were single item measures of experience[357] and moreover rather unreliable[358]. First, measuring a multifaceted construct like experience by

---

[351] See KPMG/Manchester Business School (2002), p. 4.

[352] See Soo/Devinney (2003), pp. 1ff and the sources quoted therein.

[353] The unlabeled semantic differential has been chosen due to the abstract character of information quality variables (see Garland (1990), pp. 19ff).

[354] See Chin (2000), pp. 53ff. For a discussion of the various models linking first and second order factors see Rindskopf/Rose (1988) and Chin/Gopal (1995).

[355] Chin (1998a), p. 10.

[356] The unlabeled semantic differential has been chosen due to the abstract character of the construct performance of information systems and its variables. See Garland (1990), pp. 19ff.

[357] Burgel/Murray (2000) measured experience on the basis of whether private equity firms had raised their first-time versus a follow-up fund, Kaplan/Schoar (2003) used the sequence number of a fund to measure experience and De Clercq/Sapienza (2002) measured the overall years of experience held by all private equity firm partners.

[358] The fact whether a private equity firm has raised its first or a follow-up fund (see Burgel/Murray (2000)) as well as the sequence number of a fund (see Kaplan/Schoar (2003)) is not necessarily a reliable measure of the experience of private equity professionals: a phenomenon observable in the private equity industry is that once a critical firm size is reached, some of the professionals tend to spin off and start-up their own private

only one item means neglecting a significant part of the construct's essence. Moreover, unreliable measures of a latent variable are likely to make any conclusion drawn from a structural relationship of that latent variable inadmissible. Due to the inappropriateness of prior operationalizations, the experience construct was designed starting from scratch. Given that this study focuses on the levers of post-investment value creation, the relevant experience of the partner/director mainly responsible for a portfolio company was to be measured, not the experience of private equity professionals in general. In order to identify the dimensions relevant for partners managing a portfolio company, expert interviews were conducted. The consensus of the experts interviewed was that four dimensions of experience are especially relevant for post-investment value creation. First, professional services experience was deemed valuable due to the quantitative skills that may be acquired – helping private equity partners to make decisions based on hard numbers rather than qualitative reasoning.[359] Second, private equity experience was regarded as important as private equity partners have to learn about the traps and lifelines in the daily cooperation with portfolio company management. Third, P&L responsibility of private equity partners was considered helpful in giving credibility to recommendations. Fourth, work experience in the portfolio company's industry helps private equity partners to add more value to a portfolio company and to do that quicker starting at acquisition – an inexperienced partner will require setup time in order to become familiar with a specific industry.

Concluding, the experience of private equity partners or directors relevant for post-investment value creation was operationalized in this study by four indicators identified through expert interviews.

5.2.6 Usage of External Resources

The construct "usage of external resources" was operationalized with the following four items: "management consultants", "interim managers", "industry experts", "CEOs of other portfolio companies" and "executive search firms". All five items were measured by a rating scale with seven response alternatives. The meaning of response alternatives was illuminated by a semantic differential labeling the two extreme points with "never" and "always", and the neutral response alternative with "every now and then".

---

equity firm (see Willert (forthcoming)), i.e. even private equity firms not having raised a fund so far may be led by highly experienced individuals. Moreover, the cumulative experience of a private equity firm's professionals may not result in an accurate reflection of experience: does a firm with a large number of inexperienced partners really have the same experience as a firm led by a small number of highly experienced partners?

[359] One German interviewee illustrated this argument – with respect to consulting – in a very colorful way: "In der Unternehmensberatung lernt man nach dem Prinzip 'ZDF statt ARD' zu arbeiten, d.h. Zahlen, Daten, Fakten statt alles redet Drumherum".

This operationalization is based on the study of Kraft, who analyzed the sources of management capacity for turnaround investments.[360] However, Kraft limited the analysis of external sources of management capacity to industry experts, interim managers and management consultants. The pre-testers of this study's survey instrument indicated Kraft's list as being too short and suggested, therefore, also including CEOs of other portfolio companies and executive search firms. Regular meetings among the CEOs of a private equity firm's portfolio companies may help to discuss problems on a peer-to-peer basis. Although the portfolio companies of a private equity firm will usually belong to different industries, many challenges of CEOs such as laying off employees, may be similar. Moreover, executive search firms may be helpful in finding both executives for a portfolio company and highly qualified second- and third-tier management. Concluding, the construct usage of external resources was operationalized in this study by five indicators – based both on an existing survey instrument and supplements identified with the help of pre-tests with private equity professionals.

5.2.7   Value Added to Buyout

The question how to measure value added to a buyout and how to compare value added among different buyouts is crucial, given that the goal of this study is to identify the levers of post-investment value creation.

In his study of success strategies of German venture capital firms, Schefczyk gives an overview of potential measures of portfolio company success.[361] Whereas several of Schefcyzk's measures are static in the sense that they measure only the current success of a portfolio company, this study needs dynamic measures of portfolio company success giving an indication of the value added to a buyout. More precisely, this study focuses on the cash flow growth-part of value added – other sources of value added, namely the opportunity cost of capital and the present value of financing side effects were shown above not to be relevant for a study focusing on the post-investment phase. Given that, the list of potential measures of portfolio company success given by Schefczyk will be discussed with respect to their suitability for measuring the cash flow growth-part of value added.

Seven measures of portfolio company success are given by Schefczyk:[362]

- P&L and balance sheet items and ratios: measures are return ratios (e.g. return on sales) or absolute numbers taken from the P&L or balance sheet (e.g. sales). However, P&L and balance sheet items and ratios can only be used for very homogeneous sam-

---

[360] See Kraft (2001), p. 258.
[361] See Schefczyk (2000), pp. 162ff.

ples of portfolio companies in terms of portfolio company size and industry[363] – which is not the case for this study[364]. Moreover, P&L and balance sheet items are static measures of portfolio company success that do not allow any form of inference on the value added by the private equity firm.

- Market shares: Despite the fact that market shares should only be compared for portfolio companies in similar industries and markets, market shares are a static measure of portfolio company success just as P&L and balance sheet items and therefore do not allow an inference on the value added by the private equity firm.[365]

- Growth rates on the other hand may help to measure the value added by private equity firms, as long as the measurement period of the growth rate is identical to the time that the private equity firm has been holding the portfolio company. However, growth rates of, for example, operating income can hardly be compared among different portfolio companies. This is due to the fact that growth rates are always a function of the starting value. Very small companies will therefore more easily achieve high growth rates than large corporations. It is therefore questionable whether growth rates are a realistic measure of value added by private equity firms.[366]

- Internal rate of return (IRR): In order to calculate the IRR, an interest rate has to be determined so that the present value of a series of payments between private equity firm and portfolio company is equal to zero. The IRR is useful on the one hand in that it is a dynamic measure of portfolio company success. The IRR has, however, several drawbacks inherent in its arithmetic.[367] Moreover, a reliable IRR can only be given when an investment into a portfolio company is realized. Before a portfolio company has been exited, any IRR measure is mere speculation. Then, the IRR is a measure of all sources of value added, including measures of post-investment value creation. It is therefore only a hazy measure of post-investment value creation. Therefore, the IRR,

---

[362] See Schefczyk (2000), pp. 162ff. The measures of portfolio company success given by Schefczyk are not mutually exclusive. The measures of portfolio company success given by Schefczyk are rather different (reflective) measures of the same underlying construct.

[363] See Brettel (forthcoming), pp. 200f.

[364] Although this study is homogeneous in that it focuses on portfolio companies in the buyout stage, the buyout cases provided by study participants are not homogeneous in terms of their industry focus and size.

[365] See MacMillan et al. (1987), pp. 125f.

[366] See Dubini (1989), pp. 128f.

[367] According to Brealey and Myers, the IRR is associated with four pitfalls (see Brealey/Myers (2000), pp. 101ff). First, there are projects, where the NPV increases as the discount rate increases – obviously making the IRR decision rule of accepting projects with an IRR above the opportunity cost of capital obsolete (instead, in this case, projects with an IRR below the opportunity cost of capital should be accepted). Second, there may exist multiple rates of return that make NPV equal to zero: "there can be as many different internal rates of return for a project as there are changes in the sign of the cash flows" (Brealey/Myers (2000), p. 103). Third, internal rates of return may be misleading, when a choice among mutually exclusive projects has to be made. In this case, a project A may be preferable to a project B on the basis of a higher IRR. However, at the same time project B may offer the opportunity to generate a larger NPV than project A, as more capital can be invested. This pitfall results from the inability of the IRR measure to account for the amount of capital committed. Fourth, the IRR assumes that there is no term structure of interest rates, as there is only one rate of the opportunity cost of capital used for decision.

although established as the (private equity) industry standard for performance measurement, should be used with great caution.

- Multiples: Multiples (e.g. earnings before interest and taxes (EBIT) multiple) are derived by dividing a portfolio company's (market) value by a specific value driver (e.g. EBIT). The difference between the exit and the purchase multiple of a private equity investment yields the so-called multiple expansion, a dynamic measure of portfolio company performance. Given, however, that multiple expansion is determined primarily in the deal structuring phase (purchase multiple) and in the exit phase (exit multiple), multiple expansion is not a suitable measure for post-investment value creation.[368]

- Subjective measures of portfolio company success rely on the judgment of study participants as opposed to interpersonally comparable, objective measures calculated from P&L and balance sheet data. Subjective measures of portfolio company performance may be associated with a higher measurement error than objective measures.[369] Apart from that, subjective measures have the advantage of allowing both static and dynamic measurement of portfolio company success – depending on the operationalization. Moreover, subjective measures can be operationalized so that post-investment value creation can be measured.[370] Then, subjective measures of portfolio company success have the advantage of being correlated to a large number of objective measures[371] and show a high disclosure rate, especially when compared to objective measures.[372] Subjective measures of portfolio company success are therefore ideally suited for the purposes of this survey.

- Avoidance of insolvency is a dichotomous measure of portfolio company success with the values avoidance of insolvency and insolvency. However, insolvency of portfolio companies is a relatively rare phenomenon in buyout investing – especially when compared to seed and start-up investing[373] – making its use in this study questionable.

Given the above discussion, the value added to a buyout can be measured best by subjective measures. Two subjective measures of post-investment value creation were used in this study.

---

[368] See the detailed discussion of multiples method above.
[369] See Schefczyk (2000), p. 164.
[370] See below.
[371] Dess and Robinson found that a company's subjective performance relative to its industry shows a significant positive correlation to objective measures of sales growth and return on assets (see Dess/Robinson (1984), pp. 265ff). Brush and Vanderwerf found that the subjective performance of a portfolio company relative to its industry has a high degree of correlation with various financial measures of performance (see Brush/Vanderwerf (1992), pp. 157ff). Schefczyk finds that the subjective performance relative to business plan and relative to the industry are highly and significantly correlated to the (objective) IRR (see Schefczyk (2000), p. 245).
[372] See Chandler/Hanks (1993), pp. 391ff. This characteristic is especially important for this study, given that private equity firms have a high need for secrecy.
[373] See Brettel (forthcoming), p. 202.

First, study participants were asked for the performance of their portfolio company relative to business plan on an eight-point rating scale (1: "total loss"; 2: "worse"; 5: "same"; 8: "better").[374] Second, study participants were asked for the performance of their portfolio company relative to competitors at acquisition (1: "in bankruptcy"; 2: "worse"; 5: "same"; 8: "better") and currently/at exit (1: "total loss"; 2: "worse"; 5: "same"; 8: "better"). The difference between the subjective performance relative to competitors at exit and at acquisition was used as a measure of value creation.[375]

---

[374] This measure has also been used by Schefczyk (2000), Reißig-Thust (2003) and Brettel (forthcoming).

[375] Prior studies have only asked for the current performance or the performance at exit of the portfolio company relative to its competitors (see Schefczyk (2000); Reißig-Thust (2003); Brettel (forthcoming)). In order to focus on the value added to a portfolio company, the measure used in this study asked for the performance of the portfolio company at acquisition and currently, or at exit.

6 Data Collection and Analysis

6.1 Data Collection

In order to test the structural equation model introduced above, data has to be gathered in a quantity and quality that allows the selected structural equation modeling technique to converge. In this chapter the details of data collection will therefore be described.

The survey instrument outlined above is tailored to the portfolio company as unit of analysis. It has been preferred to a fund level analysis, as private equity firms are extremely reluctant to release any information on fund performance. For example private equity firms turned down the University of California, when it recently tried to invest in several private equity funds: private equity firms were afraid that the University of California – as a public institution – would have to disclose the performance of its funds.[376]

Potential data sources for the above survey instrument are private equity firms, portfolio companies or matched pairs (dyads) of private equity firms and portfolio companies. For the current study, data was collected only among private equity firms. This choice was made due to the considerable number of realized investments that private equity professionals are usually knowledgeable about – compared to the typically single experience portfolio company management has with a private equity firm. Moreover, private equity professionals will frequently be able to report about realized investments, whereas portfolio company management can typically report only about a current investment – the portfolio company they are running. Focusing on private equity firms rather than portfolio companies or dyads of private equity firms and portfolio companies also does not give rise to any kind of bias: answers given by private equity professionals have been shown not to differ significantly from answers given by the portfolio company management.[377]

Given the specification of the portfolio company as unit of analysis and the private equity firm as data source, each private equity firm was asked to complete the questionnaire for one randomly chosen portfolio company. Information on only one portfolio company was requested due to the questionnaire length. Pre-tests had shown that private equity professionals needed about 15 minutes to fill in the questionnaire for one portfolio company, which was

---

[376] See Grimes (2004), p. A1.
[377] See Sapienza (1992), pp. 9ff.

regarded as the maximum input of time that a private equity professional would be prepared to commit. Asking study participants to complete the survey instrument for three or more portfolio companies could therefore have resulted in a sharp reduction in the number of participants.[378] It was tried to ensure the random selection of a portfolio company by asking study participants to select the portfolio company that came first alphabetically.[379] As a matter of fact choosing the portfolio company that comes first alphabetically does not necessarily imply random selection. For example portfolio companies that come first alphabetically might have a systematically higher performance than portfolio companies that come last alphabetically. However, pre-tests of the survey instrument with private equity professionals did not give rise to such a suspicion.

Two alternative ways for getting portfolio company information from private equity firms have been used in prior studies: interviews and mail surveys.[380] In the current study, a mail survey was chosen to gather information,[381] as it offers the following advantages over telephone or personal interviews: it is relatively cheap, it avoids interviewer bias or variability, it encourages respondents to communicate private information due to its relative anonymity and it tends to be more valid than interviews as respondents can double-check information and reply leisurely at their discretion. The benefits of a mail survey come at the cost of lower response rates – which can be managed, however, by following existing recommendations for cover letter and envelope design.[382]

In order to increase the typically low response rates achieved with mail surveys, several recommendations with regard to cover letter and envelope design as well as the process of conducting a mail survey were implemented. With regard to the cover letter, ten recommendations were implemented:[383]

---

[378] An extreme example is the study of Schefczyk (2000). Asking every potential study participant to give information on at least three portfolio companies, Schefczyk ended up with a total of 120 portfolio companies, completed, however, by as little as ten private equity firms. Although the absolute number of portfolio companies is a formidable basis, the fact that only ten private equity firms provided the information raises concerns with regard to the representativeness of Schefczyk's study.

[379] See De Clercq/Sapienza (2002).

[380] A third alternative for getting quantitative information is the observation (see Bortz/Döring (2002), pp. 262ff). However, the observation has not been employed by prior studies. The reasons for this practice were most probably confidentiality concerns of private equity firms: giving a researcher the possibility to observe the day-to-day interaction between private equity firm and portfolio company means losing control over the information provided. Moreover, the anonymity of a portfolio company cannot be guaranteed, if a researcher accompanies a private equity professional to a plant visit.

[381] In spite of this decision, three study participants indicated their preference for a personal interview rather than filling in a survey instrument themselves. In order not to upset study participants, this preference was met.

[382] See Kanuk/Berenson (1975), pp. 440ff.

[383] See Richter (1970), pp. 148f.

- The contact data of researchers was given. This was especially important, since a prior study had shown that surveys administered by universities had significantly higher response rates than surveys administered by other institutions.[384]
- Study participants were addressed personally. This was done using available contact information from private equity associations or the homepages of private equity firms. Typically, a partner of the private equity firm was chosen as addressee. If information on more than one partner was provided, a partner with a doctoral degree or a German sounding name was chosen to increase the likelihood of participation.
- The rationale of the study was given: academic research conducted to obtain a doctoral degree.
- An appeal to participate in the survey was made.
- A deadline was set exactly three weeks after sending out the questionnaire.
- Instructions for filling in the questionnaire were given.
- It was guaranteed that any response would be treated confidentially and data provided be processed anonymously.
- The time needed to complete the survey – 15 minutes – was made explicit.
- Thanks for study participation were included.
- Every cover letter was signed personally by both the doctoral student and the academic advisor (Prof. Dr. Malte Brettel). In addition, it was promised to study participants that they would be provided with the results of the study.

With regard to the envelope in which most of the questionnaires were sent out, the recommendation to distinguish envelopes from promotional mailings was implemented.[385] This was done by using special issue stamps with a Christmas theme.

Concerning the mail survey process, the following steps were taken. In a first step, all personally known private equity professionals were contacted via telephone or e-mail and asked to participate in the study. After that, a copy of the survey instrument was sent to the professional via e-mail. In addition to asking for participation, every personally known private equity professional was asked for recommendations to other private equity firms' professionals potentially interested in the study. This technique is called snowball sampling, which is "an empirical technique for sampling social networks that attempts to reconstruct the ego-centered network around a given actor"[386] and has the advantage of comparatively high response rates.[387] In a second step, all remaining private equity firms – unreachable via snowball sampling – received the questionnaire along with the personalized cover letter via surface mail. After three weeks, a reminder was sent out to all private equity firms that had not responded

---

[384] See Jones (1979), pp. 102ff.
[385] Kahle/Sales (1978), pp. 545ff.
[386] Newman (2003), p. 85.
[387] Brettel (forthcoming), p. 180.

in the first round. There are different views with regard to the timing of a reminder.[388] In this study, the reminder was sent out after three weeks. This timing was chosen so that every potential study participant had at least one weekend for answering the questionnaire. Given that several European countries have relatively inefficient postal services resulting in mail delivery times of up to one week, three weeks was the time frame needed. In order to use different means of written communication, the reminder was sent out via fax.[389] Taken together, all three process steps of the mail survey – snowball sampling, mail survey and fax reminder – were completed between October and December of 2003.

6.2 Data Analysis

The data obtained was analyzed with PLS on the basis of the following steps (see also figure 9): First, the representativeness of data was tested to ensure that any conclusions drawn are based on a sample of buyout firms that represents the characteristics of the underlying population sufficiently well. Second, the sample was tested for a potential non-response bias to exclude the possibility that non-respondents are significantly different from respondents and for an informant bias implying that informant reports and actual events are significantly different. Third, the reliability and validity of the measurement model was evaluated to ensure that latent variables are adequately measured and avoid systematic measurement errors. Fourth, a significance criterion was determined. Finally, the structural model was assessed by testing the significance of path relationships between latent variables and analyzing the explanatory power and predictive validity of the structural model.

Figure 9: Data analysis steps using PLS[390]

---

[388] There are always persons who, intending to participate in a survey, put the survey instrument aside in order to respond at a more convenient time. On the one hand, such a person may lose or discard a questionnaire as time passes, and will therefore be grateful for a reminder – indicating that the reminder is the more effective, the earlier it is sent. If the reminder is sent too early, however, a person – having intended to answer a questionnaire – may be annoyed due to the researchers not respecting a potential study participant's time constraints.

[389] One study participant indicated that a fax may be the most suitable means of written communication in research on private equity firms. The reason given was that both e-mail and surface mail are usually screened by the secretary of a private equity professional – with the risk that secretaries may discard the material received. A fax on the other hand creates a sense of urgency and may therefore be handed directly to the private equity professional without the scrutiny applied to e-mails or surface mail.

[390] See Hänlein (forthcoming), pp. 84ff.

6.2.1 Representativeness of Study

Representative samples are characterized by the fact "dass sie hinsichtlich möglichst vieler Merkmale und Merkmalskombinationen der Population gleichen"[391]. Prior studies on private equity firms have analyzed the representativeness of their samples with the help of response rates achieved and a comparison of sample and real distribution of number and volume of investments by industry and financing stage.[392]

Study participation was high in this survey: more than 22% of all European private equity firms focusing on buyout investments agreed to participate. With regard to the private equity firms addressed by this study, a number of restrictions were made. As outlined in detail in chapter 2.2.1, only independent, semi-captive or captive private equity firms engaging in buyout financing in Europe were included. Moreover, only major European buyout markets were included in this study.[393] Based on the information provided by private equity & venture capital associations as well as additional sources, initially 500 private equity firms were identified that seemed to match the criteria. Unfortunately 46 private equity firms had to be dropped from that list as they were either a fund of funds, had not completed a buyout investment yet or did not exist any more. This left a total of 454 private equity firms forming the basic population of this study. Out of that basic population, 101 private equity firms agreed to participate in the study, which corresponds to a response rate of 22%. Splitting up the response rate by country, a relatively homogeneous picture emerges.[394] There is strong study participation across all countries surveyed – the only exception being Germany with a response rate of more than 40%. This exceptionally high response rate can be attributed to the fact that snowball sampling was concentrated by and large on Germany: the researcher's personal network of private equity professionals was restricted largely to Germany. Summarizing, the overall response rate as well as the country-specific response rates do not give rise to concerns regarding the representativeness of this study.

---

[391] Bortz/Döring (2002), p. 400.

[392] See e.g. Schefczyk (2000), pp. 228ff; Reißig-Thust (2003), p. 144. Analyzing the distribution of number and volume of investments by financing stage does not make sense in the context of this study, as only buyout stage investments were included.

[393] Major buyout markets were defined as such, if they had a share in cumulated buyout investments (2000-2002) in excess of 5% (see EVCA (2003)). Based on this definition, the major buyout markets in Europe are the UK, France, Italy, Germany, Sweden and the Netherlands (sorted by their respective importance). In order to cover all German speaking countries, moreover Switzerland and Austria were included in this study. The eight countries included in this study represent 96% of cumulated buyout investments (2000-2002) in Europe.

[394] See figure 10.

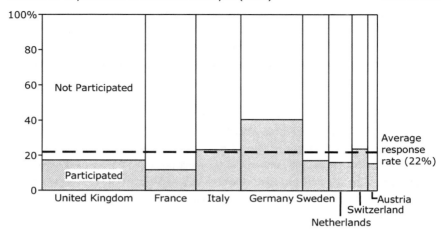

Figure 10: Response rate by country surveyed.

A more specific proof of the representativeness of this study would be a comparison of sample and real distribution of number and volume of investments by industry sector. However, the EVCA yearbook does not offer a separate statistic on the distribution of buyouts by industry.[395] Therefore this test of representativeness could not be included.

6.2.2 Analysis of Non-response and Informant Bias

Non-response bias refers to the problem that "persons who respond differ substantially from those who do not"[396]. In this case "the results do not directly allow one to say how the entire sample would have responded"[397]. Testing a sample for non-response bias is therefore an important step before generalizing a sample to the population. Three alternative methods are suggested to test for non-response bias. First, responses obtained can be compared with known values for the population. This approach cannot be used in the current study, given that known values do not exist for the population surveyed. Second, subjective estimates of non-response bias have been proposed, although it is relatively unclear, how such subjective estimates should be obtained. A third method of estimating the non-response bias is the extrapolation method. It assumes that persons who answer later are similar to non-respondents. Based on this logic, a researcher can identify a non-response bias, if answers of early and late respondents are significantly different. Due to the infeasibility of comparisons with known values and the ambiguity of subjective estimates of non-response bias, the extrapolation

---

[395] See EVCA (2003).
[396] Armstrong/Overton (1977), p. 396.
[397] Armstrong/Overton (1977), p. 396.

method was adopted by this study. In a first step, the sample was divided into a group of early respondents and a group of late respondents. On the basis of the two samples obtained, two sided t-tests were conducted for a total of 57 variables, testing whether the mean responses of both groups were significantly different. Significant differences arose in the case of nine out of 57 variables, indicating that this study's sample is not affected by a material non-response bias.[398]

An informant bias implies that "there may be little correspondence between informant reports and actual events."[399] Informant bias may arise, if a survey is conducted among individuals of one corporate function[400] or one hierarchy[401] only. This is due to the fact that individuals filter information on the basis of their functional and hierarchical point of view. For example members of the marketing function in a corporation have been shown to have a different view on the success factors of innovation than members of the research and development or operations function.[402] It is recommended therefore – with regard to studies conducted in corporations – that multiple informants, i.e. informants from different functions and hierarchies, be included in a survey. Private equity firms, however, are usually lacking functional divisions and rigorous hierarchies.[403] It is therefore likely that different professionals of one private equity firm will filter information similarly. Including only one professional per private equity firm, as done by the current study, is therefore not likely to result in a material informant bias.[404]

6.2.3   Evaluation of the Measurement Model: Validation of Constructs

Once a sample has been shown to be representative and unbiased, it is crucial to ensure that the indicators and constructs used are sufficiently reliable and valid.[405] "Reliability can be defined broadly as the degree to which measures are free from error and therefore yield consistent results"[406]. More precisely, the variance of a construct or an individual indicator is assumed to consist of a true component and an error component, which is due to measurement error. An indicator or a construct is therefore the more reliable, the smaller the share of error variance in total observed variance.[407] To provide an example, a reliable bathroom scale will give the same weight consistently – assuming that a person's true weight remains unchanged. Whether or not the weight displayed consistently by the scale is correct, is not relevant with

---

[398] An overview of literature on non-response bias is provided by Armstrong/Overton (1977). The arithmetic of the extrapolation method used in this thesis is based on Brettel (forthcoming), p. 183.

[399] Kumar et al. (1993), p. 1634.

[400] See Ernst (2003), pp. 1253f.

[401] See Seidler (1974), pp. 816ff; Phillips (1981), pp. 395ff; Ernst (2003), pp. 1255f.

[402] See Ernst (2003), pp. 1260f.

[403] For the hierarchies in a private equity firm see chapter 5.1.4.

[404] For a current overview on literature on the informant bias see Ernst (2003), pp. 1249ff. A discussion of the consequences of not identifying a key informant bias can be found in Kieser/Nicolai (2002), p. 504.

[405] See Hildebrandt (1984), p. 41.

[406] Peter (1979), p. 6.

[407] See Peter (1979), p. 7.

respect to its reliability – displaying the correct weight refers to the bathroom scale's validity. Validity "is the degree to which a measure assesses the construct it is purported to assess"[408]. The reliability of a measurement model is a necessary, but not sufficient condition for its validity. For example a test on a person's reaction time may be very reliable in that it returns consistent reaction times for the same person taking the test at different points in time. It is rather improbable, however, that the test will accurately measure the driving capabilities of an individual.[409]

Only after the reliability and validity of a measurement model have been shown, can the relations of a structural model be tested. The importance of construct evaluation is re-emphasized by Peter – focusing on the validity of a measurement model: "valid measurement is the sine qua non of science. In a general sense, validity refers to the degree to which instruments truly measure the constructs that they are intended to measure. If the measures used in a discipline have not been demonstrated to have a high degree of validity, that discipline is not a science."[410] In PLS, the reliability and validity of a measurement model can be assessed in terms of its content validity, indicator and construct reliability, convergent validity, discriminant validity and nomological validity.[411]

Content validity is defined to exist "when a measure 'looks as if' it should indicate a particular variable or concept"[412]. Churchill suggests ensuring content validity by first specifying the domain of a construct, and second designing items that capture the domain as specified. The domain of a construct can be specified by describing precisely what is included and excluded in its definition. The design of items capturing the domain can be based on "exploratory research, including literature searches, experience surveys, and insight-stimulating examples"[413]. Content validity can be evaluated by having experts review whether or not the items used for measuring a construct are appropriate. The judgment of experts with regard to the suitability of a measure can be quantified in the form of a content validity ratio, which is proportional to the share of experts deeming an indicator essential for measuring a construct.[414]

Indicator and construct reliability as well as convergent and discriminant validity are also referred to as components of the trait validity of a construct.[415] Traditional methods of examining the trait validity of a construct are based on an analysis of the correlations between different indicators of the same construct. More precisely, traditional methods of examining trait

---

[408] Peter (1981), p. 134.
[409] This example is taken from Bortz/Döring (2002), p. 199.
[410] Peter (1979), p. 6.
[411] See Chin (1998b), pp. 316ff; Hulland (1999), pp. 198ff; Hänlein (forthcoming), pp. 96ff.
[412] Heeler/Ray (1972), p. 361.
[413] Churchill (1979), p. 67.
[414] See Lawshe (1975), p. 567.

validity assume "that indicators of the same construct should be positively correlated with each other, an assumption which is only given in the case of reflective indicators."[416] Formative indicators, however, can be correlated with each other positively, negatively or not at all.[417] Therefore the trait validity of formative indicators needs to be determined with completely different methods than the trait validity of reflective indicators: "reliability in the internal consistency sense and construct validity in terms of convergent and discriminant validity are not meaningful when indexes are formed as a linear sum of measurements"[418].

Distinguishing formative and reflective indicators is intricate – a recent study shows that 29% of the latent constructs with multiple measures found in the top-four marketing journals during the past 24 years were specified incorrectly.[419] The "algorithm" chosen most frequently to distinguish formative and reflective indicators is the mental experiment. Jarvis et al. suggest four decision rules to distinguish formative and reflective indicators with the help of mental experiments. First, the direction of causality between a construct and its indicators has to be analyzed: e.g. if the researcher imagines a change in the construct and expects a resulting shift in its indicators, this would be consistent with a reflective specification of indicators. Second, the interchangeability of indicators has to be examined: e.g. if the conceptual domain of a construct is not changed by dropping an indicator, this would be consistent as well with a reflective specification of indicators. Third, the covariation among indicators has to be studied: if a change in one of a construct's indicators results in a change of another indicator, this would suggest the existence of reflective indicators. In addition to this mental experiment, the covariance or correlation matrix of a construct's indicators can be analyzed as well. Fourth, the nomological net of a construct's indicators needs to be investigated: if indicators need to have the same antecedents and consequences, reflective indicator specification would be suggested.[420] The results of mental experiments can be ambiguous, however, and "do not provide an empirical means to check the specification"[421].

Therefore Bollen and Ting developed a confirmatory tetrad analysis test determining whether a formative or reflective indicator specification is appropriate.[422] A tetrad "refers to the differ-

---

[415] See Peter (1981), p. 135.
[416] Hänlein (forthcoming), p. 99.
[417] See chapter 4.2.
[418] Bagozzi (1994), p. 333. Determining whether the indicators of a construct are formative or reflective is not only necessary to use the right tests with regard to the trait validity of indicators. Even more importantly, model misspecification, i.e. modeling reflective indicators as formative or modeling formative indicators as reflective, can have very serious consequences with regard to the validity of a structural equation model. "More specifically, the results indicate that paths emanating from a construct with a misspecified measurement model are likely to be substantially inflated, thus leading to Type I errors. However, paths leading into a construct with a misspecified measurement model are likely to be deflated, thus leading to Type II errors" (Jarvis et al. (2003), p. 212).
[419] Jarvis et al. (2003), p. 207.
[420] See Jarvis et al. (2003), p. 203.
[421] Bollen/Ting (2000), p. 4.
[422] See Bollen/Ting (2000) and Bollen/Ting (1998).

ence between the product of a pair of covariances and the product of another pair among four random variables."[423] To provide an example, three tetrads can be constructed on the basis of four variables and six associated covariances: $\tau_{1234} = \sigma_{12}\sigma_{34} - \sigma_{13}\sigma_{24}$, $\tau_{1342} = \sigma_{13}\sigma_{42} - \sigma_{14}\sigma_{32}$ and $\tau_{1423} = \sigma_{14}\sigma_{23} - \sigma_{12}\sigma_{43}$, where σ refers to the population covariance of the two variables indexed below and a vanishing tetrad is characterized by $\tau_{ghij} = 0$. In general, for models with n observed indicators there will be $n!(n-4)!4!$ sets of tetrads.[424]

Bollen and Ting have shown mathematically that reflective indicators imply all possible vanishing tetrads, whereas formative indicators imply that none of the tetrads vanish. Whether the indicators of a construct are formative or reflective can therefore be determined quantitatively. The only exception "occurs, when some of the causal indicators are not linearly related, that is, their covariances tend toward zero. If both sides of the tetrad difference have one or more covariances equal to zero, the tetrad vanishes"[425]. Vanishing tetrads may therefore falsely indicate reflective indicators, whenever both sides of the tetrad difference have one or more covariances equal to zero.

Fortunately enough, tetrad values do not have to be computed manually. Ting designed a SAS program performing a simultaneous vanishing tetrad test.[426] The SAS program requires the user to enter the covariance matrix of all indicators of a construct as well as the sample size N. The SAS program then calculates a simultaneous test statistic for vanishing tetrads that "asymptotically approximates a chi-square variate with degrees of freedom equal to the number of vanishing tetrads considered in the test"[427]. A non-significant value of the so-called confirmatory tetrad analysis (CTA) test statistic "suggests that the observed tetrad differences are not significantly different from zero"[428] indicating reflective indicators. The CTA test statistic derives from asymptotic theory. Therefore the CTA test statistic follows the χ^2 distribution under the conditions of a large sample size and a small number of indicators. More precisely, given this study's sample size of 101, the CTA test statistic approaches the χ^2 distribution only for constructs with five or less indicators:[429] the properties of constructs with more than five indicators have to be checked with "traditional" mental experiments. Given that the CTA test statistic is based on tetrads, constructs need to have at least four indicators to be able to calculate the CTA test statistic. Whenever the properties of a construct with fewer than four indicators are to be tested, indicators from another construct have to be added. A t-test then

---

[423] Bollen/Ting (2000), p. 5.

[424] See Bollen/Ting (2000), p. 7.

[425] Bollen/Ting (2000), p. 7.

[426] The CTA-SAS program can be downloaded from http://www.cuhk.edu.hk/soc/ting/. The program also handles redundancy problems arising among a set of vanishing tetrads. See Ting (1995) for a detailed description of the program.

[427] Bollen/Ting (2000), p. 12.

[428] Bollen/Ting (2000), p. 12.

[429] See Bollen/Ting (1998), p. 84.

helps to determine whether the tetrads are vanishing. If none of the tetrads vanish, this would be consistent with a formative indicator specification.[430]

A non-significant CTA test statistic does not necessarily imply reflective indicators. As discussed above, a non-significant CTA test statistic may also be due to zero covariances among the indicators of a construct – consistent with formative indicators, but not with reflective indicators. In this case, the CTA test statistic falsely suggests the existence of reflective indicators. The covariance matrix of a set of indicators has therefore to be checked for near-zero covariances.

A summary of the criteria identifying formative indicators is given in table 5.

Criteria	Requirement
4 or more indicators	
Multiple vanishing tetrad test p-value	Significant
Correlations among indicators*	Not significantly different from zero
3 indicators	
Vanishing tetrads**	0
Correlations among indicators*	Not significantly different from zero
2 indicators	
Vanishing tetrads***	0
Correlations among indicators*	Not significantly different from zero

* tested only, if vanishing tetrad test suggests reflective indicators
** using one additional formative indicator from a different construct
*** using two additional formative indicators from a different construct

Table 5: Criteria for the identification of formative indicators

Once the properties of a construct's indicators (formative versus reflective) are determined, the trait validity of a construct can be tested. As underlined above, the trait validity of formative and reflective indicators has to be determined with completely different methods. Therefore, tests of the trait validity of reflective indicators will be discussed first and then, in a second part, tests of the trait validity of formative indicators.

Reflective indicators are considered to be reliable if they share more variance with their underlying construct than with error variance.[431] "This implies that standardized loadings should be greater than 0.707"[432]. Low loadings can be attributed to "(1) a poorly worded item, (2) an inappropriate item, (3) an improper transfer of an item from one context to another. The first

---

[430] Bollen and Ting illustrate at length, which vanishing tetrads are implied by formative versus reflective indicators in the case of constructs with fewer than four indicators (see Bollen/Ting (2000), pp. 21f).

[431] See Carmines/Zeller (1979), p. 27.

[432] Chin (1998b), p. 325. For a derivation see Fornell et al. (1982), pp. 405ff.

problem leads to low reliability, the second to poor content (and construct) validity, and the last to nongeneralizability of the item across contexts and/or settings."[433] Indicators with loadings of less than 0,7 should therefore be dropped, as their explanatory contribution to the construct is limited, while attenuating the associated construct.

A reflective construct is considered to be reliable, if the indicators share more variance with the construct than with error variance. This is the case, if "independent but comparable measures of the same trait or construct of a given object agree"[434]. Researchers using PLS are generally employing three measures of construct reliability: Cronbach's alpha, composite reliability and average variance extracted.[435] Both Cronbach's alpha and composite reliability are measures of the agreement of indicators, the so-called internal consistency of a reflective construct. Average variance extracted on the other hand measures the amount of indicator variance captured by a construct relative to error variance. First, Cronbach's coefficient alpha is the mean of all inter-item correlations in a construct: $\alpha = \left(\dfrac{K}{K-1} \right) \left(1 - \sum\limits_{k=1}^{K} \dfrac{\sigma_k^2}{\sigma_s^2} \right)$ or

$\alpha = \dfrac{K\bar{r}}{1 + \bar{r}(K-1)}$ [436], where α is Cronbach's alpha, K is the number of indicators in a construct, σ_k is the variance of indicator k in a construct, σ_s is the variance of the scale, and $\bar{r}$ is the average inter-indicator correlation. In general, a Cronbach's alpha of 0,7 or above is regarded to indicate an acceptable level of construct reliability.[437] Second, the composite reliability measure developed by Werts, Linn and Jöreskog is another measure of construct reliability: $\rho_c = \dfrac{\left(\sum\limits_{k=1}^{K} \lambda_k \right)^2}{\left(\sum\limits_{k=1}^{K} \lambda_k \right)^2 + \sum\limits_{k=1}^{K} Var(\varepsilon_k)}$ [438], where ρ_c is the composite reliability, K is the number of indicators in a construct, λ_k is the component loading to indicator k of a construct and $Var(\varepsilon_k)$ is the error variance defined by $Var(\varepsilon_k) = 1 - \lambda_k^2$. Again, a composite reliability coefficient of 0,7 or above is regarded to indicate a sufficient degree of construct reliability. The composite reliability coefficient differs from Cronbach's alpha in so far as it does not assume equally weighted indicators. ρ_c is therefore a closer approximation of construct reliability, whereas Cronbach's alpha tends to be a lower bound estimate of construct reliability.[439] Finally, average variance extracted "attempts to measure the amount of variance that an LV

[433] Hulland (1999), p. 198.
[434] Churchill (1979), p. 65.
[435] See e.g. Hulland (1999), pp. 199f; Hanlon (2001); Roldan/Leal (2003), p. 76.
[436] See Peterson (1994), p. 382. For a derivation see Cronbach (1951), pp. 297ff.
[437] See Nunally (1978), pp. 245f; Kaplan/Saccuzzo (1982), p. 106; Murphy/Davidshofer (1988), p. 89.
[438] See Fornell/Larcker (1981), p. 45. For a derivation see Werts et al. (1974), pp. 25ff.
[439] Chin (1998b), p. 320.

component captures from its indicators relative to the amount due to measurement error"[440]:

$$AVE = \frac{\sum_{k=1}^{K} \lambda_k^2}{\sum_{k=1}^{K} \lambda_k^2 + \sum_{k=1}^{K} Var(\varepsilon_k)}$$ [441], where AVE is the average variance extracted, λ_k is the compo-

nent loading to indicator k of a construct and $Var(\varepsilon_k)$ is the error variance defined by $Var(\varepsilon_k) = 1 - \lambda_k^2$. As indicated above, whereas Cronbach's alpha and composite reliability are measures of the association between individual indicators, average variance extracted shows the amount of true variance explained by a construct in relation to total observed variance. Average variance extracted should be higher than 0,5 implying that 50% or more of construct variance is accounted for.[442]

Convergent validity can be defined as "the degree to which two or more attempts to measure the same concept through maximally different methods are in agreement."[443] At first sight the definition of convergent validity seems to be very similar to the definition of reliability. The difference between convergent validity and reliability lies in the formulation "maximally different methods". Whereas reliability "is the agreement between two efforts to measure the same trait through maximally similar methods"[444], convergent validity "is represented in the agreement between two attempts to measure the same trait through maximally different methods."[445] Venkatraman and Grant mention as "illustrative methods in a strategy research context interviews, questionnaires, archival data, participant observation, multiple managers in different key functions, published secondary data, expert opinion, and use of different types of scales."[446] It is doubtful, however, whether those methods are really maximally different. Says Peter: "Different forms of paper and pencil self-rating scales are clearly not maximally different methods, [...] such approaches more closely assess internal consistency or alternative form reliability than convergent validity."[447] The discussion so far illustrates that reliability and convergent validity are "regions on a continuum"[448]. As mentioned above the current study made use of only one method, the questionnaire, and is therefore unable to test the convergent validity of constructs with the help of, for example, a multitrait-multimethod matrix. The decision to focus on the questionnaire method only was made first due to the ambiguity of the term maximally different methods: administering a study with multiple methods is associated with significantly increased effort but an uncertain return. Second, the use of different methods would have been impracticable with regard to the portfolio companies of private

---

[440] Chin (1998b), p. 321.
[441] See Fornell/Larcker (1981), p. 46.
[442] See Chin (1998b), p. 321.
[443] Bagozzi/Phillips (1982), p. 468.
[444] Campbell/Fiske (1959), p. 83.
[445] Campbell/Fiske (1959), p. 83.
[446] Venkatraman/Grant (1986), p. 82.
[447] Peter (1981), p. 137.
[448] Campbell/Fiske (1959), p. 83.

equity firms, chosen above as the unit of analysis. Private equity firms participated in the study only under the condition of providing data on anonymous portfolio companies. Analyzing published secondary data, archival data or conducting interviews would have made an anonymous data analysis impossible. Third, using only one method is also in line with prior research on private equity firms.[449]

Discriminant validity refers to "the degree to which measures of distinct concepts differ. This means that measures of different concepts should share little common variance (in a relative sense) and that too high a covariation casts doubt on the uniqueness of the measures and/or the concepts."[450] It can be inferred from the definition that discriminant validity has to be given both at an indicator and a construct level. At an indicator level, discriminant validity means that each indicator reflects only the construct it is intended to measure – and no other construct. This is given, if no reflective indicator loads more highly on any other construct than it does on the one it intends to measure.[451] At a construct level, discriminant validity implies that every reflective construct differs significantly from all other constructs. This is the case if the average variance extracted of reflective constructs is higher than the square of the correlations with any other construct.[452]

---

[449]   See e.g. Schefczyk (2000); Reißig-Thust (2003). Please note that several studies employing a PLS methodology claim to test convergent validity of constructs (see Amoroso/Cheney (1991), p. 79; Cool/Dierickx (1989), pp. 514f; Hulland (1999), p. 199; Yi/Hwang (2003), p. 440). They do so analyzing Cronbach's alpha, internal consistency or average variance extracted of their reflective constructs –measures designed to evaluate construct reliability and not convergent validity. Testing a construct for its convergent validity would require maximally different methods such as comparing two constructs based on questionnaire data and publicly available secondary data, respectively. The above studies therefore do not test the convergent validity – as they claim to do – but rather construct reliability.

[450]   Bagozzi/Phillips (1982), p. 469.

[451]   See Chin (1998b), pp. 325f.

[452]   This evaluation of discriminant validity has been proposed by Fornell/Larcker (1981), p. 46. See also Fornell/Cha (1994), p. 69; Chin (1998b), pp. 321ff.

Criteria	Requirement
Reliability	
Item loading	$\geq 0{,}707$
Cronbach's alpha	$\geq 0{,}7$
Composite reliability	$\geq 0{,}7$
Average variance extracted (AVE)	$\geq 0{,}5$
Discriminant validity	
Item discriminant validity	No item should load more highly on another construct than it does on the construct it intends to measure
Construct discriminant validity	AVE of each of two constructs should be larger than the squared correlation between them

Table 6: Criteria for the assessment of reflective constructs' trait validity

So far, the trait validity of reflective indicators and constructs has been discussed.[453] Unfortunately, conventional procedures used to assess the validity and reliability of constructs composed of reflective indicators are not appropriate for constructs with formative indicators. As a consequence, alternative methods have to be used in order to evaluate the trait validity of formative indicators and constructs. Hänlein suggests evaluating formative indicators by testing for indicator collinearity.[454]

As shown above, the scores of formative constructs are obtained on the basis of multiple regressions with their respective indicators. Excessive collinearity among the independent variables of a multiple regression are associated with a number of problems, "such as parameters estimated with wrong signs, theoretically important variables with insignificant coefficients, the inability to determine the relative importance of collinear variables – all factors which encumber the interpretation of unobservable variables based on indicator weights"[455]. This means that excessive collinearity has to be excluded, if researchers want to interpret the

---

[453] See table 6.

[454] See Hänlein (forthcoming), p. 102. Aside from specifying constructs and indicators as well as excluding multicollinearity, Diamantopoulos and Winklhofer suggest examining the external validity of constructs by including both formative and reflective indicators for each construct and estimating a multiple indicators and multiple causes (MIMIC) model (see Diamantopoulos/Winklhofer (2001), p. 272f). Unfortunately, PLS is not able to solve a MIMIC model. However, a so-called redundancy analysis can be conducted between two constructs, one with the formative and the other with the reflective operationalization of the same construct (see Chin (1998b), pp. 323f). Assuming that the reflective operationalization of the construct is sufficiently reliable, a path coefficient of 0,8 between the reflective and formative construct would be suggestive of the external validity of formative indicators. Although this approach to formative construct validation sounds intriguing, significant complexity is associated with including both formative and reflective operationalizations of every construct in a survey instrument. As a result, PLS researchers only rarely evaluate the external validity of formative constructs with the help of redundancy analysis (to the knowledge of the author so far only one study has tested the external validity of formative constructs (see Reinartz et al. (2003), pp. 18f)).

[455] Hänlein (forthcoming), p. 102.

weights of formative indicators.[456] Although numerous approaches exist to detect the presence of multicollinearity,[457] PLS researchers usually examine the variance inflation factor (VIF) for each indicator included in the causal model.[458] The VIF can be calculated by regressing each formative indicator on all remaining indicators of a certain construct. The resulting coefficient of determination R^2 is then used to determine the VIF as $1/(1-R^2)$.[459] Due to the fact that "the variance inflation factors are not usually equal for all parameters, since the inflation factors depend on the partial correlation of each x with the other xs", the VIF had to be calculated for every single formative indicator of a construct. The minimum value of the VIF is 1 indicating that the formative indicator in question is linearly independent from all other indicators. A common rule of thumb for the presence of harmful multicollinearity is that the VIF in question exceeds a value of 10. However, the threshold of 10 is only a rule of thumb and researchers should be cautious about interpreting the weights of formative indicators, if several indicators of the same construct show elevated VIFs.

Nomological validity "is based on the explicit investigation of constructs and measures in terms of formal hypotheses derived from theory."[460] More precisely, nomological validity refers "to the degree to which predictions in a formal theoretical network containing a construct of interest are confirmed"[461]. This can be done with the help of SEM techniques that analyze the association and significance of relationships between the constructs of a structural equation model.

The process of testing construct reliability and validity in PLS models is summarized in figure 11. For this study all dimensions of construct reliability and validity will be evaluated – excluding, however, tests of convergent validity due to their vagueness and inappropriateness in a private equity setting.[462]

---

[456] "Lack of multicollinearity is important if the researcher is concerned with understanding the formation process of the LV. Otherwise, it can be ignored if the focus is on the structural path relations" (Chin (1998b), p. 307).
[457] See Mason/Perreault (1991), p. 270 for an overview.
[458] See e.g. Reinartz et al. (2003), p. 18.
[459] See Mason/Perreault (1991), p. 270.
[460] Peter (1981), p. 135.
[461] Bagozzi (1981b), p. 327.
[462] See above.

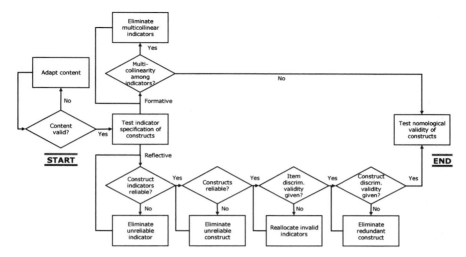

Figure 11: Process of validating formative and reflective constructs in PLS structural equation models

The content validity of this study's survey instrument can be assumed to be sufficiently high. First, the domain of all constructs has been specified (see chapter 4). Second, all of the indicators used to operationalize constructs were based on prior research (see chapter 5.2). Third, the survey instrument was refined on the basis of pre-tests that led to a significant improvement of the survey instrument. Pre-tests were conducted first with fellow researchers. After implementing their recommendations, pre-tests with a Bain & Company partner specializing on the private equity industry and a panel of four private equity professionals were conducted.

Given that the trait validity of constructs has to be evaluated with different methods for formative and reflective constructs, each construct had to be tested for its formative or reflective properties. This was done with the vanishing tetrad test introduced above. Given that the tetrad test can only be applied to constructs with five or less indicators with the given sample size of 101, the properties of the construct "activities of private equity firms" – operationalized by 22 indicators – had to be evaluated on the basis of mental experiments.[463] First, the direction of causality – clearly from indicators to constructs – points toward a formative indicator specification. For example a higher value of the indicator "focusing or consolidating operations" should result in a higher involvement score of the respective private equity firm. Second, indicators are not interchangeable, which is another piece of evidence for a formative indicator specification. For example, the involvement of a private equity firm with "focusing or consolidating operations" says nothing about the involvement of a private equity firm in "obtaining alternative sources of debt or equity financing". Third, however, there is signifi-

---

[463] The mental experiments used are based on the suggestions of Jarvis et al. (2003), pp. 199ff.

cant covariation among indicators, suggesting a reflective indicator specification: out of a total of 231 correlations, 168 or 73% are significant. Fourth, the nomological net of indicators differs: indicators do not have the same antecedents and consequences, which, again, suggests a formative indicator specification. For example the consequence of intensive monitoring of financial performance is a hands-off management strategy, whereas the consequence of intensive involvement in focusing or consolidating operations of a portfolio company is a hands-on management style. Summarizing, three out of the four decision criteria of Jarvis et al. support a formative indicator specification. The large number of significant correlations indicates the case of a formative construct affected by multicollinearity problems among several of its indicators.[464]

The construct "organization of involvement" has a total of three indicators, which would in principle allow one to conduct a tetrad test by adding one formative indicator. However, all indicators of the construct "organization of involvement" are nominal variables. Applying the tetrad test, which is based on an analysis of a covariance matrix, to nominal variables would not yield meaningful results. Therefore the properties of the construct "organization of involvement" had to be analyzed with mental experiments. Although the covariation of nominal indicators cannot reasonably be calculated, the three remaining decision criteria developed by Jarvis et al. point toward a formative indicator specification. First, the direction of causality is from the indicators to the construct. For example, it is more likely that carrying out management tasks results in a formal organization of the relationship with a portfolio company than a formal organization resulting in carrying out management tasks. Second, none of the indicators is interchangeable. For example board membership does not give any information about whether or not consulting tasks are carried out. Although the covariation among indicators cannot be analyzed, the variables have, finally, different antecedents and consequences. Private equity firms will, for example, have considerably different rationales for joining the board as opposed to carrying out management tasks. Besides, the consequences of carrying out consulting tasks as opposed to carrying out management tasks are different.

The construct "completeness and intensity of portfolio company reporting" cannot be tested with the multiple vanishing tetrad test, as its six indicators exceed the maximum number of indicators allowed given the limited sample size of 101. Therefore mental experiments had to be conducted to find out about the construct's formative or reflective properties. First, the direction of causality seems to support a reflective operationalization: it is from the construct to its indicators: high intensity portfolio company reporting will be associated with frequent reports of revenue, balance sheet and P&L, cash flows, interim qualitative reports on business situation, reports on planned investments and reports on R&D or other projects. Second, the indicators are more or less interchangeable. For example, revenue and cash flow reporting will occur in the same report pointing toward similar reporting frequencies. Third, 11 out of

---

[464] The multicollinearity problems will be dealt with when validating the formative construct "activities of pri-

the total of 15 intra-indicator correlations are significant. Fourth, the indicators of reporting intensity have similar antecedents – the private equity firm's need for information – and consequences – a more or less intense reporting. A reflective indicator specification is therefore adopted.

With regard to the construct "frequency of interaction between private equity firm and portfolio company", the problem arises that the construct has only three indicators. Adding a fourth (formative) indicator from another construct allows one to conduct the vanishing tetrad test.[465] The tetrad test results in none of the three tetrads vanishing – compatible only with a formative indicator specification.[466]

The construct "performance of information systems" has only one indicator. Unfortunately, a construct operationalized by a single item cannot be tested for its formative or reflective properties. Fortunately enough, however, this does not matter in a PLS analysis. For constructs measured by single items, both formative and reflective indicator specifications yield the same results: in both specifications, the value of the latent variable is determined by a simple regression between indicator and construct. For this study, a reflective indicator specification has been chosen for the construct performance of information systems. This choice is, however, arbitrary, as a formative indicator specification would have yielded identical results.

The construct "quality of portfolio company information" also has only three indicators. Again, adding a fourth (formative) indicator from another construct allows one to conduct the vanishing tetrad test. Given that all three tetrads vanish, a reflective indicator specification has to be chosen.

The construct "experience of private equity professionals" has four indicators, allowing one to apply the multiple vanishing tetrad test. The resulting insignificant p-value of 0,46 suggests that the observed tetrad differences are not significantly different from zero. Before adopting a reflective indicator specification, the covariance or correlation matrix has to be checked for near-zero values.[467] With regard to the construct "experience of private equity professionals", only two out of six correlations are significantly different from zero. As discussed above, one or more near-zero covariances on both sides of the tetrad difference may result in vanishing tetrads, falsely pointing towards reflective indicators. Although the multiple tetrad test yields an insignificant p-value, several near-zero correlations are consistent only with formative indicators but not with reflective indicators. A formative indicator specification is chosen therefore.

---

vate equity firm" below.

[465] In this specific case, an indicator from the activity construct has been added.

[466] A simultaneous or so-called multiple vanishing tetrad test cannot be conducted due to the fact that an external indicator has been added. As a result, the properties of individual tetrads have to be analyzed.

[467] The correlation is calculated by standardizing the covariance of two variables with their respective standard deviation coefficients. A near zero correlation coefficient is therefore attributable to near zero covariance of two variables. If the covariance matrix of a set of indicators is not at hand, the correlation matrix can be used instead to check for near-zero values.

The construct "usage of external resources" has five indicators, which permits using the multiple vanishing tetrad test. An insignificant p-value of 0,53 implies that none of the tetrad differences is significantly different from zero. Given that the correlation matrix does not show any near-zero value – all correlations are significant on a five percent level – a reflective indicator model can be adopted.

The construct "value added to buyout" has two indicators. In order to conduct a tetrad test, two (formative) indicators were added from another construct.[468] The tetrad test conducted on the set of four indicators returned one vanishing tetrad. This is compatible only with a reflective indicator specification – formative indicators would have been characterized by none of the tetrads vanishing. Therefore a reflective indicator specification is chosen.

Once the formative or reflective properties of constructs are revealed, the trait validity of constructs can be tested. Starting with the evaluation of reflective constructs, first, reliability and second, discriminant validity will be evaluated. The reliability coefficients of the construct "completeness and intensity of portfolio company reporting" are shown in table 7. Out of the six indicators intended to measure the construct, three had to be eliminated due to insufficient loadings. The remaining indicators are characterized by strong item loadings. The construct shows a good level of reliability, given that all three construct reliability measures are well above their respective thresholds.

"Completeness and intensity of portfolio company reporting"			
Item reliability			
Indicator		Loading	
Revenue		*0,84*	
Balance sheet and P&L		*0,83*	
Cash flows		*0,78*	
Interim qualitative reports on business situation		*removed*	
Reports on planned investments		*removed*	
Reports on R&D or other projects		*removed*	
Construct reliability			
Cronbach's alpha	*0,76*	Composite reliability	*0,86*
AVE	*0,67*		

Table 7: Reliability coefficients of the construct "completeness and intensity of portfolio company reporting"

---

[468] In this case, two indicators were taken from the activity construct.

The indicators of the second reflective construct, "quality of portfolio company information", have all satisfactory item loadings. The construct reliability coefficients indicate good construct reliability as well.[469]

"Quality of portfolio company information"			
Item reliability			
Indicator		Loading	
Timeliness		*0,75*	
Appropriateness/suitability for your information needs		*0,86*	
Reliability		*0,88*	
Construct reliability			
Cronbach's alpha	0,78	Composite reliability	0,87
AVE	0,70		

Table 8: Reliability coefficients of the construct "quality of portfolio company information"

Regarding the construct "performance of portfolio company information systems", both item and construct reliability coefficient show optimal values. This is, however, due to the single item operationalization of the construct. In this case, construct and item are identical, resulting in optimal indicator and construct reliability.[470]

"Performance of portfolio company information systems"			
Item reliability			
Indicator		Loading	
Portfolio company kept you well-informed		*1,00*	
Construct reliability			
Cronbach's alpha	*1,00*	Composite reliability	*1,00*
AVE	*1,00*		

Table 9: Reliability coefficients of the construct "performance of portfolio company information systems"

The indicators of the fourth reflective construct, "usage of external resources", had to be significantly adjusted to match reliability requirements. Out of five reflective indicators, three had to be eliminated due to low loading coefficients. The resulting composite reliability as well as AVE point towards satisfactory construct reliability, while Cronbach's alpha indicates insufficient construct reliability. Given that Cronbach's alpha is a lower boundary of construct reliability, overall a satisfactory reliability of constructs can be assumed.[471]

---

[469] See table 8.
[470] See table 9.
[471] See table 10.

101

"Usage of external resources"		
Item reliability		
Indicator		Loading
Management consultants		*removed*
Interim managers		*removed*
Industry experts		*0,88*
CEOs of other portfolio companies		*removed*
Executive search firms		*0,67*
Construct reliability		
Cronbach's alpha	*0,39*	Composite reliability *0,76*
AVE	*0,61*	

Table 10: Reliability coefficients of the construct "usage of external resources"

The fifth and last reflective construct, "value added to buyout" shows adequate levels of item and construct reliability.[472] Again, Cronbach's alpha raises suspicion of inadequate construct reliability. However, composite reliability and AVE are well above the thresholds defined above, indicating satisfactory construct reliability.

"Value added to buyout"		
Item reliability		
Indicator		Loading
Performance relative to business plan		*0,92*
Increase/decrease in performance relative to competitors		*0,74*
Construct reliability		
Cronbach's alpha	*0,60*	Composite reliability *0,82*
AVE	*0,70*	

Table 11: Reliability coefficients of the construct "value added to buyout"

Concluding, all reflective constructs show satisfactory levels of item and construct reliability after removing several items with low loading coefficients.

Moving on to discriminant validity, item discriminant validity is given, if no reflective item loads more highly on any other construct than on the one it intends to measure.[473] Table 12

---

[472] See table 11.
[473] Please note that discriminant validity can only be evaluated for reflective items. Formative indicators can be correlated with their respective constructs negatively, positively or not at all. Therefore it is not wise to require high correlations of formative indicators with the construct intended to measure.

shows that every single reflective indicator has the highest loadings with the construct it is intended to measure. Item discriminant validity is therefore given.

	Act	Org	Int	Frq	Qua	Perf	Exp	Ext	Val
Int 1	0,27	-0,13	**0,84**	-0,17	0,27	0,27	0,08	0,17	0,13
Int 2	0,23	-0,11	**0,83**	-0,04	0,19	0,18	-0,03	0,05	-0,06
Int 3	0,34	-0,23	**0,78**	-0,08	0,22	0,16	0,03	0,22	0,10
Qua 1	0,22	-0,01	0,28	-0,17	**0,75**	0,56	0,12	-0,02	0,24
Qua 2	0,06	-0,11	0,27	-0,10	**0,86**	0,68	0,03	-0,04	0,24
Qua 3	0,02	-0,04	0,17	-0,01	**0,88**	0,67	-0,03	-0,07	0,22
Perf 1	0,09	0,02	0,26	-0,24	0,77	**1,00**	0,15	-0,07	0,33
Ext 1	0,23	-0,01	0,14	0,01	0,01	-0,05	0,20	**0,89**	0,21
Ext 2	0,30	-0,09	0,15	-0,06	-0,13	-0,07	0,04	**0,67**	0,13
Val 1	0,08	-0,02	0,02	-0,04	0,30	0,33	0,13	0,12	**0,74**
Val 2	0,46	-0,18	0,10	-0,14	0,20	0,26	0,19	0,23	**0,92**

Table 12: Correlations of constructs and reflective indicators (correlations of indicators with their respective constructs in bold)[474]

Moreover, construct discriminant validity can be assumed for all five reflective constructs. The square roots of AVE are all higher than the respective construct's correlations with other constructs.[475] More precisely, the square root of a construct's AVE is compared with the correlation values in the same row and column. If the square root of the AVE in question is higher than correlations in the same row and column, construct discriminant validity is given, which is the case in this study.

---

[474] The following abbreviations were used in order to display correlations in a readable way: Act: activities of private equity firms; Org: organization of involvement; Int: completeness and intensity of portfolio company reporting; Frq: frequency of interaction between private equity firm and portfolio company; Qua: Quality of portfolio company information; Perf: performance of portfolio company information systems; Exp: experience of private equity professionals; Ext: usage of external resources; Val: value added to buyout. Reflective indicators consist of a prefix indicating which construct is reflected and a suffix number indicating the identity of the indicator. The sequence of indicators is identical with the sequence used in the reliability evaluations above.

[475] See table 13.

	Act	Org	Int	Frq	Qua	Perf	Exp	Ext	Val
Act	**n.a.**								
Org	-0,27	**n.a.**							
Int	0,34	-0,19	**0,82**						
Frq	-0,06	-0,01	-0,14	**n.a.**					
Qua	0,11	-0,06	0,29	-0,11	**0,84**				
Perf	0,09	0,02	0,26	-0,24	0,77	**1,00**			
Exp	0,18	-0,09	0,04	-0,12	0,04	0,15	**n.a.**		
Ext	0,32	-0,05	0,18	-0,02	-0,05	-0,07	0,17	**0,78**	
Val	0,37	-0,14	0,08	-0,12	0,28	0,33	0,20	0,22	**0,84**

Table 13: Square root of average variance extracted (diagonal) and correlations of constructs (off-diagonal)[476]

Concluding, all of the reflective constructs used by this study show satisfactory levels of item and construct reliability and discriminant validity.

With regard to formative constructs, an evaluation is limited to excluding multicollinearity among indicators. Starting with the first formative construct "activities of private equity firms", all VIFs are below the threshold of 10, suggesting that multicollinearity problems are not present. However, when testing the construct's properties above, 168 of 231 correlations among indicators were significant, suggesting the presence of some degree of multicollinearity. Taking a closer look at the VIFs, it appears that they are in fact below 10, but several VIFs are only slightly below this threshold. Given that the VIF threshold of 10 is rather a rule of thumb than carved out of stone, multicollinearity problems may be suspected. The easiest way to identify the indicators that cause multicollinearity problems would be to set a somewhat lower threshold than 10 and eliminate all indicators above that threshold. A less arbitrary way to eliminate multicollinearity problems was chosen in this thesis. First, the factors contained in the 22 indicators of private equity firm activities were identified. A total of six factors were extracted with the help of a Varimax rotation of principal components: a sales&marketing and operations factor, a management recruiting factor, a management coaching factor, a controlling factor, a finance factor and a business development factor. In a second step, all six factors were tested for their formative or reflective properties with the help of the tetrad test. It turned out that all six factors had reflective properties. In a third step, a PLS model was estimated with the six exogenous constructs identified by the above factor analysis and the construct "value added to buyout" as endogenous variable. From each exogenous construct, the indicator loading highest on its respective latent variable was chosen for the construction of the latent variable "activities of private equity firms". The resulting VIFs of the construct "activities of private equity firms" all have near-one values affirming that multicol-

---

[476] In order to display the correlations of constructs in a readable way, abbreviations were used for construct names. The abbreviations are identical with the construct abbreviations used above.

linearity problems were eliminated. Eliminating multicollinearity problems allows the inter-preting of indicator weights.[477] Based on the magnitude of significant weight coefficients, the indicator "focusing or consolidating operations" has a positive impact on the latent variable "activities of private equity firms", whereas the indicator "optimizing reporting systems" has a negative impact. All other indicators have a nonsignificant impact on the construct "activities of private equity firms". Indicators with nonsignificant weights are not eliminated, "as excluding or adding a formative indicator changes the composition of the unobservable variable"[478].

"Activities of private equity firms"		
Indicator	Weight	VIF
Focusing or consolidating operations	*0,88*	*1,19*
Linking incentives to performance measures (n.s.)	*0,21*	*1,30*
Directing business plan (n.s.)	*0,16*	*1,41*
Selling non-required assets (n.s.)	*0,15*	*1,19*
Interviewing and selecting members of management team (n.s.)	*0,03*	*1,33*
Motivating members of management team (n.s.)	*-0,07*	*1,33*
Optimizing reporting systems	*-0,31*	*1,17*

Table 14: Weights and VIFs for the construct "activities of private equity firms"[479]

With regard to the construct "organization of involvement", near-one VIFs show that multi-collinearity problems are not present. Based on the magnitude of significant weight coefficients, "carrying out management tasks" has the largest positive influence on "organization of involvement" followed by "board membership".

"Organization of involvement"		
Indicator	Weight	VIF
Carrying out management tasks	*0,85*	*1,01*
Board membership	*0,44*	*1,02*
Carrying out consulting tasks (n.s.)	*0,17*	*1,01*

Table 15: Weights and VIFs for the construct "organization of involvement"

---

[477] In order not to burden this text with too much unnecessary information, the weights and VIFs are only shown for indicators that were not eliminated for the subsequent PLS analysis.

[478] Hänlein (forthcoming), pp. 104-105. See also Bollen/Lennox (1991), pp. 305ff. Eliminating multicollinear formative indicators is different in so far as redundant indicators are removed, which does not change the composition of an unobservable variable. Removing non-redundant formative indicators – which would be the case of the nonsignificant indicators above – would certainly change the composition of a latent variable.

[479] The abbreviation n.s. refers to a non-significant indicator.

The construct "frequency of interaction between private equity firm and portfolio company" does not seem to be affected by multicollinearity problems, which can be inferred from low VIFs. The importance of individual indicators can again be assessed based on the magnitude of their respective weight coefficients. Interestingly enough, "personal meetings with management" has a large and significant positive impact on "frequency of interaction between private equity firm and portfolio company", whereas "telephone calls, video conferences" has a large and significant negative impact. The indicator "written contacts" in turn has a non-significant negative impact on its latent variable.

"Frequency of interaction between private equity firm and portfolio company"		
Indicator	Weight	VIF
Personal meetings with management	*1,26*	*1,87*
Written contacts (n.s.)	*-0,32*	*1,18*
Telephone calls, video conferences	*-0,87*	*2,08*

Table 16: Weights and VIFs for the construct "frequency of interaction with the portfolio company"

The construct "experience of private equity professionals" is not affected by multicollinearity problems either, due to VIFs that are close to one. Based on the magnitude of weight coefficients, "work experience in professional services" has the largest positive impact on "experience of private equity professionals" followed by "P&L experience", the weight coefficient of which is, however, non-significant. "Work experience in the portfolio company's industry" has the largest negative impact on "experience of private equity professionals" followed by "private equity experience".

"Experience of private equity professionals"		
Indicator	Weight	VIF
Work experience in professional services	*0,71*	*1,01*
P&L experience (n.s.)	*0,35*	*1,10*
Private equity experience	*-0,43*	*1,09*
Work experience in the portfolio company's industry	*-0,74*	*1,10*

Table 17: Weights and VIFs for the construct "experience of private equity professionals"

6.2.4 Determination of the Significance Criterion: Statistical Power Analysis

Classical statistical tests put forward a null hypothesis of no relationship between two variables of interest. Researchers hope to reject that null hypothesis in order to prove the existence of a certain relationship. With regard to accepting or rejecting a null hypothesis, two types of errors can be made.[480] First, the Type I error is defined as the probability of incor-

---

[480] See figure 12.

rectly rejecting a true null hypothesis, "that is, of finding an effect or relationship where none exists. The risk associated with committing Type I errors is represented by α, the significance criterion"[481]. Second, the Type II error is defined as the probability of incorrectly accepting a false null hypothesis, "that is, of failing to detect an effect or relationship when one exists. The risk associated with committing Type II errors is represented by β."[482] The concept of statistical power is closely linked to β. The statistical power of a test is defined as $1-\beta$, "the probability that a statistical test will correctly reject a false null hypothesis"[483].

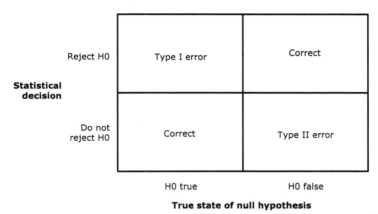

Figure 12: Type I and Type II errors

Interestingly enough, "textbooks on classical statistics, for instance, indicate that the alpha error is generally and arbitrarily set at 5 or 1 percent in hypothesis testing."[484] The requirement of an α of 5% "as the maximum acceptable probability for determining statistical significance was established, somewhat arbitrarily, by Sir Ronald Fisher when he developed his procedures for the analysis of variance."[485] However, "to set α at the same level, say, 0.05 for all hypothesis testing situations is hardly rational. Rather, for some actions the probability of not taking the right action when the hypothesis is true should be small such as once out of 100 times; while for other statistical inference problems this alpha error level should be rather large such as 30 or 40 percent."[486] Despite the widespread assumption of an α of 5% or smaller, researchers usually ignore the Type II error. Myers and Melcher refer to this conven-

[481] Baroudi/Orlikowski (1989), p. 88.
[482] Baroudi/Orlikowski (1989), p. 88.
[483] Baroudi/Orlikowski (1989), p. 88.
[484] Myers/Melcher (1969), p. B31.
[485] Cowles/Davis (1982), p. 553.
[486] Myers/Melcher (1969), p. B35.

tion as "the almost I don't care β error level"[487]. However, Type II errors should not be ig-nored. Mazen et al. present an illuminating example surrounding the ill-fated Challenger space shuttle, where the cost of committing a Type II error by far outweighs that of a Type I error: "decision makers at the National Aeronautics and Space Administration faced a choice between two types of assumptions, each with a distinctive risk and cost. The first was that the shuttle was unsafe to fly because the performance of the O-ring in the rocket-booster was dif-ferent from that used on previous missions. The second was that the shuttle was safe to fly because there would be no difference between the performance of the O-rings in this and pre-vious missions. If the mission had been aborted and the O-ring had indeed been functional, Type I error would have been committed. Obviously, the cost of the Type II error, launching with a defective O-ring, was much greater than the cost that would have been incurred with Type I error."[488]

Statistical power analysis helps to define a precise requirement for α and β levels. Statistical power analysis "exploits the relationships among the four variables involved in statistical in-ference: sample size (N), significance criterion (α), population effect size (ES), and statistical power"[489]. The significance criterion (α) refers, as stated above, to the risk of incorrectly re-jecting a true null hypothesis. Effect size "represents the magnitude of a phenomenon in a population. If all else is constant, the larger the effect size, the greater the degree to which a phenomenon manifests itself and the greater the probability it will be detected and the null hypothesis rejected."[490] Finally, the statistical power ($1-\beta$) has been defined above as the probability that a false null hypothesis will correctly be rejected. For any statistical model, the relationships among the four variables sample size, significance criterion, effect size and sta-tistical power "are such that each is a function of the other three."[491] In the case of a fixed sample size due to resource constraints and a given effect size, "the targeted level of power can be maintained by manipulating alpha"[492], i.e. for any given test statistic, α can be deter-mined for given N, ES and statistical power.[493] Given that a Type II error is at least as serious as a Type I error in an early stage of research,[494] it can be assumed that α has to be just as high as β. Compromise power analysis[495] allows researchers to specify "the size of the effect to be detected, the maximum possible sample size, and the ratio $q: = \beta/\alpha$, which defines the

---

[487] Myers/Melcher (1969), p. B39.
[488] Mazen et al. (1987), p. 370.
[489] Cohen (1992), p. 156.
[490] Mazen et al. (1987), p. 370.
[491] Cohen (1992), p. 156.
[492] Cascio/Zedeck (1983), p. 518.
[493] See figure 13.
[494] Whereas a Type I error – finding a relationship, where none exists – will usually be corrected by subsequent studies, a Type II error "may result in [...] researchers prematurely abandoning what may be promising ar-eas of research" (Baroudi/Orlikowski (1989), p. 97).
[495] See Erdfelder (1984), pp. 18ff.

relative seriousness of both types of errors"[496]. Given these specifications, the associated critical value for the test statistic and the associated α and β values can be determined.

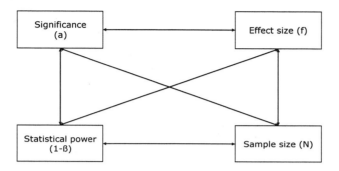

Figure 13: Statistical power analysis.

The relationship among N, α, ES and statistical power is not linear. The relationship is rather governed by the respective test statistic, which in the case of the t-test – used to test the significance of structural paths – is non-linear. Unfortunately, available "power tables are typically based on conventional α levels (i.e., $\alpha \leq .1$) exclusively and therefore do not provide the information necessary to arrive at a reasonable power value."[497] GPOWER is a high-precision software tool for compromise power analysis that allows one to determine α and β values for any given N, ES and q.[498] The N of this survey was equal to 101. With regard to the effect size, usually the following are distinguished in statistical power analyses: small, medium and large effect sizes.[499] With regard to the choice of an effect size, especially one issue has an important impact. Given that there are always errors in the measurement of a variable due to the process of operationalization and the imperfect reliability of measures, there is an upper bound on the size of effects that will be detected. O'Grady notes that behavioral sciences will usually "produce small measures of explained variance because of measurement problems alone"[500]. The argument of O'Grady suggests that also the effects analyzed in this dissertation are unlikely to be large and that therefore a small to medium effect size should be expected.[501] Assuming an ES of 0,20, which is between small (0,10) and medium (0,25) effect sizes,[502] and

---

[496] Erdfelder et al. (1996), p. 2.
[497] Erdfelder et al. (1996), p. 2.
[498] Information on GPOWER can be found at http://www.psycho.uni-duesseldorf.de/aap/projects/ gpower/how_to_use_gpower.html.
[499] Cohen (1992), p. 157.
[500] O'Grady (1982), p. 770.
[501] See for example Baroudi/Orlikowski (1989), p. 90.
[502] See Hänlein (forthcoming), p. 111; Baroudi/Orlikowski (1989), p. 90. The ES of 0.10 and 0.25 for small and medium effects are taken from the effect size conventions given in GPOWER for the so-called other t-tests.

a beta-to-alpha ratio of 1 results in a significance criterion α of 21,91% for a two-tailed[503] t-test with 99 degrees of freedom. Setting α equal to 22% may seem extraordinarily high when compared to conventional α levels of 5% or less. However, with an α at 5%, the statistical power of the analysis would be only 51% – implying that there is only a 51% chance of correctly rejecting a false null hypothesis or – put differently – a 51% probability that existing relationships between latent variables will actually be detected. Setting α to 22% on the other hand is associated with a statistical power of 78%, implying that there is a 78% probability of detecting existing relationships between latent variables. Therefore an α of 22% seems to be a rational compromise between N, ES and statistical power of the test.

6.2.5   Estimation of the Structural Model: PLS analysis

The structural model was estimated using PLS-Graph version 3.00 build 1060, a beta license that was kindly provided by Wynne Chin for beta testing purposes. The beta version of PLS-Graph was chosen, as it is the most highly developed software package available for PLS analyses and as a result also the software package most heavily used by researchers for PLS analyses. The path weighting scheme – using the multiple regression coefficient as a weight for all variables impacting the target latent variable and the correlation coefficient for weighting all latent variables dependent on it – was chosen for inner weighting, as it is the only inner weighting scheme taking into account the directionality of structural relationships.[504] The structural model was then estimated using the available sample of 101 buyout portfolio companies.[505]

Similar to traditional regression analysis, the coefficient of determination (R^2) can be used to evaluate the explanatory power of a structural model. R^2 is defined as "the proportion of the total variation of y (about its mean $\bar{y}$) that is explained (accounted for) by the fitted model."[506] Given that PLS calculates case values for all latent variables, R^2 can be calculated

as $R^2 = 1 - \dfrac{\sum\limits_{n=1}^{N}(y_n - \hat{y}_n)^2}{\sum\limits_{n=1}^{N}(y_n - \bar{y})^2}$ [507], where y_n is the construct score of the endogenous variable esti-

mated with the nth set of its indicators, $\bar{y}$ the arithmetic mean of all construct scores y_n, and

---

[503] A t-test is conducted to find out whether the path coefficients in the structural model are significantly different from zero. The hypothesis tested is non-directional, i.e. the path coefficient may be either significantly smaller or larger than zero. In the case of non-directional hypothesis testing, a two-sided t-test (rather than a one-sided t-test) has to be used (see Backhaus et al. (1996), p. 42).

[504] Inner weighting schemes are defined and contrasted in chapter 4.3.

[505] The PLS algorithm converged at iteration cycle number 17. For all calculations – despite bootstrapping – PLS-Graph default options were used. With regard to bootstrapping, the individual sign changes preprocessing option was chosen. No anomalies were encountered during the analytic process.

[506] Kvalseth (1985), p. 281.

[507] See Goldberger (1964), pp. 160 and 166.

$\hat{y}_n$ is the construct score calculated on the basis of the case values of the nth exogenous variable. In general, R^2 of 1 indicates that all of the variance of the endogenous variable can be explained by the exogenous variables. R^2 of 0 on the other hand implies that exogenous variables are unable to explain any of the variance of the endogenous variable in question. In this study, two endogenous variables are included – "performance of information systems" and "value added to buyout" – that have an R^2 of 62% and 26%, respectively. Although it is difficult to interpret absolute values of R^2,[508] the coefficient of determination for "performance of information systems" indicates good model fit. The R^2 for "value added to buyout" points toward limited model fit. However, it has to be taken into account that not only private equity firms add value to a buyout post-investment – the management team of a portfolio company is at least equally important. Explaining the levers of post-investment value creation available to private equity firms, an R^2 of 26% therefore indicates a satisfactory model fit.

The coefficient of determination (R^2) is calculated using the entire sample. R^2 indicates therefore, how well a structural model fits sample data. Whether or not a structural model is able to correctly predict, cannot be inferred from R^2. The so-called predictive relevance of a structural model can be determined, however, with the help of a sample reuse technique developed by Stone and Geisser.[509] This technique is based on the idea that "the prediction of observables or potential observables is of much greater relevance than the estimation of what are often artificial construct-parameters"[510]. Put very simply, the PLS implementation of the Stone-Geisser test criterion (Q^2) "follows a blindfolding procedure that omits a part of the data for a particular block of indicators during parameter estimations and then attempts to estimate the omitted part using the estimated parameters. This procedure is repeated until every data point has been omitted and estimated."[511] The general form of the Stone-Geisser test criterion is

$$Q^2 = 1 - \frac{\sum_{d=1}^{D} E_d}{\sum_{d=1}^{D} O_d}$$, where E_d is defined as the sum of squares of prediction errors, O_d as the sum

[508] See Backhaus et al. (1996), pp. 23ff.
[509] See Stone (1974), pp. 111ff and Geisser (1975), pp. 320ff.
[510] Geisser (1975), p. 320.
[511] Chin (1998b), p. 317. More precisely, "the blindfolding procedure takes a block of say N cases and K indicators and takes out a portion of the N by K data points. Using an omission distance D, we would omit the first point (case 1 indicator 1) and then omit every other D data point as we move across each column and row. This continues until we reach the end of the data matrix. With the remaining data points, estimates are obtained by treating the missing values via pairwise deletion, mean substitution, or an imputation procedure. The sum of squares of prediction error (E) is calculated when the omitted data points are then predicted. The sum of squares errors using the mean for prediction (O) is also calculated. The omitted data points are returned and we shift over to the next data point in the data matrix [...] as the starting point for a new round of omission. A new E and O are calculated. This continues until D sets of Es and Os are obtained" (Chin (1998b), p. 317).

of squares of errors using the mean for prediction and D is the omission distance.[512] In general, $Q^2>0$ points toward predictive relevance of a structural model, whereas $Q^2<0$ suggests lack of predictive relevance.[513] Using an omission distance of seven[514] results in a Q^2 of 0,17 for the endogenous variable "value added to buyout" implying predictive relevance of this study's causal model.[515]

In addition to the analysis of fit and predictive relevance of a structural model, the magnitude and significance of path coefficients can be analyzed in order to find out, which exogenous constructs have the strongest impact on endogenous latent variables. Whereas the size of the path coefficients in a PLS model is part of the output generated by the PLS algorithm, the significance of path coefficients has to be evaluated separately. Unlike "traditional regression analysis, where standard errors and corresponding t-values can be determined analytically, the nature of PLS requires the use of resampling techniques, such as the jackknife or bootstrap"[516]. For this study, the bootstrap is chosen as resampling technique, as the jackknife is only an approximation to the bootstrap taking less computational time.[517] The bootstrap can be described as follows: "the bootstrap procedure is a means of estimating the statistical accuracy of [...] the data in a single sample. The idea is to mimic the process of selecting many samples [...] in order to find the probability that the values of their (test statistic) fall within various intervals. The samples are generated from the data in the original sample [...]. The data are copied an enormous number of times, say a billion (for each group). [...] Samples [...] are then selected at random and the (test statistic) is calculated for each sample. [...] The distribution of the (test statistic) for the bootstrap samples can be treated as if it were a distribution constructed from real samples."[518] In order to determine the significance of the path coefficients in this survey's structural model, a bootstrap analysis was conducted based on 100 generated samples.[519] As can be inferred from figure 14, only three out of the five path coefficients relating to "value added to buyout" are significant, using the significance criterion of 22% identified through statistical power analysis. With regard to the path coefficients relating to "performance of information systems" as endogenous variable, two out of the three are

---

[512] See Chin (1998b), p. 317.

[513] See Fornell/Cha (1994), p. 73; Chin (1998b), p. 318.

[514] The omission distance should be a prime integer between the number of indicators K and the number of cases N (see Chin (1998b), p. 318).

[515] The Q^2 coefficient cannot be calculated for the endogenous variable "performance of information systems" due to its single item operationalization: omitting a data point from a single-item construct makes the causal model unsolvable, as no dependent variable is available any more.

[516] Hänlein (forthcoming), p. 111.

[517] See Efron/Tibshirani (1993), p. 145f.

[518] Diaconis/Efron (1983), p. 120. For a formal discussion of the bootstrap see Efron (1979), pp. 1ff.

[519] Given that the bootstrap samples are drawn at random from an extremely large population of scores (billions as Diaconis/Efron (1983) put it), it is the researcher that determines the number of bootstrap resamples. For this study a number of 100 bootstrap samples was chosen, although a significantly larger number of bootstrap samples – say several hundred – would have been possible. The limited number of bootstrap samples was drawn in order not to artificially magnify the significance of path coefficients in the structural model.

significant using a threshold of 22% for the significance criterion. Based on the magnitude of the path coefficients shown in figure 14, "performance of information systems" has the largest influence on "value added to buyout" followed by "activities of PE firm" and "usage of external resources". With regard to the endogenous variable "performance of information systems", "quality of portfolio company information" has the strongest impact followed by "frequency of interaction between private equity firm and portfolio company". The magnitude of significant path coefficients is in all cases in line or sufficiently close to the recommendation of Chin that "standardized paths should be at least 0,20 and ideally above 0,30 in order to be considered meaningful."[520] It is only the paths emanating from the constructs "completeness and intensity of portfolio company monitoring", "frequency of interaction between private equity firm and portfolio company", "organization of involvement" and "experience of private equity professionals" that have path coefficients below 0,20. Given that the paths emanating from the first three constructs are not only below the threshold criterion with regard to the magnitude of path coefficients but also insignificant in addition, their impact on the respective dependent variables can be regarded as not meaningful. The path emanating from "frequency of interaction between private equity firm and portfolio company" is below the threshold criterion of 0,20, but only slightly so. Given that the path is in addition highly significant it will be regarded meaningful.

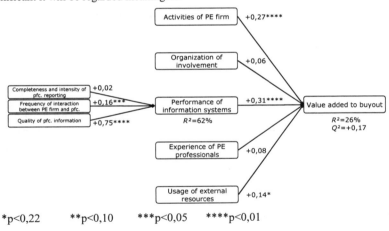

*p<0,22   **p<0,10   ***p<0,05   ****p<0,01

Figure 14: R^2, Q^2, significance and size of path coefficients of structural model.

---

520   Chin (1998a), p. 8.

7 Discussion

7.1 Interpretation of Results

The findings of the previous chapter can be used to answer all three of the research questions put forward in chapter 1.2:

- First, how can private equity firms add value to a buyout post-investment?
- Second, what is the relative importance of different post-investment concepts?
- And third, what are suitable indicators measuring post-investment concepts?

7.1.1 Influence of Post-Investment Concepts on Post-Investment Value Creation

The estimation of the structural equation model in chapter 6.2.5 shows – with regard to the first research question – that only three out of five post-investment concepts are actually adding value to a buyout. In the order of their importance (answering the second research question) – which can be derived from the magnitude of path coefficients – high-performing portfolio company information systems are the most important lever in adding value to portfolio companies, followed by hands-on involvement and finally usage of external resources. Interestingly enough, the organization of the relationship between private equity firm and portfolio company as well as the experience of private equity professionals have no significant impact on "value added to buyout".

The "performance of portfolio company information systems" has, as expected, a positive impact on "value added to buyout". High-performing information systems help private equity firms to identify developing issues faster and to make better decisions. Hypothesis 3 can therefore be accepted. Three dimensions were suggested above to remain well-informed about a portfolio company: "completeness and intensity of portfolio company reporting", "frequency of interaction between private equity firm and portfolio company" and finally "quality of portfolio company information". Consistent with Hypothesis 3a, "completeness and intensity of portfolio company reporting" has no significant impact on the "performance of portfolio company information systems". Private equity professionals require current information triggering actions. This is seemingly incompatible with written reports. Not surprisingly, the "frequency of interaction between private equity firm and portfolio company" has, consistent with Hypothesis 3b, a significantly positive impact on "performance of portfolio company information systems". Besides making the information provided more current, frequent interaction will also serve as a basis for a trustful relationship and give private equity professionals a deeper understanding of a portfolio company's business and industry – thereby increasing

114

the perceived performance of information systems. In accordance with Hypothesis 3c, "quality of portfolio company information" has a positive and significant impact on the "performance of portfolio company information systems". The importance of quality information is relatively easy to understand. If private equity firms interact frequently with their portfolio companies, but receive, however, only poor quality information, the perceived performance of portfolio company information systems will be low. That is, high frequency of interaction will only be helpful, if information of sufficiently high quality is transmitted.

Provided that high-performing portfolio company information systems are in place, private equity firms may deduce suitable action implications. This study supports the notion that hands-on involvement of private equity firms actually does add value to a buyout. Consistent with Hypothesis 1, there is a positive and significant relationship between the activity level of private equity firms and "value added to buyout".

Due to their small personnel base, private equity firms have neither the management capacity nor all of the capabilities needed to adequately support portfolio company management. As a consequence, external resources have to be used. The results of the above PLS analysis show – consistent with Hypothesis 5 – that external resources are adding significant value to a buyout. Private equity firms should therefore actively use external resources to boost their management capacity and to complement their capabilities.

The construct "organization of the relationship between private equity firm and portfolio company" is not significantly related to "value added to buyout". This implies that neither informal nor formal modes of organization have a significant impact on post-investment value creation – thereby contradicting all but one prior study. Reißig-Thust, unable as well to find a significant relationship between informal organization of involvement ("Beratungsunterstützung i.e.S.") and value added, gives the following rationale for her research findings: "In der vorliegenden aktuellen Stichprobe leistet inzwischen die große Mehrheit der Gesellschaften inhaltsorientierte Beratungsunterstützung. Es ist also denkbar, dass bei den VC-Gesellschaften ein Lernprozess eingesetzt hat, der dazu geführt hat, dass die Beratungsunterstützung i.e.S. mittlerweile zu den Standardleistungen der Gesellschaften gehört. Dies hat zur Folge, dass sich einzelne VC-Gesellschaften durch die Leistung dieser Form der Beratungsunterstützung nicht mehr von anderen Gesellschaften differenzieren können und somit keine signifikanten Unterschiede im Beteiligungserfolg auftreten."[521] Concluding, an informal organization of the relationship between private equity firm and portfolio company may indeed be relevant for adding value to a portfolio company – the findings of this study can not, however, find evidence of its significance.

---

[521] Reißig-Thust (2003), p. 206. The abbreviation VC refers to the term venture capital.

Contrary to common industry beliefs, "experience of private equity professionals" is not significantly related to "value added to buyout". Although this result seems to be counter-intuitive at first sight, it can be understood applying prior research in judgment and decision making.[522] On the one hand, increased experience of private equity professionals may be associated with various benefits improving decision quality, e.g. by focusing on the key dimensions of a problem and ignoring extraneous variables. That is, experienced private equity professionals may be able to filter information provided by the portfolio company more efficiently and to draw substantiated conclusions. On the other hand, increased experience of private equity professionals may also be detrimental – resulting in poorer decision quality, e.g. by inducing a private equity professional to be overconfident, overestimating the likelihood of certain events. That is, experienced private equity professionals may become overconfident with regard to the realization of stretched business plan goals taking excessive risks. As a consequence of effects pulling in opposite directions, no relationship between "experience of private equity professionals" and "value added to buyout" can be observed. Actually, there might be a curvilinear relationship between "experience of private equity professionals and "value added to buyout": the decision quality of private equity professionals may increase during their first years in a private equity firm; beyond a certain threshold, however, the decision quality of private equity professionals may actually decrease. A curvilinear relationship between experience and decision performance is not unheard of in research on private equity firms. For example, Shepherd et al. were able to prove a curvilinear relationship between experience of private equity professionals and decision quality in screening business plans.[523] In the case of a curvilinear relationship, SEM techniques – based on linear or quasi-linear relationships – would point toward no relationship between "experience of private equity professionals" and "value added to buyout".

7.1.2 Operationalization of Post-Investment Concepts

The third research question – which indicators should be used to operationalize post-investment constructs – will be answered in the following by a detailed interpretation of those exogenous constructs that had a significant influence on the endogenous variables "performance of portfolio company information systems" and "value added to buyout".[524] It is important to note that formative and reflective indicators have to be interpreted differently. In the case of formative indicators, weight coefficients may be used to determine the relative importance of individual indicators in forming a latent variable: "since a construct measured by formative indicators is always a composite (i.e. weighted average) of its items, an interpreta-

---

[522] See chapter 5.1.4.
[523] See Shepherd et al. (2003), pp. 381ff.
[524] Exogenous constructs having a significant impact on their respective endogenous variables are obviously the most important ones. Indicator weights and loadings for the remaining post-investment concepts as well as for the success measure can be found in chapter 6.2.3.

tion of the weight each indicator has with respect to the underlying unobservable variable shows which indicators influence the latent variable score more than others. Indicators with higher weights have a higher importance for the determination of the underlying construct score than indicators with lower weights."[525]

In the case of reflective indicators, the loading coefficient only allows one to judge whether or not an individual indicator is adequately reflecting its underlying construct. The loading coefficient "is proportional to the amount of variance in that indicator that the LV is able to account"[526]. Given that each indicator has to tap into the same latent variable, the magnitude of a loading coefficient can only be used as a cut-off criterion to determine whether or not an indicator is adequately reflecting its latent variable.

The construct "activities of private equity firms" was shown above to have formative properties. It is formed by a total of seven indicators. Two indicators, namely "focusing or consolidating operations" and "optimizing reporting systems" had a significant impact with weight coefficients of 0,88 and -0,31, respectively. This suggests that high involvement in the operations of a portfolio company is indicative of a hands-on private equity firm. Involvement in the controlling of a portfolio company on the other hand is indicative of a hands-off private equity firm. Five indicators, namely "linking incentives to performance measures", "directing business plan", "selling non-required assets", "interviewing and selecting members of management team" and "motivating members of management team" had no significant impact. This finding may be due to the fact that private equity firm involvement in business development, finance, management recruiting or management coaching is relatively common and therefore not suitable as a criterion to distinguish hands-on and hands-off private equity firms.

Proceeding to information systems, two constructs, namely "frequency of interaction between private equity firm and portfolio company" and "quality of portfolio company information" turned out to have a significant influence on "performance of portfolio company information systems". The construct "frequency of interaction between private equity firm and portfolio company" was shown above to have formative properties. It is formed by three indicators. Out of the three indicators, only the indicators "personal meetings with management" and "telephone calls, video conferences" turned out to have a significant influence with weight coefficients of 1,26 and -0,87, respectively. This result seems puzzling at first sight: frequent personal meetings are indicative of frequent interaction, whereas frequent telephone calls or video conferences point toward infrequent interaction. A clearer view of this puzzle can be gained by including the endogenous variable "performance of portfolio company information systems" in the discussion – that is, by analyzing which type of frequent interaction actually

---

[525] Hänlein (forthcoming), p. 120. See also Chin (1998b), p. 307.
[526] Chin (1998b), p. 305.

keeps a private equity professionals well-informed.[527] Inferring from weight coefficients, frequent telephone calls or video conferences surely do not inform private equity professionals adequately. In order to remain well-informed about a portfolio company, frequent personal meetings with portfolio company management are needed.

With regard to the construct "quality of portfolio company information", indicators were demonstrated to be reflective. All three indicators – "timeliness", "appropriateness/suitability for your information needs" and "reliability" – significantly reflect the latent variable "quality of portfolio company information" with loading coefficients of 0,75, 0,86 and 0,88, respectively. This result suggests that quality portfolio company information is reflected by timeliness of information provision, appropriateness and suitability of information and reliability of information given.

With regard to the reflective indicators of the construct "usage of external resources", indicators were demonstrated to be reflective as well. Out of the five indicators used for operationalization, only two turned out to adequately reflect the underlying latent variable. The two indicators were "industry experts" and "executive search firms" with loading coefficients of 0,88 and 0,67, respectively. This implies that the degree of external resource usage of private equity firms is measured ideally by the usage of industry experts and executive search firms. The usage of management consultants, interim managers or CEOs of other portfolio companies does not adequately reflect the latent variable "usage of external resources".

7.2   Implications for Practitioners

Based on the findings regarding the influence of post-investment concepts on value creation and the findings with regard to the operationalization of post-investment concepts, a post-investment strategy can be derived that demonstrably creates value.

A value adding post-investment strategy consists of three elements. First of all, private equity firms should make sure to be well-informed by their portfolio company. As one of the study participants put it, "you cannot add value if you do not know precisely how your business is working". This can be achieved on the one hand by frequent interaction between private equity firm and portfolio company. Keeping "close contact to [the] portfolio company [is important] in order to be able to react quickly". However, frequent e-mail contact, telephone calls or video conferences are not enough. Personal meetings between private equity professionals

---

[527]   Including an endogenous variable in the discussion of latent variable indicators is legitimate in a PLS analysis, given that the PLS algorithm determines indicator weights in a way that results in optimal prediction of endogenous variables. For details see chapter 4.3.

and portfolio company management are required to convey all relevant information. Study participants warned against "remote control" of portfolio companies and advised not to "neglect on-site plausibility checks". Even if private equity professionals may regard travel times as unproductive use of limited time budgets, the additional information provided by personal meetings will be worth the effort. On the other hand, being well-informed by the portfolio company requires maintaining high quality standards with regard to the information provided. Put very simply, private equity professionals should "avoid strong visions without seeing strong figures at all." More precisely, information provided by the portfolio company has to be tailored to the information needs of the private equity professional and, besides that, free from any sort of error, and has to be delivered punctually to the minute. This implies that the quality of a portfolio company's finance director is of considerable importance. "Changing a poor finance director" can be a measure adding considerable value to an investment.

Second, based on the information provided by the portfolio company, private equity firms can derive suitable action implications. Whatever the action implications are, private equity firms should be sure to vigorously implement them: hands-on involvement actually does add value to a portfolio company. Any "delay in gaining hands-on involvement" or "waiting if tough measures have to be taken", as study participants put it, will result in sub-optimal post-investment value creation. Hands-on involvement is not easy to implement, however. It implies dealing with portfolio company issues on a continual basis, dedicating a significant amount of time and applying specialist know-how beyond the financial skills readily available in any private equity firm. More precisely, hands-on private equity firms are involved in a remarkable breadth and depth of portfolio company issues, down to operational questions identified in this study as key characteristics of hands-on private equity firms. Focus on the operational improvement of a portfolio company implies that a private equity firm actively supports management in key value creation initiatives targeting top-line growth or gross margin improvement. Several participants stated that momentum can be gained by "creating a sense-of-urgency in the company" and "asking the team to start implementing the key actions straight away, we lost about a year".

Third, once individual action items are defined, private equity firms should make active use of qualified external resources. Saving the – admittedly – sizeable fees charged by qualified external resources will backfire in terms of less value added. External resources used by private equity firms on a regular basis include industry experts and executive search firms. Industry experts help a private firm to understand the traps and life belts of a portfolio company's industry, especially in cases in which private equity professionals do not know an industry very well. Besides advising the private equity firm, industry experts may also help to coach the management team. Due to their industry experience, industry experts have the necessary standing to discuss critical issues with management on a level playing field. A key success factor for private equity firms is therefore maintaining a pool of highly qualified industry experts. Caution has to be applied, however, with regard to the number of private equity executives or industry experts interacting with management. As one of the study participants put it, it may be detrimental to "involve too many different people [...] – concentrate this responsibility on few shoulders". In addition, executive search firms are helpful in defining positions of portfolio company executives, identifying potential candidates and selecting those that are best suited.

The findings presented above are relevant not only for private equity firms, but also for buyout fund investors. Private equity firms may use the findings of this study to achieve an edge over their competitors' fund performance. Pension funds, high net worth individuals or other buyout fund investors may include the findings of this study to identify private equity firms with post-investment strategies promising above average post-investment value creation. The findings of this study are also relevant to corporate parent companies that aim at creating value through non-synergistic factors. This so called "stand-alone influence is about the parent's impact on the strategies and performance of each business in the parent's ownership, viewed as a stand-alone profit center."[528] This study may therefore also indicate practical ways through which diversified companies can rejuvenate their subsidiaries.

7.3 Limitations of the Analysis and Areas of Further Research

Given that the results of this study are based on empirical research, certain limitations need to be taken into account that are implied by the research format. Limitations of this study and areas of further research are therefore closely related to the empirical research format adopted along the lines methodology of data analysis, design of the survey instrument and data collection.

First, with respect to the methodology of data analysis adopted by this study, PLS analysis, only linear or quasi-linear relationships can be identified. That is, whatever relationships there may be between post-investment concepts and value added, a PLS analysis will only be able to detect the linear or quasi-linear relationships among them. The experience construct included in this study may, however, have a non-linear impact on value added to buyout. Prior research indicates that there might be a curvilinear relationship. Therefore further research analyzing the impact of experience on value added should use a methodology that allows the identification of curvilinear relationships.

Second, regarding the survey instrument, the experience construct measured only the experience of the private equity partner responsible for the portfolio company. As discussed above, in the post-investment phase, the experience of the partner responsible for the portfolio company is most relevant. Further research may be interested, however, in analyzing the impact of private equity professional experience on value creation more broadly, including all steps of the private equity investment process. In this case, not only the experience of one private equity partner can be taken into account – the experience of entire private equity teams – managing a deal from screening to exit – will have to be measured. Further research analyzing the impact of experience on value creation may, therefore, want to measure the experience of entire teams of private equity firms. Still with regard to the survey instrument, the construct "value added to buyout" does not account for costs incurred by private equity firms as a consequence of hands-on involvement. Additional private equity professionals backing a hands-on involvement strategy should therefore be employed with prudence. Future research might analyze the impact of employing additional private equity professionals on the implementation of a hands-on involvement strategy and the resulting improvement of private equity fund performance.

Third, with regard to data collection, the post-investment phase was analyzed only from the point of view of private equity firms. Although a prior study had shown that there are no significant differences in responses provided by private equity firms and portfolio company executives, it cannot be excluded that this type of informant bias may exist with regard to buyout investing. In order to exclude potential informant bias, further research should analyze the impact of the post-investment concepts of this study on value added to buyouts from the portfolio company's point of view.

In addition, the unit of analysis used by this study was the individual portfolio company rather than the fund – thereby limiting the achievable sample size: whereas a portfolio company perspective will yield an N of 1 portfolio company for each participating private equity firm, a fund level perspective will yield a significantly larger N – equal to the number of portfolio companies held by that specific private equity firm. Although a fund level perspective is unsuitable for several of the constructs of this study – for example the constructs "activities of private equity firm" or "performance of portfolio company information systems" are portfolio company specific – a fund level perspective is well-suited to analyze the experience construct: the experience of a team of private equity professionals radiates to all of the portfolio companies held. It is legitimate therefore to analyze the impact of private equity professionals' experience on the respective fund's performance.

---

[528] Campbell et al. (1995), p. 81.

8 Summary

Prior research on post-acquisition involvement of private equity firms shares two shortcomings. First, studies conducted so far have focused on portfolio companies in the start-up and expansion financing stages. However, almost two thirds of all private equity investments in Europe can be attributed to the buyout financing stage. Second, most of these studies have relied on research techniques such as factor, cluster or regression analysis. However, given that variables of post-acquisition involvement are for the most part unobservable, structural equation modeling techniques should have been used. This doctoral dissertation therefore analyzes the levers of post-investment value creation using partial least squares analysis.

Data for the present study was collected on the basis of a standardized questionnaire. The questionnaire was sent to 454 European buyout houses. More than 101 buyout firms – corresponding to a 22% response rate – agreed to participate in the survey and filled in the questionnaire for the portfolio company that came first alphabetically. With the help of the data obtained, a structural equation model was tested, relating the five variables (1) activities of private equity firms, (2) organization of the relationship with the portfolio company, (3) performance of information systems, (4) experience of private equity professionals and (5) usage of external resources to portfolio company performance. The results indicate that hands-on involvement, high-performing information systems and qualified outside resources help to create value after the acquisition. Contrary to common beliefs, the experience of private equity professionals was not related to post-investment value creation. In addition, the organization of the relationship with the portfolio company was not associated with the value added.

The results of this study are relevant to both buyout firms and those investing in them.
Buyout firms should involve actively in their portfolio companies. A prerequisite for taking the right actions is, however, being well informed by the portfolio company. Greater attention should therefore be given to a portfolio company's information systems and the quality of the finance director. Finally, buyout houses should complement limitations in management capacity and capabilities by the use of qualified external resources.
Pensions funds, high net worth individuals and other buyout fund investors should make sure that they invest in a hands-on fund with access to high-quality external resources. The choice of a firm with the right post-investment strategy is considerably more important than the experience of its partners.

Appendix

Cover letter

RHEINISCH-
WESTFÄLISCHE
TECHNISCHE
HOCHSCHULE
AACHEN

Lehrstuhl Wirtschaftswissenschaften für Ingenieure und
Naturwissenschaftler
Templergraben 64
D-52056 Aachen
Mobil: 0173-7133206
Fax: 0241-3674010
E-Mail: degenhard.meier@rwth-aachen.de

Prof. Dr. Malte Brettel / D. Meier, RWTH Aachen, Lehrstuhl WIN
Templergraben 64, D-52056 Aachen, Deutschland

Aachen, 17.11.2003

Forschungsprojekt "Post-Investment Value Addition to Buyouts"

Sehr geehrter ,

was sind die Aktivitäten, mit denen eine Private Equity-Gesellschaft die größten Wertsteigerungen bei ihren Portfoliounternehmen erzielen kann?

Diese und weitere Fragen zum Thema „Post-Investment Value Addition" wollen wir im Rahmen eines Dissertationsvorhabens durch eine europaweite empirische Untersuchung klären. Die Ergebnisse dieser Studie werden sich in der Zusammenarbeit mit Ihren Portfoliounternehmen gewinnbringend einsetzen lassen und selbstverständlich allen Teilnehmern zur Verfügung gestellt.

Partner und Principals von Clayton Dubilier & Rice, Electra Europe, Investcorp, Warburg Pincus und über 60 weiteren Private Equity-Gesellschaften haben sich bislang bereiterklärt, an dieser Untersuchung teilzunehmen. Um die Aussagekraft weiter steigern zu können, würden wir uns auch über Ihre Beteiligung sehr freuen.

Wir bitten Sie deshalb um 15 Minuten Ihrer Zeit, um den beiliegenden Fragebogen auszufüllen. Ihre Angaben werden selbstverständlich streng vertraulich behandelt und anonym ausgewertet. Vielen Dank für Ihre Kooperation!

Mit freundlichen Grüßen,

Degenhard Meier   Prof. Dr. Malte Brettel

Anlage

124

Survey instrument

Questionnaire

Post-Investment Value Addition to Buyouts

- **15 minutes of your time** would be needed to fill in this questionnaire. **In exchange** for your effort you will be provided with the results of this study and offered **recommendations** on value-adding post-investment activities, organizational designs, instruments and resources

- **Questionnaire structure** is as follows:
  - Part 1 focuses on your firm
  - Part 2 focuses on one specific buyout or buyin of your portfolio

- All data provided in this questionnaire will be treated **confidentially** and processed **anonymously**

- Should you **not know the precise answer** to a specific question, please provide an **estimate**. Should you not be able or willing to fill in parts of this questionnaire, do not hesitate to **return an incomplete questionnaire**

- Please **return the questionnaire** by mail or fax **before December 12**[th] to:

Prof. Dr. M. Brettel / D. Meier
RWTH Aachen, Lehrstuhl WIN
Templergraben 64
D-52056 Aachen
Germany
Fax: 0049-241-3674010 or 0049-89-5123-1302

Part 1: Private equity firm

1.	How would you describe your firm's **investment focus**? *(Please check all that apply)*		
• Deal size focus	*Small cap (€5-50M)* ☐	*Mid cap (>€50-250M)* ☐	*Large cap (>€250M)* ☐
• Corporate control focus	*Hands-off* ☐	*Supporting* ☐	*Hands-on* ☐
• Company focus	*Well-managed* ☐	*Underperforming* ☐	*Restructuring* ☐

2.	What is your firm's **experience and size**?	
•	Funds raised so far	(# of funds)
•	Total capital under management/advised	(Euro million)
•	Funds invested in buyouts and buyins by your local office	(Euro million)

3. What is your firm's **ownership structure**? *(Please check only one box)*			
Independent (capital raised mainly from outside investors)	*Semi-captive (capital raised both from outside investors and parent company)*	*Captive (capital raised mainly from parent company)*	*Public (capital raised mainly from public sources or publicly held companies)*
☐	☐	☐	☐

Adding value to buyouts – a study on European private equity firms' post-investment value addition to their portfolio companies   Page 1 of 5

126

Important: For answering the following questions, please refer to **one specific, preferably realized, buyout/buyin**. Among the portfolio companies with which you are familiar, please choose the buyout/buyin that comes **first alphabetically**.

Section 1   Portfolio company characteristics

4.   What were the volume and timing of the investment in the portfolio company?

Capital invested (equity supplied by your funds)	Year of first investment	Year of exit (if exit has occurred already)
Euro million		

5.   What share of the portfolio company's voting rights do/did you own?

0-25%	>25%-50%	>50%-75%	>75-100%
☐	☐	☐	☐

6.   What is/was the portfolio company's industry? *(Please check only one box)*

• Communications and media	☐	• Manufacturing	☐
• Computer related and other electronics	☐	• Finance, insurance and real estate	☐
• Biotechnology, medical/health related	☐	• Other services	☐
• Consumer related	☐	• Other (please specify):	☐

7.   How did the portfolio company perform at acquisition?

	In bank-ruptcy	Worse			Same			Better
• relative to competitors	☐	☐	☐	☐	☐	☐	☐	☐

8.   How does/did the portfolio company perform currently/at exit?

	Total loss	Worse			Same			Better
• relative to business plan	☐	☐	☐	☐	☐	☐	☐	☐
• relative to competitors		☐	☐	☐	☐	☐	☐	☐

9.   Which internal rate of return did your investment in the portfolio company achieve?
(If exit has occurred already. Please give approximate gross IRR on realized investments, from time of investment in the portfolio company to the exit)

%

Adding value to buyouts – a study on European private equity firms' post-investment value addition to their portfolio companies   Page 2 of 5

127

Part 2: Portfolio company (continued)

Section 2 — Tasks

10. For **each of the following activities** directed to the portfolio company, please indicate the degree of **involvement that your firm had?**	*Low involvement*						*High involvement*
Business development/partnerships							
• Defining acquisition and divestment program	☐	☐	☐	☐	☐	☐	☐
• Identifying and organizing partnerships and alliances	☐	☐	☐	☐	☐	☐	☐
• Directing business plan	☐	☐	☐	☐	☐	☐	☐
Sales&Marketing							
• Formulating marketing & sales plans	☐	☐	☐	☐	☐	☐	☐
• Testing or evaluating marketing & sales plans	☐	☐	☐	☐	☐	☐	☐
• Soliciting customers or distributors	☐	☐	☐	☐	☐	☐	☐
Operations							
• Focusing or consolidating operations	☐	☐	☐	☐	☐	☐	☐
• Soliciting suppliers	☐	☐	☐	☐	☐	☐	☐
• Optimizing working capital	☐	☐	☐	☐	☐	☐	☐
Management recruiting							
• Searching for candidates of management team	☐	☐	☐	☐	☐	☐	☐
• Interviewing and selecting members of management team	☐	☐	☐	☐	☐	☐	☐
• Negotiating employment terms with management team	☐	☐	☐	☐	☐	☐	☐
Management coaching							
• Serving as sounding board to management team	☐	☐	☐	☐	☐	☐	☐
• Motivating members of management team	☐	☐	☐	☐	☐	☐	☐
• Managing crises and problems	☐	☐	☐	☐	☐	☐	☐
Finance							
• Obtaining alternative sources of debt or equity financing	☐	☐	☐	☐	☐	☐	☐
• Selling non-required assets	☐	☐	☐	☐	☐	☐	☐
• Finding the right mix between debt and equity as well as short and long-term financing	☐	☐	☐	☐	☐	☐	☐
• Monitoring financial performance	☐	☐	☐	☐	☐	☐	☐
Controlling							
• Designing management team performance measures and setting targets	☐	☐	☐	☐	☐	☐	☐
• Optimizing reporting systems	☐	☐	☐	☐	☐	☐	☐
• Linking incentives to performance measures	☐	☐	☐	☐	☐	☐	☐

11. How would you characterize your firm's **overall level of post-investment involvement** in the portfolio company?	*Low involvement*						*High involvement*
	☐	☐	☐	☐	☐	☐	☐

Adding value to buyouts – a study on European private equity firms' post-investment value addition to their portfolio companies

Page 3 of 5

128

Section 3   Organization

12. How did your firm interact with the portfolio company?

• Carrying out consulting tasks	☐ Yes	☐ No
• Carrying out management tasks	☐ Yes	☐ No

13. What was the participation of your firm in the board of directors/supervisory board?

• Total size of the board	(# of people)
• Professionals from your firm represented on the board	(# of people)
• Chairman of the board is/was a member of your firm	☐ Yes ☐ No

Section 4   Instruments

14. How often were you or your colleagues supplied with the following **types of information** by the portfolio company?	Never	On request	Yearly	Half-yearly	Quar-terly	Month-ly	Weekly
• Revenue	☐	☐	☐	☐	☐	☐	☐
• Balance sheet and P&L	☐	☐	☐	☐	☐	☐	☐
• Cash flows	☐	☐	☐	☐	☐	☐	☐
• Interim qualitative reports on business situation	☐	☐	☐	☐	☐	☐	☐
• Reports on planned investments	☐	☐	☐	☐	☐	☐	☐
• Reports on R&D or other projects	☐	☐	☐	☐	☐	☐	☐

15. How often did your firm interact with the portfolio company?	Never	Yearly	Half-yearly	Quar-terly	Month-ly	Weekly	Daily
• Written contacts	☐	☐	☐	☐	☐	☐	☐
• Telephone calls, video conferences	☐	☐	☐	☐	☐	☐	☐
• Personal meetings with management	☐	☐	☐	☐	☐	☐	☐

16. How would you rate the **quality of information** provided by your portfolio company?	Poor						Good
• Timeliness	☐	☐	☐	☐	☐	☐	☐
• Appropriateness/suitability for your information needs	☐	☐	☐	☐	☐	☐	☐
• Reliability	☐	☐	☐	☐	☐	☐	☐

17. Overall, do you feel that your portfolio company kept you well informed?	Not at all						Abso-lutely
	☐	☐	☐	☐	☐	☐	☐

Adding value to buyouts – a study on European private equity firms' post-investment value addition to their portfolio companies   Page 4 of 5

129

Section 5 | **Resources**

18. Which of the following <u>external resources</u> did you use to complement your portfolio company's own management team?	*Never*			*Every now and then*			*Al-ways*
• Management consultants (If used, which one: _____)	☐	☐	☐	☐	☐	☐	☐
• Interim managers	☐	☐	☐	☐	☐	☐	☐
• Industry experts	☐	☐	☐	☐	☐	☐	☐
• CEOs of other portfolio companies	☐	☐	☐	☐	☐	☐	☐
• Executive search firms	☐	☐	☐	☐	☐	☐	☐

19. What was the <u>age</u> (at the time of acquisition) of the <u>partner/director</u> mainly responsible for the portfolio company?	*<35 years*	*35-39 years*	*40-44 years*	*45-49 years*	*50-54 years*	*55-59 years*	*>59 years*
	☐	☐	☐	☐	☐	☐	☐

20. What was the prior <u>work experience</u> (at the time of acquisition) of the <u>partner/director</u> mainly responsible for the portfolio company?	*0-6 months*	*6-12 months*	*1-2 years*	*2-4 years*	*4-8 years*	*8-16 years*	*>16 years*
• Work experience in professional services (e.g. accounting, consulting, investment banking)	☐	☐	☐	☐	☐	☐	☐
• Private equity experience	☐	☐	☐	☐	☐	☐	☐
• P&L responsibility	☐	☐	☐	☐	☐	☐	☐
• Work experience in the portfolio company's industry	☐	☐	☐	☐	☐	☐	☐

Section 6 | **Lessons learned**

21. Based on your experience with the portfolio company, what was the main measure to drive value added?

22. Based on your experience with the portfolio company, what would you avoid doing in the future?

If you are interested in receiving this study's results please fill in your name and e-mail address.
(This part of the questionnaire will be detached in order to ensure the anonymity of your response)

• Name (optional)	
• E-Mail Address (optional)	

Thank you for your participation!

Adding value to buyouts – a study on European private equity firms' post-investment value addition to their portfolio companies   Page 5 of 5

130

References

Achleitner, A.-K. (2001): Entrepreneurial Finance - eine konzeptionelle Einführung, EF Working Paper Series, Nr. 01-01, München.

Achleitner, A.-K./ Fingerle, C. H. (2003): Unternehmenswertsteigerung durch Management Buyout, EF Working Paper Series, Nr. 01-03, München.

Akerlow, G. (1970): The market for "lemons": quality uncertainty and the market mechanism; in: Quarterly Journal of Economics, Vol. 84, Iss. 3, pp. 488-500.

Alchian, A. A. (1965): Some economics of property rights ; in: Il Politico, Vol. 30, Iss. 4, pp. 816-829.

Alchian, A. A. (1984): Specificity, specialization and coalitions; in: Journal of Institutional and Theoretical Economics, Vol. 140, Iss. 1, pp. 34-49.

Allen, F./Santomero, A. M. (1997): The theory of financial intermediation; in: Journal of Banking and Finance, Vol. 21, Iss. 11/12, pp. 1461-1485.

Amoroso, D. L./Cheney, P. H. (1991): Testing a causal model of end-user application effectiveness; in: Journal of Management Information Systems, Vol. 8, Iss. 1, pp. 63-89.

Anderson, E./Gatignon, H. (1986): Model of foreign entry: a transaction cost analysis and propositions; in: Journal of International Business Studies, Vol. 17, Iss. 3, pp. 1-26.

Armstrong, J. S./Overton, T. S. (1977): Estimating nonresponse bias in mail surveys; in: Journal of Marketing Research, Vol. 14, Iss. 3, pp. 396-402.

Asquith, P./Wizman, T. (1990): Event risk, wealth redistribution, and the return to existing bondholders in corporate buyouts; in: Journal of Financial Economics, Vol. 27, Iss. 1, pp. 195-214.

Backhaus, K./Erichson, B./Plinke, W. /Weiber, R. (1996): Multivariate Analysemethoden - eine anwendungsorientierte Einführung, 8th edition, Berlin [and others].

Bader, H. (1996): Private Equity als Anlagekategorie, Bern/Switzerland.

Bagozzi, R. P. (1981a): Evaluating structural equation models with unobservable variables and measurement error: a comment; in: Journal of Marketing Research, Vol. 18, Iss. 3, pp. 375-381.

Bagozzi, R. P. (1981b): An examination of the validity of two models of attitude; in: Multivariate Behavioral Research, Vol. 16, Iss. 3, pp. 323-359.

Bagozzi, R. P. (1994): Structural equation models in marketing research - basic principles; in: Bagozzi, R. P. (editor): Principles of Marketing Research, Oxford/UK, pp. 317-385.

Bagozzi, R. P./Phillips, L. W. (1982): Representing and testing organizational theories: a holistic construal; in: Administrative Science Quarterly, Vol. 27, Iss. 3, pp. 459-489.

Bain&Company (2003): Private equity: the rising demand for strategy in LBO deals, unpublished document, Bain&Company, Boston/MA/USA.

Barger, T. (2002): Issues in private equity funds, unpublished document, International Finance Corporation, Washington/DC/USA.

Barney, J. (1991): Firm resources and sustained competitive advantage; in: Journal of Management, Vol. 17, Iss. 1, pp. 99-120.

Barney, J./Busenitz, L./Fiet, J./Moesel, D. (1996): New venture team's assessment of learning assistance from venture capital firms; in: Journal of Business Venturing, Vol. 11, Iss. 4, pp. 257-272.

Baroudi, J. J./Orlikowski, W. J. (1989): The problem of statistical power in MIS research; in: MIS Quarterly, Vol. 13, Iss. 1, pp. 87-106.

Barry, C. B./Muscarella, C. J./Peavy, J. W./Vetsuypens, M. R. (1990): The role of venture capital in the creation of public companies; in: Journal of Financial Economics, Vol. 27, Iss. 2, pp. 447-471.

Barry, C. B. (1994): New directions in research on venture capital finance; in: Financial Management, Vol. 23, Iss. 3, pp. 3-15.

Becker, R. (2000): Buy-outs in Deutschland, Köln.

Bentler, P. M./Chou, C.-P. (1988): Practical issues in structural modeling; in: Long, J. S. (editor): Common problems/proper solutions: avoiding error in quantitative research, Newbury Park/CA/USA, pp. 161-192.

Berg, A./Gottschalg, O. (2003): Understanding value generation in buyouts, INSEAD Working Paper, Fontainebleau/France.

Berger, M. (1993): Management buy-out und Mitarbeiterbeteiligung - finanzwirtschaftliche Analyse von Konzepten zur Übernahme von Unternehmen durch Management und Belegschaft, Köln.

Bhattacharya, S./Thakor, A. V. (1993): Contemporary banking theory; in: Journal of Financial Intermediation, Vol. 3, Iss. 1, pp. 2-50.

Bilo, S. (2002): Alternative asset class - publicly traded private equity - performance, liquidity, diversification potential, and pricing characteristics, Bamberg.

Blair, M. (1995): Ownership and control: rethinking corporate governance for the twenty-first century, Washington/DC/USA.

Bollen, K. A./Lennox, R. (1991): Conventional wisdom on measurement: a structural equation perspective; in: Psychological Bulletin, Vol. 110, Iss. 2, pp. 305-314.

Bollen, K. A./Ting, K.-F. (1998): Bootstrapping a test statistic for vanishing tetrads; in: Sociological Methods & Research, Vol. 27, Iss. 1, pp. 77-102.

Bollen, K. A./Ting, K.-F. (2000): A tetrad test for causal indicators; in: Psychological Methods, Vol. 5, Iss. 1, pp. 3-22.

Boomsma, A. (1983): On the robustness of LISREL (maximum likelihood estimation) against small sample size and nonnormality, Amsterdam/Netherlands.

Boomsma, A. (1985): Nonconvergence, improper solutions, and starting values in LISREL maximum likelihood estimation; in: Psychometrika, Vol. 52, pp. 345-370.

Boomsma, A./Hoogland, J. J. (2001): The robustness of LISREL modeling revisited; in: Cudeck, R./du Toit, S./Sörbom, D. (editors): Structural equation models: present and future. A Festschrift in honor of Karl Jöreskog, Chicago/IL/USA, pp. 139-168.

Bortz, J./Döring, N. (2002): Forschungsmethoden und Evaluation für Human- und Sozialwissenschaftler, 3rd edition, Berlin [and others].

Botta, V. (1994): Ausgewählte Probleme des Beteiligungscontrollings; in: Schulte, C. (editor): Beteiligungscontrolling - Grundlagen, strategische Allianzen und Akquisitionen, Erfahrungsberichte, Wiesbaden, pp. 25-40.

Brannick, M. T. (1995): Critical comments on applying covariance structure modeling; in: Journal of Organizational Behavior, Vol. 16, Iss. 3, pp. 201-213.

Brealey, R. A./Myers, S. C. (2000): Principles of corporate finance, 6th edition, Boston [and others].

Brettel, M. (2002): Entscheidungskriterien von Venture Capitalists: eine empirische Analyse im internationalen Vergleich; in: Die Betriebswirtschaft, Vol. 62, Iss. 3, pp. 305-325.

Brettel, M. (forthcoming): Der informelle Beteiligungskapitalmarkt - eine empirische Analyse, Wiesbaden.

Brettel, M./Meier, D./Reißig-Thust, S. (2004): Vertragsgestaltung von Venture Capitalists und Business Angels im Vergleich; in: Die Betriebswirtschaft, Vol. 64, Iss. 4, pp. 431-447.

Breuer, W. (1998): Finanzierungstheorie - eine systematische Einführung, Wiesbaden.

Brinkrolf, A. (2002): Managementunterstützung durch Venture-Capital-Gesellschaften, Wiesbaden.

Bruton, G. D./Keels, J. K./Scifres, E. L. (2002): Corporate restructuring and performance: an agency perspective on the complete buyout cycle; in: Journal of Business Research, Vol. 55, Iss. 9, pp. 709-724.

Bull, I. (1989): Financial performance of leveraged buyouts: an empirical analysis; in: Journal of Business Venturing, Vol. 4, Iss. 4, pp. 263-279.

Burgel, O./Murray, G. C. (2000): The impact of fund size and investment preferences on venture capitalists' returns, in: Proceedings of the Twentieth Annual Entrepreneurship Research Conference, Wellesley/MA/USA.

Busenitz, L. W./Fiet, J. O./Moesel, D. D. (2004): Reconsidering the venture capitalists' "value added" proposition: an interorganizational learning perspective; in: Journal of Business Venturing, Vol. 19, Iss. 6, pp. 787-807.

Bygrave, W. D./Timmons, J. A. (1992): Venture capital at the crossroads, Boston/Massachusetts/USA.

Campbell, D. T./Fiske, D. W. (1959): Convergent and discriminant validation by the multitrait-multimethod matrix; in: Psychological Bulletin, Vol. 56, Iss. 2, pp. 81-105.

Cannell, C. F./Kahn, R. L. (1968): Interviewing; in: Lindzey, G./Aronsson, E. (editors): The handbook of social psychology, Reading/MA/USA, pp. 526-595.

Carmines, E. G./Zeller, R. A. (1979): Reliability and validity assessment, Beverly Hills/CA/USA.

Cascio, W. F./Zedeck, S. (1983): Open a new window in rational research planning: adjust alpha to maximize statistical power; in: Personnel Psychology, Vol. 36, Iss. 3, pp. 517-526.

Cassel, C. M./Hackl, P./Westlund, A. H. (1999): Robustness of partial least-squares method for estimating latent variable quality structures; in: Journal of Applied Statistics, Vol. 26, Iss. 4, pp. 435-446.

Chandler, G. N./Hanks, S. H. (1993): Measuring the performance of emerging business: a validation study; in: Journal of Business Venturing, Vol. 8, Iss. 5, pp. 391-408.

Chase, W./Simon, H. (1973): Perception in chess; in: Cognitive Psychology, Vol. 4, pp. 55-81.

Chin, W. W. (1998a): Issues and opinion on structural equation modeling; in: MIS Quarterly, Vol. 22, Iss. 1, pp. 7-16.

Chin, W. W. (1998b): The partial least squares approach to structural equation modeling; in: Marcoulides, G. A. (editor): Modern methods for business research, Mahwah/NJ/USA, pp. 295-336.

Chin, W. W. (2000): Partial least squares for researchers: an overview and presentation of recent advances using the PLS approach, unpublished document, Bauer College of Business, University of Houston,

Chin, W. W./Gopal, A. (1995): Adoption intention in GSS: relative importance of beliefs; in: Data Base, Vol. 2, Iss. 3, pp. 42-63.

Chin, W. W./Marcolin, B. L./Newsted, P. R. (1996): A partial least squares latent variable modeling approach for measuring interaction effects: results from a monte carlo simulation study and voice mail emotion/adoption study; in: DeGross, J. I./Jarvenpaa, S./Srinivasan, A. (editors): Proceedings of the seventeenth international conference on information systems, Cleveland/Ohio/USA, pp. 21-41.

Choo, F./Trotman, K. T. (1991): The relationship between knowledge structure and judgement for experienced and inexperienced auditors; in: Accounting Review, Vol. 66, Iss. 3, pp. 464-485.

Churchill, G. A. Jr. (1979): A paradigm for developing better measures of marketing constructs; in: Journal of Marketing Research, Vol. 16, Iss. 1, pp. 64-73.

Coase, R. H. (1937): The nature of the firm; in: Economica, Vol. 4, pp. 386-405.

Coase, R. H. (1960): The problem of social cost; in: Journal of Law and Economics, Vol. 3, Iss. 1, pp. 1-44.

Coase, R. H. (1984): The new institutional economics; in: Journal of Institutional and Theoretical Economics, Vol. 140, pp. 229-231.

Cohen, J. (1992): A power primer; in: Psychological Bulletin, Vol. 112, Iss. 1, pp. 155-159.

Cohen, R. (1985): What a hands-on venture capitalist offers beyond money; in: Pratt, S. E./Lloyd, S. E. (editors): Guide to European venture capital sources, London, pp. 37-39.

Conner, K. R./Prahalad, C. K. (1996): A resource-based theory of the firm: knowledge versus opportunism; in: Organization Science, Vol. 7, Iss. 5, pp. 477-501.

Cool, K./Dierickx, I. (1989): Business strategy, market structure and risk-return relationships: a structural approach; in: Strategic Management Journal, Vol. 10, Iss. 6, pp. 507-522.

Cooper, A. C./Weil, L. A. (2003): Entrepreneurship: the past, the present and the future, West Lafayette/IN/USA.

Cowles, M./Davis, C. (1982): On the origins of the .05 level of statistical significance; in: American Psychologist, Vol. 37, Iss. 5, pp. 553-558.

Cox, E. P. I. (1980): The optimal number of response alternatives for a scale: a review; in: Journal of Marketing Research, Vol. 17, Iss. 4, pp. 407-422.

Cronbach, L. J. (1951): Coefficient alpha and the internal structure of tests; in: Psychometrika, Vol. 16, Iss. 3, pp. 297-334.

Cui, W. W. (2003): Reducing error in mail surveys; in: Practical Assessment, Research and Evaluation, Vol. 8, Iss. 18, pp. 1-7.

Cullinan, G./Le Roux, J.-M./Weddigen, R.-M. (2004): When to walk away from a deal; in: Harvard Business Review, Vol. 82, Iss. 4, pp. 96-104.

De Clercq, D./Sapienza, H. J. (2002): Knowledge-based antecedents of venture capital firm value added, in: Proceedings of the Twenty-Second Annual Entrepreneurship Research Conference, Wellesley/MA/USA.

Demsetz, H. (1964): The exchange and enforcement of property rights; in: Journal of Law and Economics, Vol. 7, Iss. 1, pp. 11-26.

Demsetz, H. (1966): Some aspects of property rights; in: Journal of Law and Economics, Vol. 9, Iss. 1, pp. 61-70.

Demsetz, H. (1967): Toward a theory of property rights; in: American Economic Review, Vol. 57, Iss. 2, pp. 347-359.

Denis, D. J. (2004): Entrepreneurial finance: an overview of the issues and evidence; in: Journal of Corporate Finance, Vol. 10, Iss. 2, pp. 301-326.

Dess, G. G./Robinson, R. B. (1984): Measuring organizational performance in the absence of objective measures: the case of the privately held firm and conglomerate business unit; in: Strategic Management Journal, Vol. 5, Iss. 3, pp. 265-273.

Deutsche Bundesbank (2004): Neue Eigenkapitalanforderungen für Kreditinstitute; in: Monatsbericht, Iss. 9, pp. 75-100.

Diaconis, P./Efron, P. (1983): Computer-intensive methods in statistics; in: Scientific American, Vol. 248, Iss. 5, pp. 116-129.

Diamantopoulos, A. (1994): Modeling with LISREL: A guide for the uninitiated; in: Journal of Marketing Management, Vol. 10, Iss. 1-3, pp. 105-136.

Diamantopoulos, A./Winklhofer, H. M. (2001): Index construction with formative indicators: an alternative to scale development; in: Journal of Marketing Research, Vol. 38, Iss. 2, pp. 269-277.

Diamond, D. (1984): Financial intermediation and delegated monitoring; in: Review of Economic Studies, Vol. 51, Iss. 166, pp. 393-414.

Dijkstra, T. (1983): Some comments on maximum likelihood and partial least squares methods; in: Journal of Econometrics, Vol. 22, Iss. 1/2, pp. 67-90.

Dillon W. R./Kumar, A./Mulani, N. (1987): Offending estimates in covariance structure analysis: comments on the causes of and solutions to Heywood cases; in: Psychological Bulletin, Vol. 101, Iss. 1, pp. 126-135.

Dionne, G. (1991): Contributions to insurance economics, Dordrecht/Netherlands.

Dixit, A./Jayaraman, N. (2001): Internationalization strategies of private equity firms; in: Journal of Private Equity, Vol. 5, Iss. 1, pp. 40-54.

Dubini, P. (1989): Which venture capital backed entrepreneurs have the best chances of succeeding?; in: Journal of Business Venturing, Vol. 4, Iss. 2, pp. 123-132.

Dyckhoff, H./Ahn, H. (2001): Sicherstellung der Effektivität und Effizienz der Führung als Kernfunktion des Controlling; in: Kostenrechnungspraxis, Vol. 45, Iss. 2, pp. 111-121.

Easterwood, J./Seth, A./Singer, R. (1989): The impact of leveraged buyouts on strategic direction; in: California Management Review, Vol. 32, Iss. 1, pp. 30-43.

Efron, B. (1979): Bootstrap methods: another look at the jackknife; in: Annals of statistics, Vol. 7, Iss. 1, pp. 1-26.

Efron, B./Tibshirani, R. J. (1993): An introduction to the bootstrap, New York/NY/USA.

Ehrlich, S. B./De Noble, A. F./Moore, T./Weaver, R. R. (1994): After the cash arrives: a comparative study of venture capital and private investors' involvement in entrepreneurial firms; in: Journal of Business Venturing, Vol. 9, Iss. 1, pp. 67-82.

Eisenhardt, K. M. (1989): Agency theory: an assessment and review; in: Academy of Management Review, Vol. 14, Iss. 1, pp. 57-74.

Elango, B./Fried, V./Hisrich, R./Polonchek, A. (1995): How venture capital firms differ; in: Journal of Business Venturing, Vol. 10, Iss. 2, pp. 157-179.

Erdfelder, E. (1984): Zur Bedeutung und Kontrolle des Beta-Fehlers bei der inferenzstatistischen Prüfung log-linearer Modelle; in: Zeitschrift für Sozialpsychologie, Vol. 15, Iss. 1, pp. 18-32.

Erdfelder, E./Faul, F./Buchner, A. (1996): GPOWER: a general power analysis program; in: Behavior Research Methods, Instruments & Computers, Vol. 28, Iss. 1, pp. 1-11.

Ernst, H. (2003): Ursachen eines Informant Bias und dessen Auswirkung auf die Validität empirischer betriebswirtschaftlicher Forschung; in: Zeitschrift für Betriebswirtschaft, Vol. 73, Iss. 12, pp. 1249-1275.

EVCA (1997): EVCA yearbook 1997, Zaventem/Belgium.

EVCA (1998): EVCA yearbook 1998, Zaventem/Belgium.

EVCA (2001): Survey of the economic and social impact of management buyouts & buyins in Europe, Zaventem/Belgium.

EVCA (2003): EVCA yearbook 2003, Zaventem/Belgium.

EVCA (2004): Private equity, unpublished document, http://www.evca.com/html/ PE_industry/glossary.asp.

Fama, E. F. (1970): Efficient capital markets: a review of theory and empirical work; in: Journal of Finance, Vol. 25, pp. 383-417.

Fama, E. F. (1980): Banking in the theory of finance; in: Journal of Monetary Economics, Vol. 6, Iss. 1, pp. 39-58.

Fama, E. F. (1991): Efficient capital markets II; in: Journal of Finance, Vol. 46, pp. 1575-1614.

Fenn, G. W./Liang, N./Prowse, S. (1997): The private equity market: an overview; in: Financial Markets, Institutions and Instruments, Vol. 6, Iss. 4, pp. 1-105.

Fornell, C. (1987): A second generation of multivariate analysis: classification of methods and implication for marketing research; in: Houston, M. (editor): Review of Marketing, Chicago/IL/USA, pp. 407-450.

Fornell, C./Bookstein, F. L. (1982): Two structural equation models: LISREL and PLS applied to consumer exit-voice theory; in: Journal of Marketing Research, Vol. 19, Iss. 4, pp. 440-453.

Fornell, C./Cha, J. (1994): Partial least squares; in: Bagozzi, R. P. (editor): Advanced methods of marketing research, Malden/MA/USA [and others], pp. 52-78.

Fornell, C./Larcker, D. F. (1981): Evaluating structural equation models with unobservable variables and measurement error; in: Journal of Marketing Research, Vol. 18, Iss. 1, pp. 39-50.

Fornell, C./Lorange, P./Roos, J. (1990): The cooperative venture formation process: a latent variable structural modeling approach; in: Management Science, Vol. 36, Iss. 10, pp. 1246-1255.

Fornell, C./Tellis, G./Zinkhan, G. M. (1982): Validity assessment: a structural equations approach using partial least squares , in: American Marketing Association Educators' Proceedings, Chicago/IL/USA, pp. 405-409.

Foss, K./Foss, N. (2000): Learning in firms: knowledge-based and property rights perspectives, Working Paper, Nr. 2000-2, Frederiksberg/Denmark.

Foss, N. (1993): Theories of the firm: competence and contractual perspectives; in: Journal of Evolutionary Economics, Vol. 3, Iss. 2, pp. 127-144.

Fredriksen, O./Olofsson, C./Wahlbin, C. (1991): The role of venture capital in the development of portfolio firms, in: Proceedings of the Eleventh Annual Babson College Entrepreneurship Research Conference, Wellesley/MA/USA, pp. 435-444.

Fredriksen, O./Olofsson, C./Wahlbin, C. (1997): Are venture capitalists firefighters? A study of the influence and impact of venture capital firms; in: Technovation, Vol. 17, Iss. 9, pp. 503-532.

Freeman, R. (1984): Strategic management: a stakeholder approach, London.

Fried, V. H./Bruton, G. D./Hisrich, R. D. (1998): Strategy and the board of directors in venture capital-backed firms; in: Journal of Business Venturing, Vol. 13, Iss. 6, pp. 493-503.

Fried, V. H./Hisrich, R. D. (1988): Venture capital research: past, present and future; in: Entrepreneurship Theory and Practice, Vol. 13, Iss. 1, pp. 15-28.

Fried, V. H./Hisrich, R. D. (1992): Venture capital and the investor; in: Management Research News, Vol. 15, Iss. 4, pp. 28-39.

Fried, V. H./Hisrich, R. D. (1995): The venture capitalist: a relationship investor; in: California Management Review, Vol. 37, Iss. 2, pp. 101-113.

Furubotn, E. G./Pejovich, S. (1972): Property rights and economic theory: a survey of recent literature; in: Journal of Economic Literature, Vol. 10, Iss. 4, pp. 1137-1162.

Furubotn, E. G./Pejovich, S. (1974): The economics of property rights, Cambridge.

Garland, R. (1990): A comparison of three forms of the semantic differential; in: Marketing Bulletin, Vol. 1, Iss. 1, pp. 19-24.

Garver, M. S./Mentzer, J. T. (1999): Logistics research methods: employing structural equation modeling to test for construct validity ; in: Journal of Business Logistics, Vol. 20, Iss. 1, pp. 33-58.

Gebhardt, G. (1995): Marktwertorientiertes Beteiligungscontrolling; in: Der Betrieb, Vol. 48, pp. 2225-2231.

Geisser, S. (1975): The predictive sample reuse method with applications; in: Journal of the American Statistical Association, Vol. 70, Iss. 350, pp. 320-328.

Goldberger, A. S. (1964): Econometric theory, New York/NY/USA.

Gompers, P. A./Lerner, J. (1999a): An analysis of compensation in the U.S. venture capital partnership; in: Journal of Financial Economics, Vol. 51, Iss. 1, pp. 3-44.

Gompers, P. A./Lerner, J. (1999b): The venture capital cycle, 2nd edition, Cambridge/MA/USA.

Gorman, M./Sahlman, W. A. (1989): What do venture capitalists do?; in: Journal of Business Venturing, Vol. 4, Iss. 4, pp. 231-248.

Gottschalg, O./Kreuter, B./Zollo, M. (2005): Myths and truths about determinants of buyout performance, unpublished document, Strategy Department, INSEAD Feri Trust, Fontainebleau/France.

Gottschalg, O./Phalippou, L./Zollo, M. (2003): Performance of private equity funds: another puzzle?, Fontainebleau/France.

Gräper, M. (1993): Management-Buy-Out - eine empirische Analyse zur deutschen Entwicklung bis 1990, Kiel.

Graf, S./Gruber, A./Grünbichler, A. (2001): Der Private Equity Markt in Europa; in: Grünbichler, A./Graf, S./Gruber, A. (editors): Private Equity und Hedge Funds, Zürich/Switzerland, pp. 21-42 .

Gregory, H. J./Simmelkjaer, R. T. I. (2001): Comparative study of corporate governance codes relevant to the European Union and its member states: on behalf of the European Commission, Internal Market Directorate General, unpublished document, Weil, Gotshal & Manges, Brussels/Belgium [and others].

Grimes, A. (5.11.2004): Publicity shy: venture capitalists scramble to keep their numbers secret - public university discloses data after court fight, is barred from new funds - 'saddest business letter ever'; in: Wall Street Journal, pp. A1.

Grochla, E. (1959): Polarität in betriebswirtschaftlicher Forschung und Lehre; in: Zeitschrift für Betriebswirtschaft, Vol. 29, pp. 65-76.

Grochla, E. (1976): Praxeologische Organisationstheorie durch sachliche und methodische Integration; in: Zeitschrift für betriebswirtschaftliche Forschung, Vol. 28, pp. 617-637.

Gros, S. (1998): Das Management-Buyout-Konzept als Instrument der Unternehmensprivatisierung bei der Transformation einer Planwirtschaft in eine Marktwirtschaft, Frankfurt am Main.

Gurley, J. G./Shaw, E. S. (1960): Money in a theory of finance, Washington/DC/USA.

Häckner, E./Hisrich, R. D. (2001): Editorial: contemporary entrepreneurial finance research; in: Venture Capital, Vol. 3, Iss. 3, pp. 183-185.

Hänlein, M. (forthcoming): An exploratory investigation of e-Business success factors using partial least squares analysis, Vallendar.

Hänlein, M./Kaplan, A. M. (forthcoming): A beginner's guide to partial least squares (PLS) analysis; in: Understanding Statistics, pp. 1-31.

Hagenmüller, M. (2004): Investor Relations von Private Equity Partnerships, Sternenfels.

Hammer, M./Champy, J. (1993): Reengineering the corporation: a manifesto for business revolution, New York.

Hamprecht, M. (1996): Controlling von Konzernplanungssystemen, Wiesbaden.

Hanlon, D. (2001): Vision and support in new venture start-ups, in: Proceedings of the Twenty-First Annual Entrepreneurship Research Conference, Wellesley/MA/USA.

Harrison, R. T./Mason, C. M. (1992): The roles of investors in entrepreneurial companies: a comparison of informal investors and venture capitalists, in: Proceedings of the Twelfth Annual Babson College Entrepreneurship Research Conference, Wellesley/MA/USA, pp. 388-404.

Haynes, M./Thompson, S./Wright, M. (2002): The impact of divestment on firm performance: empirical evidence from a panel of UK companies; in: Journal of Industrial Economics, Vol. 50, Iss. 2, pp. 173-196.

Heeler, R. M./Ray, M. L. (1972): Measure validation in marketing; in: Journal of Marketing Research, Vol. 9, Iss. 4, pp. 361-370.

Hellmann, T./Puri, M. (2002): Venture capital and the professionalization of start-up firms: empirical evidence; in: Journal of Finance, Vol. 57, Iss. 1, pp. 169-198.

Hildebrandt, L. (1984): Kausalanalytische Validierung in der Marketingforschung; in: Marketing - Zeitschrift für Forschung und Praxis, Vol. 6, Iss. 1, pp. 41-51.

Hoffmann, F. (1972): Merkmale der Führungsorganisation amerikanischer Unternehmen - Auszüge aus den Ergebnissen einer Forschungsreise 1970; in: Zeitschrift Führung + Organisation, Vol. 41, pp. 3-8, 85-89 and 145-148.

Hoffmann, P./Ramke, R. (1992): Management buy out in der Bundesrepublik Deutschland - Anspruch, Realität und Perspektiven, 2nd edition, Berlin.

Horne, A./Morgan, J./Page, J. (1973): Where do we go from here?; in: Journal of the Market Research Society, Vol. 16, Iss. 3, pp. 157-182.

Horváth, P. (1978): Entwicklung und Stand einer Konzeption zur Lösung der Adaptions- und Koordinationsprobleme der Führung; in: Zeitschrift für Betriebswirtschaft, Vol. 48, pp. 194-208.

Horváth, P. (2001): Controlling, 8th edition, München.

Howorth, C./Westhead, P./Wright, M. (2004): Buyouts, information asymmetry and the family management dyad; in: Journal of Business Venturing, Vol. 19, Iss. 4, pp. 465-613.

Huang, K.-T./Lee, Y. W./Wang, R. Y. (1998): Quality information and knowledge, Upper Saddle River/NJ/USA.

Hui, B. S. (1982): On building partial least squares models with interdependent inner relations; in: Jöreskog, K. G./Wold, H. (editors): Systems under indirect observations: causality, structure, prediction, Amsterdam/Netherlands, pp. 249-272.

Hulland, J. (1999): Use of partial least squares (PLS) in strategic management research: a review of four recent studies; in: Strategic Management Journal, Vol. 20, Iss. 2, pp. 195-204.

Jacoby, J. (1978): Consumer research: a state of the art review; in: Journal of Marketing, Vol. 42, Iss. 2, pp. 87-96.

Jacoby, S. (2000): Erfolgsfaktoren von Management Buyouts in Deutschland - eine empirische Untersuchung, Lohmar.

Jarvis, C. B./Mackenzie, S. B./Podsakoff, P. M. (2003): A critical review of construct indicators and measurement model misspecification in marketing and consumer research; in: Journal of Consumer Research, Vol. 30, Iss. 2, pp. 199-218.

Jensen, M. C. (1989): Active investors, LBOs, and privatization of bankruptcy; in: Journal of Applied Corporate Finance, Vol. 2, Iss. 1, pp. 35-44.

Jensen, M. C./Kaplan, S./Stiglin, L. (1989): Effects of LBOs on tax revenues of the U.S. treasury; in: Tax Notes, Vol. 42, Iss. 6, pp. 727-733.

Jensen, M. C./Meckling, W. H. (1976): Theory of the firm: managerial behavior, agency costs and ownership structure; in: Journal of Financial Economics, Vol. 3, Iss. 4, pp. 305-360.

Jöreskog, K. G. (1967): Some contributions to maximum likelihood factor analysis; in: Psychometrika, Vol. 32, Iss. 4, pp. 443-482.

Jöreskog, K. G. (1969): A general approach to confirmatory maximum likelihood factor analysis; in: Psychometrika, Vol. 34, Iss. 2, pp. 183-202.

Jöreskog, K. G. (1970): A general method for analysis of covariance structures; in: Biometrika, Vol. 57, Iss. 2, pp. 239-251.

Jöreskog, K. G. (1973): A general method for estimating a linear structural equation system; in: Goldberger, A. S./Duncan, O. D. (editors): Structural equation models in the social sciences, New York/NY/USA, pp. 85-112.

Jöreskog, K. G./Sorbom, D. (1982): Recent developments in structural equation modeling; in: Journal of Marketing Research, Vol. 19, Iss. 4, pp. 404-416.

Jones, W. H. (1979): Generalizing mail survey inducement methods: population interactions with anonymity and sponsorship; in: Public Opinion Quarterly, Vol. 43, Iss. 1, pp. 102-111.

Jost, P.-J. (1998): Strategisches Konfliktmanagement in Organisationen: eine spieltheoretische Einführung, Wiesbaden.

Jost, P.-J. (1999): Organisation und Führung, unpublished document, WHU, Vallendar.

Judge, W. Q. Jr./Zeithaml, C. P. (1992): Institutional and strategic choice perspectives on board involvement in the strategic decision process; in: Academy of Management Journal, Vol. 35, Iss. 4, pp. 766-794.

Kahle, L. R./Sales, B. D. (1978): Personalization of the outside envelope in mail surveys; in: Public Opinion Quarterly, Vol. 42, Iss. 4, pp. 547-550.

Kanuk, L./Berenson, C. (1975): Mail surveys and response rates: a literature review; in: Journal of Marketing Research, Vol. 12, Iss. 4, pp. 440-453.

Kaplan, R. W./Saccuzzo, D. P. (1982): Psychological testing: principles, applications, and issues, Monterey/CA/USA.

Kaplan, S. N. (1988): Sources of value in management buyouts, Cambridge/MA/USA.

Kaplan, S. N. (1989): Management buyouts: evidence on taxes as a source of value; in: Journal of Finance, Vol. 44, Iss. 3, pp. 611-632.

Kaplan, S. N./Schoar, A. (2003): Private equity performance: returns, persistence and capital flows, NBER Working Paper, Nr. 9807,

Kaplan, S. N./Strömberg, P. (2003): Financial contracting theory meets the real world: evidence from venture capital contracts; in: Review of Economic Studies, Vol. 20, Iss. 2, pp. 281-315.

Katz, D. (1942): Do interviewers bias poll results?; in: Public Opinion Quarterly, Vol. 6, Iss. 2, pp. 248-268.

Keesling, J. W. (1972): Maximum likelihood approaches to causal analysis, Chicago/IL/USA.

Kieser, A./Nicolai, A. (2002): Trotz eklatanter Erfolglosigkeit: Die Erfolgsfaktorenforschung weiter auf Erfolgskurs; in: Die Betriebswirtschaft, Vol. 62, Iss. 6, pp. 579-596.

Kinnear, T. C./Taylor, J. R. (1971): Multivariate methods in marketing research - a further attempt at classification; in: Journal of Marketing, Vol. 35, Iss. 4, pp. 56-59.

Kleinschnittger, U. (1993): Beteiligungs-Controlling, München.

Knoblauch, B. (2002): Value creation strategies for companies in private equity portfolios, unpublished document, Hicks, Muse, Tate & Furst Center for Private Equity Finance, McCombs School of Business, The University of Texas at Austin, Austin/TX/USA.

Koch, M. (1997): Eine empirische Studie über Möglichkeiten und Chancen von Management Buyouts in der Schweiz, St. Gallen/Schweiz.

Kogut, B./Zander, U. (1992): Knowledge of the firm, combinative capabilities, and the replication of technology; in: Organization Science, Vol. 3, Iss. 3, pp. 383-397.

Korsgaard, M./Schweiger, D./Sapienza, H. (1995): Building commitment, attachment, and trust in strategic decision-making teams - the role of procedural justice; in: Academy of Management Journal, Vol. 38, Iss. 1, pp. 60-84.

Korsukéwitz, C. (1975): Die Prüfung der Beteiligungswürdigkeit nicht emissionsfähiger Unternehmungen durch Kapitalbeteiligungsgesellschaften, Berlin.

KPMG/Manchester Business School (2002): Insight into portfolio management - private equity research programme, unpublished document, Manchester/UK.

Kraft, V. (2001): Private Equity für Turnaround-Investitionen, Frankfurt.

Kümmerle, W./Paul, F. M./Freye, H. (1998): Survey of private equity in Germany - summary of results and analysis, Harvard Business School Working Paper, Boston/MA/USA.

Küpper, H.-U. (1997): Controlling - Konzeption, Aufgaben und Instrumente, 2nd edition, Stuttgart.

Kumar, N./Stern, L./Anderson, J. (1993): Conducting interorganizational research using key informants; in: Academy of Management Journal, Vol. 36, Iss. 6, pp. 1633-1651.

Kvalseth, T. O. (1985): Cautionary note about R²; in: The American Statistician, Vol. 39, Iss. 4, pp. 279-285.

Landström, H. (1990): Co-operation between venture capital companies and small firms; in: Entrepreneurship and Regional Development, Vol. 2, Iss. 4, pp. 345-362.

Lawshe, C. H. (1975): A quantitative approach to content validity; in: Personnel Psychology, Vol. 28, Iss. 4, pp. 563-575.

Leibenstein, H. (1966): Allocative efficiency vs. "x-efficiency"; in: American Economic Review, Vol. 56, Iss. 3, pp. 392-415 .

Leland, H./Pyle, D. (1977): Information asymmetries, financial structure, and financial intermediation; in: Journal of Finance, Vol. 32, Iss. 2, pp. 371-387.

Lerner, J. (2000): Private equity and venture capital - a casebook, New York [and others].

Lind, E. A./Tyler, T. (1988): The social psychology of procedural justice, New York/NY/USA.

Lintner, J. (1965): The valuation of risk assets and the selection of risky investments in stock portfolios and capital budgets; in: Review of Economics and Statistics, Vol. 47, Iss. 1, pp. 13-37.

Lohmöller, J.-B. (1984): LVPLS Program Manual Version 1.6 - latent variables path analysis with partial least-squares estimation, Köln.

Lohmöller, J.-B. (1989): Latent variable path modeling with partial least squares, Heidelberg.

Luehrman, T. A. (1997): Using APV - a better tool for valuing operations; in: Harvard Business Review, Vol. 75, Iss. 3, pp. 145-154.

MacCallum, R. C./Browne, M. W. (1993): The use of causal indicators in covariance structure models: some practical issues; in: Psychological Bulletin, Vol. 114, Iss. 3, pp. 533-541.

MacCallum, R. C./Browne, M. W./Sugawara, H. M. (1996): Power analysis and determination of sample size for covariance structure modeling; in: Psychological Methods, Vol. 1, Iss. 2, pp. 130-149.

MacMillan, I. C./Kulow, D. M./Khoylian, R. (1989): Venture capitalists' involvement in their investments: extent and performance; in: Journal of Business Venturing, Vol. 4, Iss. 1, pp. 27-47.

MacMillan, I. C./Siegel, R./Subbanarasimha, P. N. S. (1985): Criteria used by venture capitalists to evaluate new venture proposals; in: Journal of Business Venturing, Vol. 1, Iss. 1, pp. 119-128.

MacMillan, I. C./Zemann, L./Narasimha, P. N. S. (1987): Criteria distinguishing successful from unsuccessful ventures in the venture screening process; in: Journal of Business Venturing, Vol. 2, Iss. 2, pp. 123-137.

Mahajan, J. (1992): The overconfidence effect in marketing management predictions; in: Journal of Marketing Research, Vol. 29, Iss. 3, pp. 329-342.

Marais, L./Schipper, K./Smith, A. (1989): Wealth effects of going private on senior securities; in: Journal of Financial Economics, Vol. 23, Iss. 1, pp. 155-191.

Marsh, H. W./Hau, K.-T./Balla, J. R. /Grayson, D. (1998): Is more ever too much?: The number of indicators per factor in confirmatory factor analysis; in: Multivariate Behavioral Research, Vol. 33, Iss. 2, pp. 181-220.

Mason, C. H./Perreault, W. D. J. (1991): Collinearity, power, and interpretation of multiple regression analysis; in: Journal of Marketing Research, Vol. 28, Iss. 3, pp. 268-280.

Masten, S. E./Meehan, J./Snyder, E. (1991): The cost of organization; in: Journal of Law, Economics and Organization, Vol. 7, Iss. 1, pp. 1-25.

Mazen, A./Graf, L./Kellogg, C./Hemmasi, M. (1987): Statistical power in contemporary management research; in: Academy of Management Journal, Vol. 30, Iss. 2, pp. 369-380.

McDonald, R. P. (1996): Path analysis with composite variables; in: Multivariate Behavioral Research, Vol. 31, Iss. 2, pp. 239-270.

McMahon, R. G. P./ Davies, L. G. (1994): Financial reporting and analysis practices in small enterprises: their association with growth rate and financial performance; in: Journal of Small Business Management, Vol. 32, Iss. 1, pp. 9-17.

Megginson, W. L. (1996): Corporate finance theory, Reading/MA/USA [and others].

Miller, M. H. (1991): Leverage; in: Journal of Finance, Vol. 46, Iss. 2, pp. 479-488.

Miller, M. H. (1999): The history of finance: an eyewitness account; in: Journal of Portfolio Management, Vol. 25, Iss. 4, pp. 95-101.

Mintzberg, H. (1972): The myths of MIS; in: California Management Review, Vol. 15, Iss. 1, pp. 92-97.

Modigliani, F./Miller, M. H. (1958): The cost of capital, corporation finance and the theory of investment; in: American Economic Review, Vol. 48, Iss. 3, pp. 261-297.

Mössle, K. (2000): Asset Management; in: von Hagen, J./von Stein, J. H. (editors): Obst/Hintner Geld-, Bank- und Börsenwesen, 40th edition, Stuttgart, pp. 872-897.

Mols, N. P. (2000): Dual channels of distribution: a transaction cost analysis and propositions; in: International Review of Retail, Distribution and Consumer Research, Vol. 10, Iss. 3, pp. 227-246.

Morris, M./Watling, J./Schindehutte, M. (2000): Venture capitalist involvement in portfolio companies: insights from South Africa; in: Journal of Small Business Management, Vol. 38, Iss. 3, pp. 68-77.

Mossin, J. (1966): Equilibrium in a capital asset market; in: Econometrica, Vol. 34, Iss. 4, pp. 768-783.

Murphy, K. R./Davidshofer, C. O. (1988): Psychological testing: principles and applications, Englewood Cliffs/NJ/USA.

Murray, G. (1995): The UK venture capital industry; in: Journal of Business Finance and Accounting, Vol. 22, Iss. 8, pp. 1077-1106.

Myers, B. L./Melcher, A. J. (1969): On the choice of risk levels in managerial decision-making; in: Management Science, Vol. 16, Iss. 2, pp. B31-B39.

n. a. (24.11.1995): KKR agrees to buyout regional newspapers; in: Wall Street Journal - Eastern Edition, pp. B2.

n. a. (30.9.1996): A 51% stake is acquired in Italian motorcycle manufacturer; in: Wall Street Journal - Eastern Edition, pp. B5.

Nagtegaal, T. (1999): Post-investment venture management; in: Bygrave, W. D./Hay, M./Peeters, J. B. (editors): The venture capital handbook, London, pp. 183-201.

Naik, P./Tsai, C.-L. (2000): Partial least squares estimator for single-index models; in: Journal of the Royal Statistical Society: Series B (statistical methodology), Vol. 62, Iss. 4, pp. 763-771.

Nelson, R. R./Winter, S. G. (1982): An evolutionary theory of economic change, Cambridge/MA/USA.

Newman, M. E. J. (2003): Ego-centered networks and the ripple-effect; in: Social Networks, Vol. 25, Iss. 1, pp. 83-95.

Noonan, R./Wold, H. (1982): PLS path modeling with indirectly observed variables: a comparison of alternative estimates for latent variables; in: Jöreskog, K. G./Wold, H. (editors): Systems under indirect observations: causality, structure, prediction, Amsterdam/Netherlands, pp. 75-94.

Norton, E./Tenenbaum, B. H. (1992): Factors affecting the structure of U.S. venture capital deals; in: Journal of Small Business Management, Vol. 30, Iss. 3, pp. 20-29.

Norton, E./Tenenbaum, B. H. (1993): Specialization versus diversification as a venture capital investment strategy; in: Journal of Business Venturing, Vol. 8, Iss. 5, pp. 431-442.

Nunally, J. C. (1978): Psychometric theory, 2nd edition, New York/NY/USA.

NVCA (2004): What is venture capital?, unpublished document, http://www.nvca.org/def.html.

O'Grady, K. E. (1982): Measures of explained variance - cautions and limitations; in: Psychological Bulletin, Vol. 92, Iss. 3, pp. 766-777.

Opler, T. C. (1992): Operating performance in leveraged buyouts: evidence from 1985-1989; in: Financial Management, Vol. 21, Iss. 1, pp. 27-34.

Osgood, E. C./Suci, G. J./Tannenbaum, P. H. (1957): The measurement of meaning, Urbana/IL/USA.

Oskamp, S. (1982): Overconfidence in case-study judgments; in: Kahneman, D./Slovic, P./Tversky, A. (editors): Judgment under uncertainty: heuristics and biases, Cambridge/UK, pp. 287-293.

Ouchi, W. G. (1977): The relationship between organizational structure and organizational control; in: Administrative Science Quarterly, Vol. 22, Iss. 1, pp. 95-113.

Ouchi, W. G. (1979): A conceptual framework for the design of organizational control mechanisms; in: Management Science, Vol. 25, Iss. 9, pp. 833-848.

Peter, J. P. (1979): Reliability: a review of psychometric basics and recent marketing practices; in: Journal of Marketing, Vol. 16, Iss. 1, pp. 6-17.

Peter, J. P. (1981): Construct validity: a review of basic issues and marketing practices; in: Journal of Marketing Research, Vol. 18, Iss. 2, pp. 133-145.

Peteraf, M. A. (1993): The cornerstones of competitive advantage: a resource-based view; in: Strategic Management Journal, Vol. 14, Iss. 3, pp. 179-191.

Peterson, R. A. (1994): A meta-analysis of Cronbach's coefficient alpha; in: Journal of consumer research, Vol. 21, Iss. 2, pp. 381-391.

Phillips, L. W. (1981): Assessing measurement error in key informant reports: a methodological note on organizational analysis in marketing; in: Journal of Marketing Research, Vol. 18, Iss. 4, pp. 395-415 .

Pichotta, A. (1990): Die Prüfung der Beteiligungswürdigkeit von innovativen Unternehmungen durch Venture Capital-Gesellschaften, Bergisch-Gladbach.

Picot, A./Bortenlänger, C./Röhrl, H. (1997): Organization of electronic markets: contributions of new institutional economics; in: Information Society, Vol. 13, Iss. 1, pp. 107-123.

Prester, M. (2002): Exit-Strategien deutscher Venture-Capital-Gesellschaften, Münster.

PrivateEquityOnline.com (2003): Sweat; in: PrivateEquityOnline.com Newsletter.

Ray, G./Hutchinson, P. J. (1983): The financing and financial control of small enterprise development, Aldershot/UK.

Rees, R. (1985): The theory of principal and agent: part 1 and 2; in: Bulletin of Economic Research, Vol. 37, Iss. 1 and 2, pp. 3-26, 75-95.

Reinartz, W./Krafft, M./Hoyer, W. (2003): Measuring the customer relationship management construct and linking it to performance outcomes, INSEAD Working Paper Series, Nr. 2003/02/MKT, Fontainebleau Cedex/France [and others].

Reißig-Thust, S. (2003): Venture-Capital-Gesellschaften und Gründungsunternehmen: empirische Untersuchung zur erfolgreichen Gestaltung der Beziehung, unpublished document.

Richter, H. J. (1970): Die Strategie schriftlicher Massenbefragungen, Bad Harzburg.

Rindskopf, D./Rose, T. (1988): Some theory and applications of confirmatory second-order factor analysis; in: Multivariate Behavioral Research, Vol. 23, Iss. 1, pp. 51-67.

Rinne, H. (1997): Taschenbuch der Statistik, 2nd edition, Frankfurt am Main.

Robbie, K./Wright, M. (1996): Management buy-ins: entrepreneurship, active investors and corporate restructuring, Manchester/UK.

Robbie, K./Wright, M./Thompson, S. (1992): Management buy-ins in the UK; in: Omega, Vol. 20, Iss. 4, pp. 445-456.

Robson, P./Bennett, R. (2000): SME growth: the relationship with business advice and external collaboration; in: Small Business Economics, Vol. 15, Iss. 3, pp. 193-208.

Rogers, P./Cullinan, G./Shannon, T. (2002a): 'Performance culture' the private equity way; in: European Business Journal, Vol. 14, Iss. 4, pp. 206-211.

Rogers, P./Holland, T./Haas, D. (2002b): Private equity disciplines for the corporation; in: Journal of Private Equity, Vol. 6, Iss. 1, pp. 6-8.

Rogers, P./Holland, T./Haas, D. (2002c): Value-acceleration: lessons from private-equity masters; in: Harvard Business Review, Vol. 80, Iss. 6, pp. 94-101.

Roldan, J. L./Leal, A. (2003): A validation test of an adaptation of the DeLone and McLean's model in the Spanish EIS field; in: Cano, J. J. (editor): Critical reflections on information systems - a systemic approach, Hershey/PA/USA, pp. 66-84.

Rosenstein, J./Bruno, A. V./Bygrave, W. D./Taylor, N. T. (1993): The CEO, venture capitalists, and the board; in: Journal of Business Venturing, Vol. 8, Iss. 2, pp. 99-113.

Ross, S. A. (1973): The economic theory of agency: the principal's problem; in: American Economic Review, Vol. 63, Iss. 2, pp. 134-139.

Ruppen, D. A. (2002): Corporate governance bei Venture-Capital-finanzierten Unternehmen, Wiesbaden.

Sahlman, W. A. (1990): The structure and governance of venture-capital organizations; in: Journal of Financial Economics, Vol. 27, Iss. 2, pp. 473-521.

Sahlman, W. A. (1997): Entrepreneurial finance - course introduction, Case Study 9-288-004, Harvard Business School.

Sapienza, H. J. (1992): When do venture capitalists add value?; in: Journal of Business Venturing, Vol. 7, Iss. 1, pp. 9-27.

Sapienza, H. J./Korsgaard, A. (1996): Procedural justice in entrepreneur-investor relations; in: Academy of Management Journal, Vol. 39, Iss. 3, pp. 544-574.

Sapienza, H. J./Manigart, S./Vermeir, W. (1996): Venture capitalist governance and value added in four countries; in: Journal of Business Venturing, Vol. 11, Iss. 6, pp. 439-469.

Sapienza, H. J./Timmons, J. A. (1989): Launching and building entrepreneurial companies, in: Proceedings of the Ninth Annual Babson College Entrepreneurship Research Conference, Wellesley/MA/USA, pp. 245-257.

Sappington, D. E. M. (1991): Incentives in principal-agent relationships; in: Journal of Economic Perspectives, Vol. 5, Iss. 2, pp. 45-66.

Schefczyk, M. (2000): Erfolgsstrategien deutscher Venture-Capital-Gesellschaften, 2nd edition, Stuttgart.

Schefczyk, M./Gerpott, T. J. (1998): Beratungsunterstützung von Portfoliounternehmen durch deutsche Venture Capital Gesellschaften. Eine empirische Untersuchung; in: Zeitschrift für Betriebswirtschaft Ergänzungsheft, Vol. 2, pp. 143-166.

Schefczyk, M./Gerpott, T. J. (2001): Qualification and turnover of managers and venture capital-financed firm performance; in: Journal of Business Venturing, Vol. 16, Iss. 2, pp. 145-163.

Schmid, H. (1994): Leveraged management buy-out: Begriff, Gestaltungen, optimale Kapitalstruktur und ökonomische Bewertung, Frankfurt am Main.

Schmidt, A. (1986): Das Controlling als Instrument zur Koordination der Unternehmensführung - eine Analyse der Koordinationsfunktion des Controlling unter entscheidungsorientierten Gesichtspunkten, Frankfurt am Main [and others].

Schmidt, A. (1989): Beteiligungscontrolling - wie man seine Tochtergesellschaft organisatorisch in den Griff bekommt; in: Controlling, pp. 270-275.

Schmidt, R. H. (1985): Venture Capital aus der Sicht der Finanzierungstheorie; in: Betriebswirtschaftliche Forschung und Praxis, Vol. 37, Iss. 5, pp. 421-437.

Schröder, C. (1992): Strategien und Management von Beteiligungsgesellschaften: ein Einblick in Organisationsstrukturen und Entscheidungsprozesse von institutionellen Eigenkapitalinvestoren, Baden-Baden.

Schwenkedel, S. (1991): Management Buyout: ein Geschäftsfeld für Banken, Wiesbaden.

Seidler, J. (1974): On using informants: a technique for collecting quantitative data and controlling for measurement error in organizational analysis; in: American Sociological Review, Vol. 39, Iss. 6, pp. 816-831.

Seraphim, R.-P./Herbst, T. (1995): Start up-Berichtswesen für das Beteiligungscontrolling; in: Controlling, pp. 22-28.

Sharpe, W. F. (1964): Capital asset pricing: a theory of market equilibrium under conditions of risk; in: Journal of Finance, Vol. 19, Iss. 3, pp. 425-442.

Shepherd, D. A./Zacharakis, A./Baron, R. A. (2003): VCs' decision processes: evidence suggesting more experience may not always be better; in: Journal of Business Venturing, Vol. 18, Iss. 3, pp. 381-401.

Sheth, J. N. (1971): The multivariate revolution in marketing research; in: Journal of Marketing, Vol. 35, Iss. 1, pp. 13-19.

Shleifer, A./Vishny, R. W. (1997): A survey of corporate governance; in: Journal of Finance, Vol. 52, Iss. 2, pp. 737-783.

Shook, C. L./Ketchen, D. J./Hult, G. T. M./Kacmar, K. M. (2004): An assessment of the use of structural equation modeling in strategic management research; in: Strategic Management Journal, Vol. 25, Iss. 4, pp. 397-404.

Simon, H. A. (1957): Administrative behavior, New York/NY/USA.

Smart, G. H./Payne, S. N./Yuzaki, H. (2000): What makes a successful venture capitalist; in: Journal of Private Equity, Vol. 3, Iss. 1, pp. 7-29.

Smith, A. J. (1990): Corporate ownership structure and performance: the case of management buyouts; in: Journal of Financial Economics, Vol. 27, Iss. 1, pp. 143-164.

Soo, C. W./Devinney, T. M. (2003): The role of knowledge quality in firm performance, unpublished document, Broadway/NSW/Australia [and others].

Spremann, K. (1987): Agent and principal; in: Bamberg, G./Spremann, K. (editors): Agency theory, information and incentives, Berlin [and others], pp. 3-37.

Steenkamp, J. B./van Trip, H. (1991): The use of LISREL in validating marketing constructs; in: International Journal of Research in Marketing, Vol. 8, Iss. 4, pp. 283-299.

Stone, M. (1974): Cross-validatory choice and assessment of statistical predictions; in: Journal of the Royal Statistical Society, Series B, Vol. 36, Iss. 2, pp. 111-133.

Sweeting, R. C. (1991): UK venture capital funds and the funding of new technology based businesses: process and relationships; in: Journal of Management Studies, Vol. 28, Iss. 6, pp. 601-622.

Sweeting, R. C./Wong, C. F. (1997): A UK 'hands-off' venture capital firm and the handling of post-investment investor-investee relationships; in: Journal of Management Studies, Vol. 34, Iss. 1, pp. 125-152.

Szyperski, N. (1980): Informationsbedarf; in: Grochla, E. (editor): Handwörterbuch der Organisation, 2nd edition, Stuttgart, columns 904-913.

Teece, D. J./Pisano, G./Shuen, A. (1997): Dynamic capabilities and strategic management; in: Strategic Management Journal , Vol. 18, Iss. 7, pp. 509-533.

Temple, P. (1999): Private Equity, Chichester/UK [and others].

Then Bergh, F. (1998): Leveraged Management Buyout, Wiesbaden.

Thibaut, J./Walker, L. (1975): Procedural justice: a psychological analysis, Hillsdale/NJ/USA.

Thomas, J./Evanson, R. V. (1987): An empirical investigation of association between financial ratio use and small business success; in: Journal of Business Finance and Accounting, Vol. 14, Iss. 4, pp. 555-571.

Ting, K. F. (1995): Confirmatory tetrad analysis in SAS; in: Structural Equation Modeling, Vol. 2, pp. 163-171.

Trester, J. J. (1998): Venture capital contracting under asymmetric information; in: Journal of Banking & Finance, Vol. 22, Iss. 6-8, pp. 675-699.

Tyebjee, T. T./Bruno, A. V. (1984): A model of venture capitalist investment activity; in: Management Science, Vol. 30, Iss. 9, pp. 1051-1066.

Valdmanis, T. (21.4.1998): Consultants opt for stakes in client's firms; in: USA Today,

Venkatraman, N./Grant, J. H. (1986): Construct measurement in organizational strategy research: a critique and proposal; in: Academy of Management Review, Vol. 11, Iss. 1, pp. 71-87.

Vest, P. (1995): Der Verkauf von Konzernunternehmen durch Management Buy-Out, Wiesbaden.

Vogel, J. (1998): Marktwertorientiertes Beteiligungscontrolling: Shareholder Value als Maß der Konzernsteuerung, Wiesbaden.

von Maltzan, B.-A. (2000): Finanzmarktanalyse; in: von Hagen, J. /von Stein, J. H. (editors): Obst/Hintner Geld-, Bank- und Börsenwesen, 40th edition, Stuttgart, pp. 860-871.

Weber, J. (1995): Einführung in das Controlling, 6th edition, Stuttgart.

Weber, J. (2002): Einführung in das Controlling, 9th edition, Stuttgart.

Weber, J./Schäffer, U. (1999): Controlling als Koordinationsfunktion - Zehn Jahre nach Küpper/Weber/Zünd, WHU-Forschungspapier, Nr. 71, Vallendar.

Weber, J./Schäffer, U. (2003): Thesen zum Controlling (II), CCM-Forschungspapier, Nr. 8, Vallendar.

Weber, J./Weißenberger, B. E. (1998): Finanzorientiertes Controlling - Band 7 der Reihe Advanced Controlling, Vallendar.

Weber, R. (1980): Some characteristics of free recall of computer controls by EDP auditors; in: Journal of Accounting Research, Vol. 18, Iss. 1, pp. 214-241.

Welpe, I. (2002): What determines the success of the cooperation between venture capital firm and portfolio company, unpublished document, Chalmers University of Technology, Göteborg/Sweden.

Werts, C. E./Linn, R. L./Jöreskog, K. G. (1974): Interclass reliability estimates: testing structural assumptions; in: Educational and Psychological Measurement, Vol. 34, Iss. 1, pp. 25-33.

Wiley, D. E. (1973): The identification problem for structural equation models with unmeasured variables; in: Goldberger, A. S./Duncan, O. D. (editors): Structural equation models in the social sciences, New York/NY/USA, pp. 69-83.

Willert, F. (forthcoming): Determinanten der Größe von Private-Equity-Fondsgesellschaften, Bamberg.

Williamson, O. E. (1975): Markets and hierarchies: analysis and anti-trust implications, New York/NY/USA.

Williamson, O. E. (1979): Transaction costs economics: the governance of contractual relations; in: Journal of Law and Economics, Vol. 22, Iss. 2, pp. 233-261.

Williamson, O. E. (1985): The economic institutions of capitalism, firms, markets, relational contracting, New York/NY/USA.

Williamson, O. E. (1991): Comparative economic organization: the analysis of discrete structural alternatives; in: Administrative Science Quarterly, Vol. 36, Iss. 2, pp. 269-296.

Wold, H. (1966): Estimation of principal components and related models by iterative least squares; in: Krishnaiah, P. R. (editor): Multivariate analysis, New York/NY/USA, pp. 391-420.

Wold, H. (1982a): Models for knowledge; in: Gani, J. (editor): The making of statisticians, London/UK, pp. 190-212.

Wold, H. (1982b): Soft modeling: the basic design and some extensions; in: Jöreskog, K. G./Wold, H. (editors): Systems under indirect observations: causality, structure, prediction, Amsterdam/Netherlands, pp. 1-54.

Wold, H. (1985): Partial least squares; in: Kotz, S./Johnson, N. L. (editors): Encyclopedia of statistical sciences, volume 6, New York/NY/USA, pp. 581-591.

Wold, H. (1989): Introduction to the second generation of multivariate analysis; in: Wold, H. (editor): Theoretical empiricism, New York/NY/USA, pp. vii-xl.

Wright, M./Robbie, K. (1998): Venture capital and private equity: a review and synthesis; in: Journal of Business Finance & Accounting, Vol. 25, Iss. 5/6, pp. 521-570.

Wright, M./Robbie, K. (1999): Management buyouts and venture capital: into the next millennium, Cheltenham/UK [and others].

Wright, M./Robbie, K./Romanet, Y./Thompson, S./Joachimsson, R./Bruining, J./Herst, A. (1993): Harvesting and the longevity of management buy-outs and buy-ins: a four-country study; in: Entrepreneurship Theory and Practice, Vol. 18, Iss. 2, pp. 90-109.

Wright, M./Robbie, K./Thompson, S./Starkey, K. (1994): Longevity and the life cycle of management buy-outs; in: Strategic Management Journal, Vol. 15, Iss. 3, pp. 215-227.

Wright, M./Thompson, S./Robbie, K. (1992): Venture capital and management-led, leveraged buy-outs: a European perspective; in: Journal of Business Venturing, Vol. 7, Iss. 1, pp. 47-71.

Yi, M. Y./Hwang, Y. (2003): Predicting the use of web-based information systems: self-efficacy, enjoyment, learning, goal orientation, and the technology acceptance model; in: International Journal of Human-Computer Studies, Vol. 59, Iss. 4, pp. 431-449.

Zacharakis, A. L./ Shepherd, D. A. (2001): The nature of information and VCs' overconfidence; in: Journal of Business Venturing, Vol. 14, Iss. 6, pp. 311-332.

Zahra, S. A./Pearce, J. A. (1989): Board of directors and corporate financial performance; in: Journal of Management, Vol. 15, Iss. 2, pp. 291-334.

Zenz, A. (1999): Strategisches Qualitätscontrolling - Konzeption als Metaführungslehre, Wiesbaden.

Zook, C./Allen, J. (2001): Profit from the core - growth strategy in an era of turbulence, Boston/MA/USA.

AUS DER REIHE — Gabler Edition Wissenschaft

„Entrepreneurship"
Herausgeber: Prof. Dr. Malte Brettel, Prof. Dr. Lambert T. Koch,
Prof. Dr. Tobias Kollmann und Prof. Dr. Peter Witt

zuletzt erschienen:

Alexander Friedrich
Auswahl von Syndikatspartnern im Private Equity-Geschäft
Eine deutschlandweite empirische Betrachtung
2005. XVIII, 249 S., 11 Abb., 17 Tab., Br. € 49,90, ISBN 3-8350-0213-9

Hans Georg Gemünden, Sören Salomo, Thilo Müller (Hrsg.)
Entrepreneurial Excellence
Unternehmertum, unternehmerische Kompetenz und Wachstum
junger Unternehmen
2005. XIII, 356 S., 36 Abb., 40 Tab., Br. € 55,90, ISBN 3-8244-8261-4

Lukas Junker
Equity Carveouts, Agency Costs, and Firm Value
2005. XXIV, 445 S., 30 Abb., 51 Tab., Br. € 59,90, ISBN 3-8350-0092-6

Degenhard Meier
Post-Investment Value Addition to Buyouts
Analysis of European Private Equity Firms
2006. XV, 157 S., 14 Abb., 17 Tab., Br. € 45,90, ISBN 3-8350-0228-7

Inga Michler
Internationaler Standortwettbewerb um Unternehmensgründer
Die Rolle des Staates bei der Entwicklung von Clustern der Informations- und
Biotechnologie in Deutschland und den USA
2005. XXII, 296 S., 33 Abb., 27 Tab., Br. € 55,90, ISBN 3-8350-0099-3

Frank Pankotsch
Kapitalbeteiligungsgesellschaften und ihre Portfoliounternehmen
Gestaltungsmöglichkeiten und Erfolgsfaktoren der Zusammenarbeit
2005. XVI, 274 S., 23 Abb., 58 Tab., Br. € 49,90, ISBN 3-8350-0107-8

Klaus Walterscheid, Klaus Anderseck (Hrsg.)
Gründungsforschung und Gründungslehre
Zwischen Identitätssuche und „Normalwissenschaft"
2005. XI, 276 S., 5 Abb., 12 Tab., Br. € 49,90, ISBN 3-8244-8258-4

www.duv.de

Änderung vorbehalten.
Stand: Februar 2006.

Deutscher Universitäts-Verlag
Abraham-Lincoln-Str. 46
65189 Wiesbaden